DEMYSTIFYING DRUGS

Demystifying Drugs

A Psychosocial Perspective

Ted Goldberg
Associate Professor
Department of Social Work
Stockholm University
Sweden

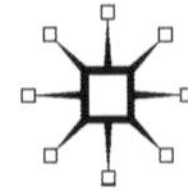

Published by PALGRAVE
Houndmills, Basingstoke, Hampshire RG21 6XS and
175 Fifth Avenue, New York, N. Y. 10010
Companies and representatives throughout the world

PALGRAVE is the new global academic imprint of
St. Martin's Press LLC Scholarly and Reference Division and
Palgrave Publishers Ltd (formerly Macmillan Press Ltd).

Outside North America

ISBN 978-0-333-72245-9 hardcover
ISBN 978-0-333-72246-6 paperback

In North America
ISBN 0-312-22312-9

This book is printed on paper suitable for recycling and made from fully managed and sustained forest sources. Logging, pulping and manufacturing processes are expected to conform to the environmental regulations of the country of origin.

A catalogue record for this book is available from the British Library.

Library of Congress Catalog Card Number: 99-11278 CIP

Transferred to digital printing 2002

Printed and bound in Great Britain by
CPI Antony Rowe, Chippenham and Eastbourne

Contents

List of Figures

Acknowledgements

This book could never have been written without assistance from a great many people. Foremost I want to thank everyone who helped me during my fieldwork. I am especially grateful to those who opened themselves as friend and confidant; giving me insight into what lies behind the façade usually shown to the straight world.

Converting their trust into a book has not been easy. The magnitude of the material was overwhelming and difficult to systematize; leading to many false starts, blind alleys and retakes. My primary critic has been Henrik Tham. Without batting an eye, he went berserk on any text I put in his path. His efforts exceeded by far the call of duty.

Bengt Börjeson helped me get past the morass of small details and to identify some of the larger issues. He also had the uncanny ability to make me feel that there really was a book at the end of the long, dark tunnel.

Leif Holgersson's enthusiasm can move mountains. His comments revitalized depreciated energy depots.

With her insight, and many references to the literature, Britt-Louise Thorberg helped me begin to understand the significance of sexual abuse for drug consumption: a belated but important awakening.

Numerous colleagues have read parts of my manuscripts and given valuable comments. Special thanks to Anders Bergmark, Sven Hessle, Börje Olsson and Lars Oscarsson.

Many people in the Netherlands helped me gain insight into Dutch narcotics policy. With great appreciation I mention Tim Boekhout van Solinge, Annemiek van Bolhuis, John Bombeeck, Peter Cohen, Roel Kerssemakers, Dany Kesteloot, Frans Koopmans, Marcel de Kort, Marieke Langemeijer, Jaap de Leeuw, Ed Leuw, C. W. Maris, Frederiek Mulder, C. M. Ottevanger, Ineke Rienks, Arjan Roskam, Gerrit van Santen, and Gust de Wit.

Jo Campling helped me find my way in the labyrinth of the British publishing industry. Without her this book might never have left Sweden.

TED GOLDBERG

Part I
On Drugs and Drug Consumers

1 Introduction

INTRODUCTORY REMARKS

This book has matured during more than thirty years of contemplation on what is often called 'the drug problem'. My curiosity about narcotics was aroused while I was in elementary school in New York City in the early 1950s. My parents warned me not to accept sweets from strangers as they might contain heroin and I would then be a slave to drugs for the rest of my life. I remember wondering what this mystical power was which could devastate my life. However, it was in 1967 that I first started reflecting on the subject more systematically. 'Flower power' was on the rise in the US and psychedelics had started to spread all over the western world. As a part of my degree in anthropology and sociology I wrote a paper comparing the use of peyote in some American Indian tribes with what I then considered to be 'hallucinogen cults' among some middle-class young Americans. Thereafter I turned my attention to narcotics consumption here in Sweden.

Since then narcotics have been my major field of interest. During a four and a half year period I did extensive participant observation research on the drug scene in Stockholm. By using this method I was able to establish meaningful relationships with problematic consumers of narcotics in their own environment. I have also been employed and done field placement in different drug care units, written books and articles, and given lectures on drugs, both for my students at Stockholm University and for the general public.

Although approximately half a century has passed since I was first warned about heroin it is clear that the belief that drugs contain mystical powers which can eradicate the individual's will and destroy lives still plays an important role in the way western policy makers envision narcotics. Thus far nobody has been able to explain exactly what this power consists of, but it seems that many conceptualize it as a result of biochemical changes in the organism. Once the chemicals get into a person's body he is thought to lose his will. The availability of *narcotics in society* is often defined as the root of the problem.

This book is written from a different perspective: to understand the effects of drugs we must learn to see *society in narcotics*. That is, to interpret people's behavior after drugs have started biochemical processes in their bodies one must have knowledge of social processes and human relationships. A primary objective of this book is to explain how I have come to this point of view.

Over the years there has often been more emotion and enthusiasm in the narcotics debate than knowledge. Not always have well-founded theories and hypotheses succeeded one another, as have prescriptions for how to deal with the problems thought to originate in drugs. There seems to be a longing to find a magic formula which in the wave of a wand will free us from narcotics. By passing the 'correct' laws, informing people through clever campaigns, finding methods of treatment which cure the disease, declaring 'war on drugs', etc., we hope to cast off the yoke. That the measures taken during the past century have not had this effect gives ample reason for reflection.

I don't believe there is any magic formula, and those looking for simple solutions will not find them in this book. I will explain why our efforts thus far have failed to free us from drugs, and why they can't succeed. However unpleasant, I believe it wise to start from the assumption that in the foreseeable future we shall have to live with narcotics.

When I have said this in public I have sometimes been met by the reaction that such statements make people passive. I am aware that since the road is long some may give up, but I believe that resignation is even more likely when people find their efforts thwarted time after time. To find measures which can have a reasonable chance of success we must redefine the problem. This is one of the principal aims of this book.

THE WAR ON DRUGS

During the 1980s and 1990s presidents Reagan and Bush declared war on drugs in the US and political leaders in many other countries followed suit. When President Clinton took office he abandoned his predecessor's rhetoric, but no global peace treaty has been signed and we can identify the thinking behind the war on drugs in many of the measures still being taken in the industrialized world. Most certainly the war on drugs will flame up again wherever and whenever someone in power deems it politically useful. In times of war, when we are fighting to eradicate evil and defend that which is good, measures are accepted which otherwise would meet considerable resistance. For instance, radical shifts in priorities are made, costs become secondary, and it is easier to dismiss rational arguments.

In some countries almost everyone and everything which claims to be against drugs is automatically deemed positive, making it difficult to rationally evaluate ideas and actions. In the words of Danish criminologist Jørgen Jepsen (1992, p. 3): 'The war on drugs is also a war against alternative definitions and descriptions of reality.' My conceptualization of the problem is vastly different from drug war rhetoric.

NARCOTICS REPRESENT MORE THAN THEMSELVES

> When strong emotions are in play, reason doesn't stand a chance. The narcotics debate provides ample proof. Olof Lagercrantz[1]

I have asked myself why so many otherwise rational people become so emotional when discussing drugs. Obviously there are many explanations, and what follows does not aspire to be a complete inventory.

Narcotics are associated with dependency, euphoria, losing control, forgoing duty, giving in to base instincts and seeking pleasure. They are therefore looked upon as a threat to the work ethic; the very fabric of industrial society. As drugs are seen as jeopardizing our survival, we are in imminent danger. With the sword of Damocles hanging over our heads there is no time for reflection or long-term solutions; we must act immediately.

Narcotics are often seen as foreign, non-western; as are the immigrants coming to the industrialized world from all over the globe. Possibly our reaction to narcotics is in part a fear of the unknown; of all that comes from afar. Foreigners bring with them cultural elements we don't understand, and many westerners interpret their feeling of being threatened and ill at ease in their own country as a result of alien influences. Racism and ethnocentrism flourish under these circumstances, and perhaps the fear of narcotics is a more socially acceptable way of venting this kind of emotion.

However, changes are not merely the result of external migration (between countries); there has also been extensive internal migration (within the same country). During the entire twentieth century western nations have experienced rapid and far ranging domestic transition. Durkheim's classical theory of anomie tells us that when a society changes rapidly, many of the norms which previously guided human behaviour are no longer relevant, leading to confusion and fear. Something does not feel right, although it is often difficult to identify what it is. By giving our fears a name, they become easier to bear. Perhaps narcotics have become a symbol for all that is unknown and frightening in our society. As drugs are defined as absolutely bad, totally lacking ameliorating qualities, we can unite with others in unreserved loathing without transgressing socially acceptable boundaries. In secularized societies the devil is no longer suitable for this function. Perhaps narcotics serve as his replacement.

TWO BASIC QUESTIONS

Some of the difference of opinion concerning narcotics is due to emphasizing different aspects of the problem. Two basic questions are:

[1] Former editor-in-chief of *Dagens Nyheter*, Sweden's largest morning newspaper.

1. What can we do to help current misusers of drugs change their behaviour?
2. How can we forestall recruitment?

The first question usually leads to a discussion of different types of treatment and/or punishment, while the second directs our interest towards preventative measures. Logically there is no contradiction between these two approaches and we should make every effort on both fronts. But in reality there is a conflict. Limited resources force us to prioritize, and it is our understanding of the problem that determines what is given precedence. In this book a theoretical approach differing from mainstream thinking will be presented. This provides a basis for questioning current countermeasures, and opens possibilities for formulating alternatives.

ON PUNISHMENT

Narcotics policy is often based on the idea that restrictive and repressive juridical measures are an efficient way to combat drugs. I shall look more closely at some of these efforts, and the secondary harm they give rise to. Here I shall merely state that there is little evidence that punishment helps those who already misuse drugs, or serves as an effective warning to those who run the risk of becoming substantial consumers.

ON TREATMENT

Heretofore published scientific evaluations of different methods of rehabilitation give little reason for optimism. While proponents of different treatment models often claim a certain (high) rate of success, there is little scientific evidence that such is the case. After examining approximately 1000 articles and books on the treatment of alcoholism, Lindström (1992, p. 255f) writes: 'the more rigorously the evaluation is designed, the less favourable are its results. Experimental studies with control or comparison groups have found only weak and short-term effects of alcoholism treatment. Moreover, in unselected groups of alcoholics very little or no outcome differences have been demonstrated between different treatment settings and orientations or between programmes of varying length and intensity.'

Two Professors of Social Work, Anders Bergmark and Lars Oscarsson (p. 170), come to a similar conclusion about narcotics: 'there is just about no evidence that there are effective methods for treating drug abuse. But governmental discussions continue to be based on the assumption that we have such knowledge and treatment methods.' The late Professor of

Medicine, Nils Bejerot (1979, p. 59) observed: 'Extensive study of the literature has taught me that treatment programs, regardless of how successful they may be... can only play a marginal role in our attempts to limit massive drug abuse.' And Professor of Social Work, Bengt Börjeson (1979, p. 49 f) writes: 'We can't eliminate narcotics misuse with treatment: or any other misuse either! Treatment can make it easier, or more difficult, to stop taking drugs. But the net result of treatment is statistically so marginal, that it hardly influences the total number of misusers.'

From my perspective, rehabilitation in itself cannot lead to a permanent reduction in the number of substantial consumers of narcotics, even if we were to develop extremely successful treatment methods in the future. This is because so many people are living in social conditions which are conducive to drug misuse. Some of these macrolevel elements will be discussed in this book. If society concentrates its efforts on rehabilitation, these macrolevel factors will produce a never ending stream of new candidates for treatment. We must therefore put far greater effort into preventative measures if we are serious about significantly reducing the number of problematic consumers of narcotics. We did not eradicate malaria by chasing mosquitoes; we drained the swamps.

In spite of the arguments presented above I am not opposed to treatment per se. But I believe that a more realistic goal is the minimization of suffering rather than getting people off drugs entirely. The labelling model presented in this book can provide important theoretical guidance towards this end. With a reasonable theoretical starting point and more limited objectives it is possible for those working with substantial consumers of narcotics to do something positive for their clients, while keeping costs at a reasonable level. Setting achievable goals also limits staff burnout as experiencing success rather than failure helps maintain motivation.

In summary, rehabilitation has a role to play but from my point of view it is more humane and we have a greater chance of significantly reducing the number of problematic consumers if we concentrate more of our efforts on preventative measures. In the long run this strategy may also prove to be cost efficient.

ON PREVENTION

Almost everyone agrees that prevention is both important and judicious. However, when this idea is translated into practical measures to be applied to narcotics, the result is usually some combination of restrictive and repressive laws, information campaigns and/or police/social workers chasing adolescents to uncover drug consumption before the youth becomes dependent. These are not the kinds of preventative measures advocated in this book.

Instead we shall discuss general political measures. In short, there are parts of the population which are subjected to so much negative societal pressure that they do not believe it possible to create a positive future for themselves and their families. This negative societal pressure originates in political decisions and macrolevel processes, both of which are related to what people must do to survive. Briefly, we live in a competitive society. Competition means that some win and others lose. The question is, what becomes of those who lose in the competition in school, on the labour market, on the housing market, etc.?

To the extent that we can reduce negative societal pressure, we shall also achieve a stable reduction in the number of people who come apart at the seams, for instance in the form of narcotics misuse. Obviously this is not a project which can be accomplished overnight. What is required is long-term planning and resolute political and economic efforts to provide an opportunity for as many people as possible to feel that they are valuable members of society. This may sound utopian, and to some extent it is, but it has also been the lodestar for European welfare states during most of the twentieth century. For instance about 100 years ago there was famine in Sweden. Many sought explanations in the starving individual's personal and moral shortcomings, and believed the problem could be solved by steps directed at the personalities and thinking patterns of these lazy and unproductive people. The founders of the welfare state, on the other hand, saw famine as a societal problem and eliminated it with political and macroeconomic measures.

Individualistic arguments similar to those once used to explain starvation are now directed at problematic consumers of narcotics. Perhaps there is something to be learned from history.

2 Assumptions and Concepts

Researchers from a number of disciplines, i.e. sociology, psychology, psychiatry, medicine, pharmacology, biology, and law, have sought answers to the question: 'Why do people take drugs?' That scientists have thus far been unable to generate a theory which explains all the known facts may come as a surprise to those who are unacquainted with the complexity of the issue. Among the major obstacles to the creation of a comprehensive theory are that different researchers

- make different *assumptions*
- ask different *questions*
- use different *concepts*
- study different *populations*

In this chapter, we shall briefly examine some difficulties in each of these areas.

ASSUMPTIONS

What are Assumptions?

'All understanding of mankind and society, be it common sense or scientific, is based on unconfirmed suppositions.... These assumptions concern (1) the nature of mankind, (2) the nature of society, (3) the relationships between humans and society.... Our theories are based upon our assumptions' (Israel, p. 16).

People with different suppositions have difficulty communicating with each other. That which is self-evident given certain assumptions is a problem in need of explanation given others. For instance, for generations astronomers had assumed that the natural trajectory of celestial bodies was orbital. When they looked in their telescopes they observed that all planets circled the sun, and all moons circled their planets. As their observations confirmed their supposition, nothing remained to be explained. Newton, however, did not accept this assumption. He believed that the natural trajectory of celestial bodies was linear. But even he observed that celestial bodies are in orbit. Based on his assumption this was a major problem; a phenomenon in need of explanation. Why don't celestial bodies act the way they 'should'? In his attempts to find an answer Newton discovered gravity. However, before Newton changed assumptions scientists didn't have a problem to work on; and nobody looks for solutions to problems they aren't aware of. Changing assumptions was a prerequisite for discovering the problem, and eventually solving it.

Drug theories are also based on assumptions. Hopefully researchers and journalists consciously choose their suppositions, but one can't be sure as it is the exception rather than the rule that assumptions are clearly stated. All too often readers are obliged to read between the lines.

Many of those who participate in the drug debate appear neither to be aware of the assumptions they have made, nor the alternatives. All too often unsubstantiated suppositions are presented as scientifically verified truths, giving the impression that nothing remains to be discussed. I shall therefore begin by making some underlying assumptions explicit.

Some Assumptions in the Drug Debate

A common supposition is that those who use narcotics do not understand their own best interests, making it necessary for others to make decisions for them; with or without their consent. One or more of the following assumptions lie behind this reasoning:

1. Those who use narcotics are *intellectually deficient*. Most often it is difficult to discern whether the problem is thought to be of biological or social origin. However, I often get the impression the deficiency is assumed to be genetic.
2. People who use narcotics are *chemically controlled*, i.e. narcotics have biochemical properties which eradicate the individual's ability to make conscious decisions.
3. Narcotics consumers are incompetent, foolhardy, impulsive, and/or have 'sensation-seeking personalities' and therefore *lack inner control*. An *outer control* (other people who make decisions for them) is therefore necessary until such time as the individual stops taking drugs (a prerequisite for developing inner control according to this assumption).

Where would it lead us if we were to abandon these suppositions? What would it imply if we instead were to assume that the range of intelligence among drug consumers approximately parallels that in the population at large, and that people who use drugs understand the consequences of their acts to about the same extent as the rest of us? What are the implications of assuming that narcotics do not control the consumer, but rather, that consumers choose both drugs and the consequences of taking them?

Assuming that an individual is capable of making his own decisions leads to questions such as: why do they make such choices? How do they perceive their alternatives? Assuming that drug consumers are active *subjects* with motives for their actions, instead of seeing them as passive *objects* who at best only react to stimuli (i.e. the chemical effects of drugs), provides an impetus for initiating a dialogue with them. Those who assume that people who use narcotics lack inner control concentrate their efforts on *controlling* consumers, rather than *communicating* with them.

In my research I have chosen to assume that it is possible to carry on a dialogue with people who use substantial quantities of narcotics. I was aware that it would take a long time to build the necessary mutual trust, and to establish a common frame of reference, but I felt that it was worth the effort. This is why I chose participant observation as a principal method. Periodically, during four and a half years, I lived on the drug scene in Stockholm, Sweden. The people I studied used narcotics on a daily or almost daily basis; most often several times a day. As much as possible (without taking drugs myself or doing anything illegal) I shared in their activities. It took time to penetrate the façade they maintain to keep at bay the 'straight' world, which rejects them and holds them in contempt. In the process of establishing close relationships my intentions were challenged and tested time and again. It was necessary to wait until people were ready to talk to me, and I also had to accept that some never let me get very close to them. But gradually many opened themselves as friends and confidants, giving me insights I previously lacked. As the barriers between us gradually eroded a landscape unfolded which had little in common with what is commonly held as true in the drug debate.

Another widespread assumption about those who use drugs is that they are untrustworthy. Most certainly many people who have come into contact with substantial consumers of narcotics would not consider this an assumption, but rather an accurate description of their experiences. Indeed, some of the things I heard during my fieldwork were untrue. There are at least two assumptions that can be made when you discover that someone is not being honest with you.

1. The other person *is* a liar, i.e. *he alone is at fault.*
2. Lies are elements in certain kinds of relationships which the participants have built up together. Deceit originates in social relations which cannot accept certain truths – i.e. *the fault is in the mutually established relationship.*

By merely assuming that those who use drugs are liars we avoid asking ourselves: 'What is it in my way of approaching this person which makes him unwilling or unable to be sincere with me?' This question is of central importance to anyone who wishes to get a glimpse of what lies behind the façade.

We also make assumptions about cause and effect. Some believe that drugs cause behaviour – such as poor schoolwork, delayed social maturation, criminality, etc. Narcotics are seen as explaining many different kinds of (negative) behaviour. For instance in a book on cannabis by Thomas Nordegren, a well-reputed journalist with narcotics as one of his specialties, and the late Kertin Tunving, senior physician at a narcotics treatment unit, readers are informed that:

> Habitual hash consumption has considerable social *consequences* for the individual. His passivity, lack of energy, and inability to meet schedules make it *difficult for him to function in school* or in working life. He *no longer* has the strength to take part in stimulating recreational activities. He often *winds up* being left out socially. While he may hang out with others who smoke, they do not spend their time enjoying common hobbies, or participating in *stimulating discussions and exchanges of opinions*. For the most part, they just sit still and listen to music, sunk in themselves and in their drug induced sensations. It is *mainly this lack of stimulation* – and want of social training – which explains why hash smokers later in life feel that it is difficult to function socially and make friends. (Nordegren and Tunving, p. 178) (my emphasis)

In this quote we can identify a number of assumptions which, from the way they are presented, can easily mislead the reader into believing that the authors are stating facts.

1. The habitual hashish smoker functioned well in school before he began using drugs.
2. He had the energy needed to take part in stimulating recreational activities before cannabis entered the picture.
3. Prior to coming into contact with hash he participated in social life in approximately the same way, and roughly to the same extent, as those who did not become substantial consumers of this drug.
4. He has neither been rejected by others nor did he actively seek out hashish and the people who smoke it; he simply *wound up* a social outcast.
5. He has previously had both the ability and the interest to participate in stimulating discussions and exchanges of opinions, but through the use of hashish, these capabilities have been lost.
6. Before he started taking cannabis he was adequately stimulated and partook in activities which gave him reasonable social training.
7. His consumption of hashish explains why he is currently understimulated, lacks social training, and has difficulty finding social acceptance.

Causation

Simple causation is when a sole factor is seen as explaining a phenomenon. In Figure 2.1, *X* represents that which causes the other things to happen (the independent variable); the arrows pointing in one direction mean 'to

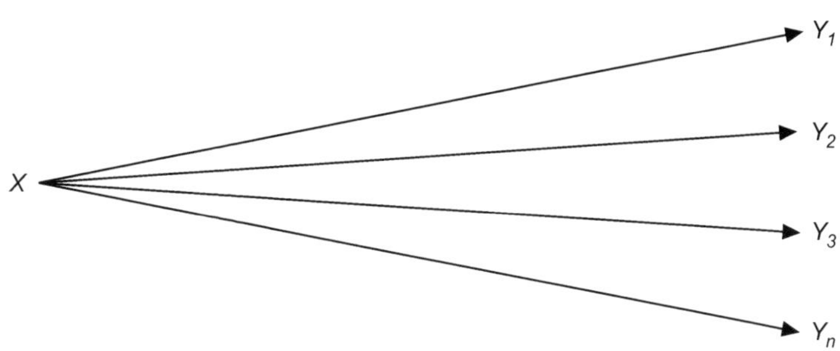

Figure 2.1 Simple causation

cause'; and the *Y*'s represent that which is believed to be the results of the actions of *X* (the dependent variables). If we apply this model to the example above, *X* represents the chemical effects of hashish, Y_1 represents passivity, Y_2 becoming a social outcast, Y_3 loss of ability to succeed in school, and Y_n lack of social maturity. Drugs and drugs alone cause it all!

If on the other hand we were to assume that drug consumption is not the cause of behaviour, but rather one of many elements in a complex behavioural pattern, we paint an entirely different picture. This assumption implies that instead of concentrating on the drugs themselves, other factors must also be taken into consideration; i.e. the individual's earlier life experiences, what type of person he was before he started taking drugs, the situations in which drugs are used, the society in which he lives, etc. In other words we reject simple causation. Instead, human behaviour is looked upon as being extremely complex and the result of different variables mutually influencing each other over an extended period of time.

In Figure 2.2, X_1, X_2, $X_3, \ldots X_n$ represent different variables, i.e. family relations, preschool experiences, school experiences, the functions of formal education in society, relations to peers, experiences with drugs, etc. Arrows pointing in both directions represent feedback relationships (the variables mutually affect each other); and in this example, *Y* is drug consumption.

In other words, through his relationships with other people and his contacts with different social institutions the individual has gained knowledge of himself, the society in which he lives, his position in society, etc. These factors affect his choice of whether to take drugs or abstain, and, if he chooses the former, his way of interpreting drug-induced experiences. This in turn influences his relations to other people and to society.

Nordegren and Tunving, and many others who write about narcotics, do in fact discuss these kinds of variables. But as we can see in the quote above, when they draw conclusions they revert to simple causation. They seem to

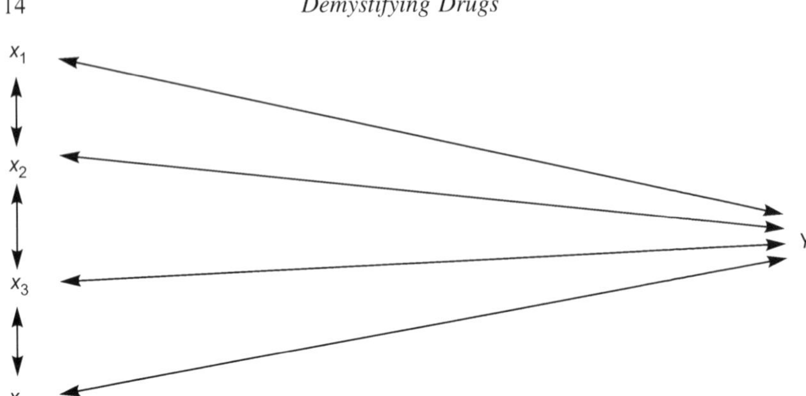

Figure 2.2 Reciprocal and circular causation

forget all of the other factors and transform drugs into *the underlying cause*. This type of oversimplification makes it more difficult to understand drug consumption and reduces our chances of finding reasonable reactions to the problems made visible by it.

In summary, some (possibly most) people assume that the drugs themselves are the root of the evil. As an alternative I propose that by studying human relationships, and the societal conditions which shape them, we can unravel the underlying causes of drug consumption.

Different Assumptions Lead to Different Conceptions of the Problem

Even if people with different assumptions were able to agree about what needs to be explained, they would still have great difficulty communicating with each other; primarily because they have different conceptual frameworks. For instance, in trying to explain how a drug abuser managed to get off drugs, a deeply religious person might speak of the work of God, Providence, a miracle, etc., while those who don't believe in God would find these concepts of little value.

I do not believe that in the foreseeable future it will be possible to create a generally accepted conceptual framework to explain narcotics consumption. But if we are going to start somewhere, it seems reasonable that we openly declare our assumptions on narcotics, and also give an account of our basic assumptions on the nature of mankind and society. In the words of philosopher Sven-Erik Liedman (p. 192f):

> [Scientists] present their results as unconditional truths, even though they, in reality, are based upon undeclared (and maybe deeply unconscious) assumptions. We speak with scientific authority and pretend (or

imagine) that science is above all conflict, while choosing sides without as much as a comment.

I will therefore account for some of the assumptions upon which this book is based.

On Human Nature

Most scientists agree that man is both a biological and a social being. But upon closer examination, we find significant differences of opinion. How much of human behaviour should be attributed to biological and social variables, respectively? Consider the following continuum:

Biological being ———————————————— Social being

The positions at either end of the continuum represent extreme viewpoints. Those who place themselves at the far left believe that social factors are irrelevant. Human behaviour is seen as solely the product of genes, instincts, metabolism, etc. Behaviour is reduced to biochemical processes. In a similar manner, those who place themselves at the extreme social end of the scale deny any influence from biological variables. Perhaps the most extreme behaviourists take this stance. Even though both of these extreme positions are probably very unusual among serious researchers today, the dispersion of positions along the continuum is extensive.

My position is based on the work of Charles H. Cooley, one of symbolic interactionism's foremost representatives. Although symbolic interactionists are well aware that biology is an essential factor in human behaviour, they emphasize social variables more than most other theoretical schools. The basic assumption is that the individual has become what he is through interaction (social contacts) with other people. To exemplify this idea Cooley constructs a pair of identical twins, born in China of Chinese parents. One of the twins remains in China, while the other is adopted and raised by a family in the US. Cooley (p. 6f) concludes:

> they would grow up alike physically, and also, probably, in temperament, as active or sluggish, thoughtful or impetuous, but would be wholly different in dress, language, and ideas. In these the child bred in America would be far more like his American foster-brothers than like his twin-brother in China.

Cooley poses the rhetorical question: 'Is the individual a product of society?' and answers:

> Yes, in the sense that everything human about him has a history in the social past. If we consider the two sources from which he draws his life,

> heredity and communication, we see that what he gets through the germ-plasma has a social history in that it has had to adapt itself to past society in order to survive: the traits we are born with are such as have undergone a social test in the lives of our ancestors. And what he gets from communication – language, education and the like – comes directly from society. Even physical influences, like food and climate, rarely reach us except as modified and adapted by social conditions. (Ibid., p. 48)

The relationship between biological and social factors has been summarized by alcohol researcher Jan Blomqvist (p. 26): Biological factors are basic potentialities

> setting the ultimate limits for the capacities, emotional reactions and ways of interacting with her/his environment which s/he may develop.... [Social factors] may be conceived of as historical and structural constraints, setting the stage for a person's construction of her/his lived reality, and setting the ultimate limits for the values s/he may acquire, and for the options of realizing these values which s/he may perceive and actually have.

Put concisely, my basic assumption on human nature is: we are all born with a wealth of biological aptitudes; which of these we shall develop, and to what extent, is dependent upon the social environment that we and our forebears have been exposed to. This implies that individuals are not predestined to any specific drug behaviour (i.e. becoming an alcoholic or a teetotaler), but that all of us can potentially use drugs in different ways. *The sum of our social relations determines how we will use drugs.*

Subject or Object?

Another essential assumption on human nature is whether people should be considered as subjects or as objects. A *subject* is an active being who creates and transforms his environment, while an *object* is passive – virtually defenceless against the influence of other agents. An object does not act – at best he reacts. In the context of drugs, the difference can be illuminated by the following quotations:

Drug consumers as objects: 'That the individual has become *chemically controlled and has serious deficiencies or completely lost self-control* vis-à-vis intoxicants is the essential nature of narcotics addiction' (Bejerot, 1979, p. 90) (my emphasis).

Drug consumers as subjects: 'The stereotypes of heroin will also depict someone's involvement with the drug as nothing more than a horrible chemical enslavement which it is impossible to throw off, whereas heroin users' own accounts are better understood as those of people *exercising choices and decisions in their lives* – even though they will often come to regret those same choices and decisions' (Pearson, 1987a, p. 5) (my emphasis).

To summarize my own position: people are objects in certain situations and during certain periods in their lives, but they almost always have some degree of freedom to choose their actions. That is, people can act, but there are limitations. Thus we are both subjects and objects. Humans are born into a society which already exists and is not a product of their own actions. They are also born in an era, a country, a social class, and a family. The individual cannot choose any of these things himself, and all of them will have an enormous impact on his life experiences. To this extent, we are all objects. However, within the framework of these limitations, there is leeway to act, and each of us is responsible for how we make use of the opportunities at our disposal. In other words, everyone is at least to some extent a subject. But we must keep in mind that there are enormous differences in the freedom of action available to different individuals. This is of vital significance for understanding drug consumption.

The Individual in Relation to Society

An important difference of opinion regarding the individual's relationship to society can be illustrated by looking at the importance attached to 'ideas'. Some people assume that thoughts in themselves are decisive in determining an individual's activities. That is, behaviour is interpreted as a process in which an individual is exposed to ideas and reacts to them.

In the context of drugs, these people focus on what they call 'the drug culture'. They believe that it is of major importance that positive statements about drugs such as those to be found in certain kinds of music, and in the lifestyles of some celebrities, entice adolescents into using drugs. In other words it is believed that the dissemination of certain ideas leads to drug abuse. For instance, Nordegren and Tunving (p. 68) write: 'To be sure, popular music... was the principal spreader of cannabis.'

An alternative way of looking at the role of ideas is to interpret thoughts and actions as emerging from, and expressing, the individual's life-situation. That is, neither deliberations nor acts are formed in a void; both evolve from the individual's experiences in society. From this perspective, emphasis is put on questions such as: What is the role of narcotics in relation to the rest of the consumer's life? How do drugs fit into his present situation, his future outlooks, and his earlier life-experiences? In other words, the idea of using drugs must be relevant to the individual's life-situation before he will act upon it. If drugs lack relevance for his life, he will either abstain or give them up after a short period of experimentation. Therefore an important task for drug research is to discover and describe the kinds of life-experiences which lead people to feel that narcotics consumption is meaningful. This will be a subject of primary concern in this book.

DIFFERENT SCIENTIFIC DISCIPLINES RAISE DIFFERENT QUESTIONS

Lettieri (p. 10) states that a theory on drug abuse must cover several of the following subjects:

1. why people begin taking drugs
2. why people continue their drug-taking behaviour
3. how or why drug taking escalates to abuse
4. why or how people stop taking drugs
5. what accounts for recidivism.

Which questions a scientist finds relevant are dependent upon his assumptions and general theoretical framework, which in turn stem from being schooled in a certain academic discipline. Furthermore, individual researchers have personal preferences and choose to emphasize different aspects of the problem. Therefore it is hardly surprising that different researchers focus on different questions.

TERMINOLOGICAL DIFFICULTIES

As drug researchers come from many different academic disciplines there is no commonly accepted terminology. Every scientist has learned the concepts and perspectives of the academic subjects he has studied prior to focusing on narcotics. Every discipline has its traditions which are passed on to the aspiring researcher during his basic education. For example, medical students are taught about the body and how it functions. A language suitable for this purpose has developed through the centuries in medical schools around the world. In a similar fashion, sociologists study societal processes, psychoanalysts emphasize the importance of the family, etc. Each discipline has different theories and terminology to describe what they are studying.

Sometimes scientists borrow concepts from other subjects and try to give them a meaning which fits into their own discipline. However, instead of simplifying matters, this usually enhances the confusion. When researchers with different backgrounds use the same concepts, they can be led to believe that they understand each other while in reality they are talking about different things. For instance, for the medical profession *pathological* refers to the human body, but sociologists use it to describe a societal process. For many psychologists, *alienation* refers to an individual's state of mind, while sociologists use it as a macroconcept. In other words, there are numerous pitfalls on the road to a generally accepted conceptual framework.

POPULATIONS

Presently drugs are used in all known cultures. However, which drugs are taken, how they are consumed, and what they are used for, varies considerably. The picture one gets depends on who is being observed, and who is observing from what vantage point. For instance, an anthropologist studying South American Indians chewing coca leaves is looking at something very different from a sociologist looking at inner-city crack consumption in the US, although coca leaves and crack originate from the same plant. A scientist doing research on heroin consumption from the vantage point of a university library does not discern the same things as a policeman pounding his beat. Observing different populations and using different methods contributes to the divergence of theories and opinions. Furthermore that which is factual in one context is not necessarily pertinent in another. For instance, the experiences of doctors working solely with the most severe cases may not be relevant for moderate consumers.

USE–ABUSE

An opinion often voiced in the drug debate is that 'all non-medical use of narcotics is abuse'. Based on the assumption that we can get people to abstain from illegal drugs by defining all consumption as abhorrent, there may be some justification for making such a statement. However, if one believes that we must understand why individuals take drugs in order to find effective countermeasures, equating all drug consumption causes more harm than good. There are two principal reasons for this.

1. *The significance and purpose of the act* – Acts which appear to be similar may have different meanings and serve disparate purposes for the individuals involved. For instance, if a young couple go to the theatre together, one of them may be there to enjoy a cultural experience and broaden his/her horizons; while the other may attend in order to become more interesting in the eyes of the former. This is so self-evident that I assume most readers feel that it is trivial and unnecessary to point it out. That I do so is because I suspect that the idea that different individuals can have different reasons for using the same drug may not be equally self-evident. We shall return to this in Chapter 4.

2. *Sliding between concepts* – By equating the meanings of two different concepts one can mistakenly conclude that what holds true for one of the concepts is also true for the other. I suspect that those who consider all *use* to be *abuse* may be sliding between the concepts *illegal* and *abuse*. It is true that possession of substances that are classified as narcotics is illegal. However, there is no logical reason to equate *illegal* with *abuse*. *Use* as well as *abuse* of both legal and illegal substances are all logically possible.

It is not only logical to differentiate between *illegal* and *abuse*; it is essential to do so to understand some of the varying meanings drug consumption can have for different people. We lose more than we gain by putting all consumption of illegal drugs into the same category. Doing so is just as absurd as calling all *use* of alcohol, *abuse*. It is easy to understand that a person sipping wine on a festive occasion has different objectives than a vagrant gulping from his bottle every day.

Many researchers who wish to emphasize that people can have different reasons for taking drugs, have created concepts to differentiate between various patterns of use. For instance, a US government report differentiates between five types of consumption (see Wurmser, p. 7). American sociologist James Inciardi (p. 95) distinguishes four categories: experimenters, social-recreational users, involved users and dysfunctional abusers. Professor of Psychiatry Norman Zinberg sees a continuum with controlled users at one end and compulsive users at the other. However, he clearly notes that 'even the most severely affected alcoholics and addicts, who may be grouped at one end of the spectrum of drug use, exhibit some control' (Zinberg, p. 7).

Most commonly two categories are distinguished, use and abuse. I have used these concepts in my earlier writings but have felt myself obliged to abandon them as they are interpreted in so many different ways that they now lack precision.

PROBLEMATIC CONSUMERS–RECREATIONAL CONSUMERS

My conceptualization is a continuum with those for whom drugs mean nothing at one end and people who make drugs their first priority at the other. I use *problematic consumer* to designate a person who allows psychoactive substances to play a dominant role in his life, i.e. those who approach the far end of my continuum. *Substantial consumer* will be used as a synonym.

Recreational consumers, on the other hand, consider drugs as one aspect among many in their lives. Borrowing an idea from Zinberg, Stanton

Peele (p. 8) writes: '[recreational consumers] subordinate their desire for a drug to other values, activities, and personal relationships. When engaged in other pursuits that they value, these users do not crave the drug or manifest withdrawal on discontinuing their drug use.'

Although frequency of consumption is a significant aspect in my definitions, it isn't a sufficient criterion. Under certain conditions it is possible to take drugs regularly without their governing one's activities. In societies where narcotics are readily accessible, socially accepted and inexpensive they can be used in this way. In the Netherlands for instance, cannabis is more or less socially accepted and can be readily and affordably purchased in any number of coffee shops. It is therefore possible to take the drug on a daily basis with a minimum of social and economic cost. Some people smoke cannabis in a manner comparable to those whose alcohol consumption primarily consists of taking a drink after work or before going to bed. To my way of thinking people who take drugs in this manner shouldn't be considered problematic consumers.

CONCLUSION

Problematic consumers and recreational consumers may well take the same psychoactive substances, but the meanings behind the act and their motives are very different. Statistically, a host of studies based on different populations show that they also have different psychosocial backgrounds. It is therefore important that drug consumption be placed in a macroperspective. But people with similar psychosocial backgrounds are not predestined to a given pattern of drug consumption. Individual social experiences and personal characteristics differentiate people from comparable environments. Therefore we must also direct our attention to drug consumers as individuals.

Accordingly, explanations for different patterns of drug consumption should principally be sought both on the macrolevel, where people are moulded by the society in which they live/have lived, and on the microlevel, where individuals are shaped through interaction with others in intimate small groups.

3 The Social Components of Drug-Influenced Behaviour

WHAT ARE NARCOTICS?

Many people believe that narcotics constitute a precise, scientifically limited category of chemical substances with objectively established (harmful) properties which clearly distinguish them from other drugs, i.e. medicine. In reality there are no chemical, biological or medical criteria that make it possible to determine whether or not a given substance is a narcotic. *Narcotic* denotes a number of drugs with nothing more in common than that they are chemical compounds which for some almost indefinable reason have been placed on a schedule entitled narcotic substances – rendering them a certain legal status. In its current usage narcotic is not a precise medical, biological or chemical concept; it is solely a legal classification.

The change in conceptual usage has been described by a Swedish government commission, The Drug Treatment Committee.

> Linguistically, the word narcotic comes from narkotikós (Gk. numbing). Biologically, narcosis means reduction of activity in cells, cell membranes, or organisms. Anaesthetics – and thereby narcotics in a strictly biological sense – are thus, those substances that bring about narcosis or general anaesthesia, i.e. ether and chloroform. However, narcotic is now often used to denote certain other substances that have an anaesthetic, soporific, or pain relieving effect. Primarily this applies to opium and its extracts, such as opium alkaloids (i.e. morphine), derivatives (i.e. heroin), and certain synthetically produced substances similar to morphine (i.e. methadone).
>
> Through international conventions narcotic gained a legal implication, and was defined as those substances which are encompassed by the conventions. It is important to note that coca leaves, cocaine, and cannabis have stimulating rather than anaesthetic effects, and in several other respects differ from the opiates. (Narkomanvårdskommittén, 1967, p. 19)

DIFFERENCES BETWEEN VARIOUS NARCOTICS

Since the 1960s, much energy has been spent discussing the biochemical effects of narcotics, their 'strength' and the dangers of usage. It takes little more than a rumour that a new drug is on its way for the discussion to start anew. Toward the end of the 1960s, it was claimed that hallucinogens such as 'STP' and 'purple haze acid' were much stronger than LSD. That the hippies who took these drugs were in great peril, was repeated time after time in the mass media. During the 1970s, the use of heroin increased in many European countries and recurrent reports implied that anyone who used it faced immediate doom. Heroin was reportedly so 'strong' that mass deaths among users were predicted. In the 1980s it was claimed that cocaine and crack would enslave a multitude of people and in the 1990s ecstasy and designer drugs were proclaimed a lethal peril to an entire generation of adolescents. The recurrent picture being painted is that narcotics threaten our civilization. When a given narcotic proves not to have this devastating effect, a new drug is soon given the same role.

In this chapter, we will discuss why placing so much emphasis on the biochemical effects of different substances leads us down a blind alley.

BIOCHEMICAL EFFECTS

When an individual takes a psychoactive drug, it sets off biochemical processes in the body. The physiological effects of a given drug vary depending on many factors: for instance, the chemical properties of the drug, the dose taken, the presence of other drugs in the body, the method of taking the drug, the body's metabolic rate, the interval between doses, the time it takes for the body to break down and excrete the substance, physiological changes in the body caused by previous consumption, i.e. tolerance, sensitizing, cell deterioration, etc.

Our understanding of what takes place in an organism on the biochemical level when drugs are induced, is far from complete, and as in all aspects of narcotics there are differences of opinion. The discourse within the different natural sciences is best presented by their own researchers and I shall not attempt to do so here. Instead I merely state that the biochemical effects of drugs are a part of the drug experience, and that they play a role in the consequent pattern of behaviour. However, these physiological effects in themselves do not constitute a sufficient explanation for behaviour exhibited after taking narcotics. If we consider this in the context of the models of causality described in the previous chapter, reducing behaviour to biochemical effects is reverting to simple causation – one factor (a chemical) is the cause of another (behaviour). Why the biochemical effects of narcotics are neither the sole nor the principal cause of subsequent behaviour is the subject of this chapter. We shall discuss why it is necessary to view the physiological changes initiated by drugs as one of several factors in an interwoven chain where a number of causes play an important role. The chain in its entirety has not as yet been fully mapped, but some of the other elements in it are known, and we shall examine them. But first we shall discuss some of the phenomena which cannot be explained by referring to drug-induced biochemical changes.

PLACEBO

The placebo effect in medicine has been defined as: 'any therapeutic procedure (or that component of therapeutic procedure) which is deliberately given to have an effect on, or does have an effect on, a symptom, syndrome or disease, but which is without specific activity for the condition to be treated' (Shapiro, 1963). 'The *normative* history of medicine, as evidenced by its therapeutic practices, was until relatively recently (eighty or ninety years ago) largely the history of the placebo effect' (Shapiro, 1960).

> . . . placebos can mimic many of the effects usually thought to be the exclusive property of active pharmacological agents. Some of these are: a *time effect curve* (a peak or maximum effect), a *cumulative effect* (increasing therapeutic effect with repeated doses), *carryover effects* (persistence of effect after cessation of treatment), and an inverse relationship between efficacy of a placebo and the severity of a symptom (a more severe symptom responds less effectively). (Jospe, p. xv) (my italics)

'The literature also shows many examples of tolerance sensitivity and idiosyncrasy to placebos, as well as increasing improvement with increasing dose of placebo' (Shapiro, 1963).

In narcotics research placebo has a somewhat different meaning. In experiments scientists have repeatedly shown that many individuals who thought they had taken narcotics or alcohol acted as if they were under the influence of drugs, although they had been given a placebo (a substance with no known psychoactive effects). Even in situations where subjects were not led to believe that they had been given psychoactive drugs, only told that there was a chance that they would be administered such substances, a significant number changed their comportment. Their behaviour was so convincing that the researchers who were observing them placed them in the experiment group when in fact they had been given a placebo.

A common method used in this kind of research is the double-blind experiment. Subjects are divided into two groups; the experiment group is administered psychoactive substances, while the control group is given a placebo such as tap water or sugar (sometimes other substances are used that give some kind of sensation on the skin or elsewhere in the body, e.g. nicotinic acid). Neither the test subjects nor the researchers who will make observations and conduct interviews know who has been given psychoactive substances. This is done to minimize the risk that the research results will be influenced by preconceived expectations of how people react to certain substances. After the subjects have reported their experiences and the researchers who have observed them have completed their evaluations, then the participants are informed as to who has received which substances.

These kinds of experiment show clearly that many subjects who had been given psychoactive substances reported no effects and behaved 'normally' enough to be classified as part of the control group by observing researchers. Many individuals in the control group became influenced by placebo substances and behaved in such a way that they convinced both themselves and the researchers evaluating them that they had received a psychoactive drug. Furthermore, it is known that some people

> can become addicted to placebos and will show many of the formal traits of drug dependence, including a tendency to increase the dose, an inability to stop taking the placebos without psychiatric help, an almost compulsive desire to take the placebos, and withdrawal or abstinence syndrome on sudden deprivation of the 'medication'. (Jospe, p. xv)

Even those with considerable experience can be fooled by placebo substances. Lasagna et al. (p. 1019) administered placebos to both detoxified problematic consumers and university students who had never tried narcotics. Approximately the same number in each group reacted to the placebo.

A problem with laboratory experiments is that we can never be sure of the extent to which behaviour exhibited in a contrived setting corresponds to the way people act in ordinary life situations. However, the placebo effect can be observed outside the laboratory. The following example is from my fieldwork.

Among the problematic cannabis consumers I studied there was a clearly pronounced norm against selling low quality hash to friends. However, selling bad drugs to outsiders was accepted. As there were so few clearly defined rules among my research subjects, I carefully examined the situation when two of them broke this norm. The situation was as follows: There was a shortage of hash in town at the time. The two men bought henna, a reddish-brown dyestuff. Henna looks like hashish, and with the help of an iron and a wet towel, it can be pressed into cakes which resemble hash. I was with them in an apartment when they made the cakes, and took it for granted that they were planning to sell them to people they didn't know. But later the same day, I observed them selling the cakes to their friends. When I asked them how they could do such a thing I was told: 'Everybody trusts us. They know that we would never sell them bad hash. When we tell them it's good, they'll believe us and get "high".'[1] Later I asked those who had smoked the henna if they got off on it. All of them said yes.

One possible interpretation is that henna is in fact a psychoactive drug. But I don't think this is plausible. I have never seen it mentioned as such in literature, nor has anyone I've met in the field made such a claim. Therefore, we must seek explanations other than henna's biochemical effects for why experienced cannabis consumers can get high after smoking it.

CONTACT HIGH

Contact high is an expression used by substantial consumers of hash which sheds some light on the placebo effect. The first time I heard the term was when one of my research subjects told me that he was going to a party that evening, but he wasn't going to smoke (hash). He said he didn't have to as everybody else would be so stoned that he would get off just by walking into the place. As he put it, he would be 'pulled up to their level'. When I replied that I didn't understand what he meant, he explained that he had been high so many times in his life that he knew what it was all about, and that he could use suggestion to get himself on to that level.

Initially I was sceptical of the idea of contact high. At the time I believed that it was the drugs themselves which caused changes in the individual's mental state. But on further contemplation contact high isn't as strange as it first appears. Perhaps a way to understand the concept is to put yourself in the following two situations. After drinking a certain amount of alcohol you arrive at a party where the participants are: (1) appreciably inebriated; (2) sober. The question is: Will you feel and act equally intoxicated in both situations? If not, why not? In both cases you have the same amount of alcohol in your blood.

Contact high is in fact a phenomenon most people recognize. We are sensitive to others in our surroundings, and we sometimes let ourselves be influenced by the prevailing mood of those we are with. Most people don't enjoy being the only one drunk at a social gathering.

[1] It is not possible to give a precise definition of slang expressions used in drug circles. As we shall see later on, ambiguity is an integral part of the drug scene. In this book, I will use the word *high* to indicate a change of sensory perception in conjunction with drug consumption. Getting off is a synonym for getting high. That getting stoned is also a synonym is significant. Getting high and getting off indicate that you are going up, while getting stoned gives the opposite impression. Perhaps in early usage stoned was used to describe the heavy feeling sometimes experienced under the influence of (large doses of) hash. However, if there ever was such a distinction, it has now disappeared, and getting high, getting off, and getting stoned are used interchangeably. Apparently it is not important to convey to yourself or others whether you are up or down, only that you are somewhere else.

PROBLEMATIC CONSUMERS OF OPIATES HARDLY TOUCH THE STUFF

Another reason for not primarily concentrating on the biochemical effects of drugs is that even those who are considered substantial consumers of opiates most often take them in small quantities. In an autobiographical novel William S. Burroughs describes his life as a heroin addict in the US during the 1930s and 1940s. Even in those days the narcotics sold on the street were so cut (diluted) that they contained only about 10 per cent heroin (Burroughs, p. 68). For economic reasons the heroin sold on the street today is often cut still further. Heroin is very expensive. The sales chain is long – from the producer, via smugglers, to larger wholesalers, to smaller wholesalers, to street dealers, and finally to the consumer. At each level profits are improved by cutting the heroin powder with another powder such as glucose.[2] According to information I've received from the police in New York City, the heroin being sold on the street there most often contains only 5 per cent heroin. That is, 95 per cent of what is injected is glucose or other non-psychoactive substances. (Talk about sugar pills!) Today's heroin addicts in NYC are in reality hardly taking any heroin at all. In fact their tolerance for the drug is so low that one way of getting rid of stool pigeons is to give them relatively pure heroin: they die from the overdose.

The situation in the UK is similar: there is not much heroin in the bags sold on the street. Based on a participant observation study of problematic consumers, Professor of Social Work Geoffrey Pearson (1987a, p. 10) relates that £5 bags of heroin are adulterated with glucose and brick-dust, and contain only milligram quantities of the drug itself.

However, the purity of heroin sold on the streets varies from country to country and from time to time. There are counteracting forces towards greater or lesser purity and what problematic consumers actually inject at any given moment is a result of the current 'balance of power' between these different elements. For instance some of the factors tending to decrease purity are cartels or monopolies dominating the market, diminished supply (if for instance the customs authorities or police have recently intercepted a large shipment), many middlemen before the drugs hit the streets, etc. Factors tending to increase purity are many suppliers competing with each other, easy accessibility, few middlemen, etc. These factors in turn are influenced by for instance the number of consumers in the area (demand), the effectiveness of the authorities, proximity to producing countries, the number of producing countries, the quantities produced, etc.

[2] Heroin is not the only drug diluted in this manner. Terry Williams (p. 6), a sociologist, who did participant observation studies among cocaine dealers in New York City, writes: 'With powder, impurity was the key to profit: cocaine brought high returns because it could be adulterated ("cut") several times.' He also gives a vivid description of how it is done.

So even if the purity of the heroin sold on the streets is commonly approximately 5 per cent, and can even be 1 per cent (Inciardi, p. 69), it can also be 40 per cent. We shall use the figure 22.5 per cent (the average of 5 and 40 per cent) for a mathematical example. An individual who takes four injections per day (a common amount for a problematic consumer when he has money and heroin is available) containing 0.2 grams of powder per injection, will inject:

> 0.2 gram powder per injection × four injections per day × 0.225 gram heroin per gram powder = 0.18 gram heroin per day.

In this case, our problematic consumer takes a daily dose of approximately 180 mg of pure heroin. I will explain shortly why this can be regarded as a relatively small dose, but first I want to emphasize that some studies indicate that substantial consumers do not have access to heroin every day. I was able to establish this during my fieldwork in Stockholm, and Windsløw (p. 154) quotes two studies, one from the USA and the other from Denmark, which indicate that on the average, heroin addicts only manage to get drugs on 40 per cent of the days when they are on drugs. If this is true, then it would mean that our calculation of the daily dose 180 mg would have to be reduced to 72 mg of heroin. But even this lower figure is more than twice as high as Windsløw's own calculations where he estimates the average daily dose for an opiate abuser in Denmark at 29 mg opiates per day (ibid., p. 152).

The idea that today's problematic consumers of opiates do not consume large amounts of narcotics is supported by two different kinds of data: comparing the amounts consumed today with those taken in the past, and by looking at withdrawal symptoms.

Windsløw refers to studies measuring the dosages taken about 100 years ago, about 70 years ago, and those of today. According to a study published in 1893, the average daily dose was 475 mg per day (ibid., p. 89), while a corresponding figure published in 1929 was about 750 mg per day (ibid., p. 18). The 180 mg per day in my example is almost certainly an overestimate, yet still far below these figures.

Another method of comparison is to look at withdrawal symptoms. The Swedish Drug Treatment Committee gives the following description of a classic withdrawal:

> 8–14 hours after the latest injection, a few insignificant symptoms are noticeable, i.e. yawning, perspiration, runny nose, tears, and uneasy sleep. After 18–24 hours, the initial symptoms are more pronounced and other symptoms appear: dilation of the pupils, goose bumps, and spasms in different muscle groups. The patient complains of back aches and muscle pains. He alternates between freezing and hot flushes. The patient

> lies hunched up in bed with his knees drawn up toward his chest. He pulls the quilts and blankets around himself in spite of the heat in the room. There are continuous spasms in the legs and feet.
>
> 36 hours after the last dose, there is pronounced and intense restlessness. The patient is constantly in motion. He feels nauseous, vomits, and has diarrhoea. There is significant weight loss. Respiration increases as does blood pressure. Body temperature is somewhat above normal. Withdrawal symptoms reach maximum intensity after 40–48 hours, and then slowly begin to subside. After seven to ten days all of the objective symptoms of withdrawal have disappeared.
>
> (Narkomanvårdskommittén, 1969, p. 80)

It would surprise me if very many people in the industrialized world in the past 20 years have seen a street addict experience the withdrawal symptoms described above. Compare the above description with what Fugelstad reports from Serafen hospital detox unit in Stockholm: 'On the basis of the physicians' diagnoses withdrawal difficulties were estimated for patients admitted to the ward.... Somewhat surprisingly, most of the withdrawals were not complicated and, *often, there were no withdrawal symptoms*' (Fugelstad, p. 10) (my emphasis). She continues: 'this was noteworthy as most of the patients were actively abusing opiates before admission. In the cases where detoxification proved difficult there was an underlying alcohol or tablet abuse, or the patients had serious psychiatric problems' (ibid.).

Researchers have been reporting similar findings for about half a century. Chein et al. (p. 163) note that in the 1950s and 1960s the heroin in New York City was so cut that severe withdrawal symptoms were unusual. In the 1970s, an American physician, Andrew Weil writes: 'In a supportive setting, with proper suggestion, a heroin addict can withdraw without medication other than aspirin and have little more discomfort than that of a moderate cold' (Weil, p. 46). Pearson (1987a, p. 150) notes that in England in the 1980s abstinence compares to 'a bad dose of influenza', and Inciardi (p. 74f) draws the same conclusion in the US in the 1990s. While today's substantial consumers may suffer psychologically when they are unable to obtain drugs, they no longer experience the lengthy physical effects described by the Drug Treatment Committee. This is because today's problematic consumers do not take particularly large quantities of opiates, even during their most active drug periods. They are substantial consumers compared to the rest of the population, but they take very little compared to their counterparts several generations ago.

One could argue that even if today's dosages are very low, 180 mg per day, or even 29 mg per day, is still enough to get high. Maybe so, but as I have already noted people get off on placebos, so for some zero mg is enough. And that is the crux of the matter. Reference to the biochemical effects of drugs is insufficient to explain the behaviour of consumers. If the biochemical effects were decisive, today's problematic consumers of opiates should find it easier to stop taking drugs than substantial consumers of yesteryear, simply because their intake is so much lower. To my knowledge, no researchers claim that such is the case.

To summarize:

- some research subjects who have been given placebos, but believe they have been given psychoactive substances, behave in such a way that researchers observing them become convinced that these people are under the influence of drugs;
- research subjects can behave as if they have taken drugs even in situations where they have merely been told that there was some chance that they might be given a psychoactive substance;
- some who have actually been given narcotics report no effects. In laboratory experiments, these subjects behave 'normally' enough to fool the researchers observing them;
- through self-suggestion, people can get high even though they know they haven't taken any drugs;
- people become addicted to substances that consist almost entirely of sugar; and even to placebos;
- today's problematic consumers of heroin use the drug in very small quantities. Still they have great difficulty in giving up narcotics.

To explain all of this, our discussion must include factors other than the biochemical effects of drugs.

SET

In the context of psychoactive substances, *set* can be defined as the sum of physiological attributes, psychological disposition, life-experiences, expectations, knowledge of drugs, etc. that the individual bears with him from the past. Set determines whether or not an individual will decide to try drugs and also plays a major role in the way he experiences these substances once he has taken them.

In most contexts when human behaviour is discussed, set is self-evident. Normally it is considered necessary to take into consideration the history of the individual when explaining their behaviour. For example, courts in many countries carefully consider such information before passing sentence.

American anthropologist Michael Montagne (p. 54f) discusses another important aspect of set – the significance of beliefs for understanding the effect of drugs. Montagne refers to different images and metaphors in conjunction with tranquillizer use. People who take these drugs can for instance regard them either as 'a ticket to normality' or 'a chemical strait-jacket'. When these metaphors become fundamental to a consumer, a conceptual transformation takes place: the 'as' becomes 'is'.

It is probably easiest to understand the importance of set if we start with an example where no drugs are involved. By doing this, it is possible to exclude biochemical effects as a possible cause of the behaviour. Let us take a look at a situation that evokes a wide range of reactions from different people – riding a roller-coaster. Some people wouldn't dream of putting their foot on one – they just say no. But even those who give it a try react differently. Everyone on the roller-coaster is subjected to the same stimuli; they are all going equally fast, climbing to the same height, are exposed for the same period of time, etc. Yet reactions differ, even for individuals of the same age, gender, weight, etc. Some interpret the situation as dangerous and responses range from nervousness to panic. Other people become happy or even exhilarated, and a certain per cent are indifferent. I don't suppose that very many fighter pilots are particularly impressed by a ride on a roller-coaster.

It is possible that some of the difference in reactions to roller-coasters may be due to differences in physiology, but this does not explain why some people never give it a try. And for those who do ride, I am certain that most readers can easily see the importance of set in determining how they interpret the experience.

To elucidate the significance of set for understanding the effects of drugs, we shall take a closer look at the mythicized 'euphoric' effect that is often attributed to opiates. If the feeling of euphoria were solely, or mainly, a result of the human body's reaction to the biochemical effects of heroin or morphine, then all of those who take these substances should experience euphoria. However, such is not the case. For instance, in a study where researchers administered opiates to naive university students (i.e. people with no previous experience of opiates), Lasagna et al. (p. 1009) found that the majority of the subjects either had negative experiences, or felt nothing at all. Only a minority had positive experiences. The same research team goes on to say: 'Such findings are in keeping with usual clinical experience, although not in accord with the statements in nearly all textbooks of pharmacology' (ibid., p. 1017). In fact, just as many of these inexperienced drug takers experienced euphoria from a placebo (in this case, one ml salt-water solution) as did from heroin or morphine (ibid., p. 1018). And equally many wanted to experience the placebo again as wanted to try heroin anew (ibid., p. 1012). Among detoxified addicts, however, there was only one person (of 30) who wanted to take the placebo again, while 14 wanted more heroin and 17 wanted more morphine. It is worth noting, however, that in this experiment, where detoxified addicts had not been informed what drugs they were given, 10 per cent did not want to take heroin again and 7 per cent said no to more morphine (ibid., p. 1016).

Chein et al. (p. 240) write: ‘a minority of naive subjects who are given opiates experimentally regard the effects as pleasant or desirable, and that, by and large, this minority consists of the psychologically most disturbed of the subjects’.

Bejerot does not agree. He writes:

> There are people who after their first heroin injection experience such an overwhelming thrill that they become psychologically conditioned before they have developed tolerance and a physical, imperative craving for the drug, and the majority of the readers of this book would become morphine and heroin addicts if these substances were administered during a certain period, a few weeks up to a month. (Bejerot, 1968, p. 241)

In other words Bejerot assumes that anybody who takes opiates for a period of time will develop a physical, imperative dependence on them. But on closer examination he contradicts himself in two different ways:

1. If there were a *physical imperative*, then *all* readers of his book would become addicts, not only the majority, as he writes. Clearly there can be no imperative, when at least some are ‘immune’. Bejerot does not discuss this resistance further but Chein et al. show that set is of vital importance for who is susceptible to opiates and who isn’t.
2. Bejerot admits that heroin addicts in New York City hardly take any heroin. He writes (ibid., p. 236): ‘The orgiastic sensations of intravenous opiate injections are well known (Möller) and often described by addicts. Whereas, opiates – but not the extremely diluted, almost heroin-free flour or glucose powder that is often sold on the streets in New York – quickly give rise to the craving for drugs and adding physical misery to the social misery of the addict’s environment.’ I agree with Bejerot that the environment of problematic consumers is destitute. What Bejerot adds is that due to their biochemical effects, opiates lead to further suffering by creating a craving for drugs. But at the same time, Bejerot states that the powder that is sold on the streets of New York is almost free from heroin and does not lead to craving. Therefore we must ask – why do problematic consumers of heroin in New York crave drugs?

One possible explanation as to how almost heroin-free glucose injections can cause craving is that it takes a longer time to develop dependency when diluted heroin is used, but that eventually, the hunger arises anyway. For this reasoning to make sense we must then explain what makes people continue to pursue the expensive and almost heroin-free powder until craving prevails. A possible answer might be that the problematic users in New York initially experience ‘the orgiastic sensations’ that Bejerot describes in conjunction with intravenous injections of opiates.

However, Bejerot himself denies that this is the case, and other researchers have come to the same conclusion. Those who have had contact with opiate addicts on the street relate an entirely different story than one of euphoria when they speak about first-time opiate users. Lasagna et al. (p. 1018) write: 'The histories of addict volunteers indicated that almost without exception they had become sick on first exposure to narcotics (even in relatively small doses)'. It takes a period of time for most people to overcome this reaction. Pearson (1987a, p. 21) writes: 'It is not uncommon . . . for opiates to make people feel terribly sick when they first use them'. 'It is common to hear it said, in fact, that you have to work quite hard in order to develop a heroin habit' (ibid., p. 37).

Unfortunately, I do not have any systematically collected data on this issue from my fieldwork, but I have listened to accounts which lend support to what Lasagna et al. and Pearson report. For example, I knew a problematic consumer who vomited after every injection during a period of about two years, and a few of my research subjects said that they never felt particularly good on opiates.

In other words, not everyone likes opiates, much less experiences euphoria and/or orgiastic sensations. A positive experience with opiates seems to be related to set. Chein et al. (p. 231f) write:

> the addict's enjoyment of the 'high' is not the enjoyment of a stirred-up, zestful state. It is not the enjoyment of intensified sensory input and orgiastic excitement, not even on a hallucinatory or fantasized level. . . . It is in fact not an enjoyment of anything positive at all, and that it should be thought of as a 'high' stands as mute testimony to the utter destitution of the life of the addict with respect to the achievement of positive pleasures and of its repletion with frustration and unresolvable tension.

I don't claim to have a scientific explanation as to why some experience euphoria from opiates while others don't, but I will take the liberty of presenting an admittedly speculative interpretation. Based on the arguments presented in this chapter, my starting point is that euphoria should not be seen merely as a result of biochemical reactions in the body, but also as having social aspects. To explain these social aspects I will borrow a basic idea from symbolic interactionism. In this academic tradition the *self* is seen as consisting of two components; the *I* which is the spontaneous side, ready to act, and the *me* which is the reflective part feeding the I with socially learned information as to the possible consequences of whatever the I is considering doing. When humans think, they hold an *inner dialogue* between the I and me.

Most people have had social experiences which they are able to incorporate into a relatively coherent me. They feel comfortable with their inner dialogue and use it as a compass to help them navigate in their environment.

The inner dialogue is a source of security giving people the feeling that they are in control of the situation. When the inner dialogue is not functioning, such as when we are in an unfamiliar environment and are uncertain if the earlier experiences being reported by our me are relevant for the current situation, we usually feel some degree of discomfort.

However, some people don't experience their me as an ally. As a result of previous chaotic, unpredictable and negative social relationships, they perceive their inner dialogue as both menacing and unreliable as a means of orienting themselves in their environment.

Based on the conjecture that one of the biochemical effects of opiates is to turn off the inner dialogue, we can use set to explain the differences in the way people react. Most will feel a loss, and maybe even insecurity if they can't define the loss of inner dialogue as temporary. However, those who normally experience their inner dialogue as threatening and chaotic may well feel relief, and in extreme cases even euphoria, when they are not being tyrannized by incomprehensible ranting inside their heads.

Regardless of whether these speculations are valid, the evidence indicates that Chein et al. (p. 348) are correct in saying: 'opiates are not inherently attractive, euphoric, or stimulant substances. The danger of addiction to opiates resides in the person, not in the drug.'

SETTING

Thus far we have discussed two groups of factors which influence the way an individual experiences a drug – the drug's biochemical effects and the individual's set. A third is *setting*, which can most simply be defined as the current circumstances. In the context of narcotics setting implies that the drug experience is influenced by how the person feels at the time the drug is taken, his relations to the people he is together with, his perception of the immediate physical surroundings through the duration of the experience, current attitudes and norms in the society in which he lives, etc.

Setting plays an important role for people's experience even when they haven't taken drugs. People are more susceptible to certain stimuli and more inclined to expressing certain emotions in one setting than in another. For instance, in familiar surroundings in the company of friends, a person's reaction to an unfamiliar stimulus will most likely be different than if he were in unknown surroundings in the midst of strangers.

Zinberg (Ch. 5) discusses another aspect of setting. Put concisely he feels that 'it is the social setting, through the development of sanctions and rituals, that brings the use of illicit drugs under control' (ibid., p. 5). Without such sanctions and rituals each consumer is left to his own devices, and few will find reasonable solutions.

The connection between that which is experienced under the influence of a drug and setting is that psychoactive drugs can alter a person's perception of his surroundings, modify his emotional state, and change his experience of any or all of the five senses. In a supportive environment where the individual feels he can get help if he should need it, and/or in a situation where rituals grant a sense of security, it is easier to deal with the sometimes dramatic changes initiated by drugs. But in an unfamiliar environment, where he may feel alone, abandoned, and insecure, the same experiences can become threatening and give rise to fear and even panic. During the 1960s and 1970s, researchers doing scientific experiments with LSD were sometimes warned not to give subjects hallucinogens in a laboratory environment. The harsh, sterile environment, with uninviting furnishings, fluorescent lighting, lack of art on the walls, unfamiliar odours, etc. typical of laboratories, combined with the presence of strangers (researchers), was thought to evoke negative interpretations of the experiences.

James B. Bakalar and Lester Grinspoon (p. 42), both at the Department of Psychiatry of Harvard University, write: 'All drugs act physically on the brain, but the brain's perceptions of reward and punishment, pleasure and pain, depend largely on what we think, and that depends largely on our culture and the company we keep.'

Weil (p. 16) takes this train of thought a step further. He believes that drug consumption is a part of a complex of behaviours and that even highly trained observers 'tend to fall into the trap of trying to explain the entire complex in terms of drug taking – that is, to make the drug a causal variable when it is not'. Weil is of the opinion that the biochemical effects of drugs have been given too prominent a role in explaining behaviour.

> the combined effects of set and setting can easily overshadow the pharmacological effects of a drug as stated in a pharmacology text. One can arrange set and setting so that a dose of an amphetamine will produce sedation or a dose of a barbiturate, stimulation. (Ibid., p. 34f)

Further on he writes: 'drug experience strongly reinforces the illusion that highs come from external, material things rather than from one's own nervous system, and it is precisely this illusion that one strives to overcome by means of meditation' (ibid., p. 71).

In other words, Weil is saying that whatever one experiences with the help of psychoactive substances can be experienced without them. He considers narcotics to be one of the many ways for an individual to get in touch with what he already bears within himself. As the perceptive reader probably has already gathered, Weil does not consider drugs as an especially good way to achieve this. Instead, he suggests non-chemical methods such as meditation, hypnosis, breathing exercises, etc. If one is taking drugs to get high, then it is possible to achieve that goal without chemicals.

To my way of thinking, Weil's alternative methods are good substitutes for narcotics if the main objective is to alter one's state of consciousness (which is often the case for recreational consumers). But, at best, this is only a part of the problematic consumer's reasons for taking drugs, and usually not the primary one. The aims of problematic consumers, which will be discussed later on, cannot be realized by the alternative methods Weil suggests.

SUMMARY

We have discussed three main groups of factors which affect the ways people experience psychoactive drugs. These are:

1. The biochemical effects of drugs, which, for instance, are influenced by:
   a. the chemical properties of the drug
   b. the quantity administered
   c. the presence of other drugs in the body simultaneously
   d. the method by which drugs are taken
   e. how quickly the drugs are absorbed
   f. the interval between dosages
   g. physiological changes in the body caused by previous consumption
2. Set, which is composed of the individual's:
   a. physical make-up
   b. general mental state
   c. life experiences
   d. expectations
   e. knowledge of the drug
3. Setting, including for instance:
   a. the physical environment in which the drug is taken
   b. the current physical and mental state of the individual
   c. social relations to others present
   d. attitudes to the drug in society

This list is incomplete. Some known variables have been omitted, and I assume that there are unknown factors which influence the drug experience.

There are also several further complications. Some of the factors influence each other, and while a certain combination may be relevant for one individual, a different combination may be necessary to understand how another person reacts to drugs. And finally, not even the same individual is necessarily affected by the same contingencies, in the same manner, every time he takes a drug.

USING SOCIAL COMPONENTS IN OUR EXPLANATIONS

From what has been said thus far, it should be clear that we cannot explain behaviour in conjunction with drug consumption by simply referring to the biochemical effects of drugs. Many factors of social origin play an important role and it is therefore essential to include them in our discussion. When we do so, new light is shed on the drug issue. To further clarify this point, I will present some interpretations that I find too dependent upon biochemical variables, and then present alternative interpretations which take social factors into consideration.

Under the heading 'Physiological damage to the psyche' Nordegren and Tunving discuss a number of problems they believe are caused by cannabis. Although they discuss set and setting in approximately the same manner as I have done in this chapter (Nordegren and Tunving, p. 107f) they fail to make use of these groups of factors in their explanations.

I shall present two arguments from Nordegren and Tunving. After each of them, I will suggest alternative explanations, taking into consideration social components.

Toxic Delirium

> During the Vietnam War, a type of acute delirium was observed among American soldiers who were heavy abusers of hashish, but who were otherwise completely healthy. The condition was similar to fever delirium characterized by paranoia and hallucinations. The delirium usually subsided after three or four days. Military physicians believed that it was caused by hashish poisoning. (Ibid., p. 136)

Nordegren and Tunving evidently believe that it is possible to be both completely healthy and a heavy abuser of hashish at the same time. I don't agree, but the difference of opinion may be due to our not having the same definitions of these concepts.

A more important difference between us is that I do not share Nordegren and Tunving's opinion that the use of a narcotic is sufficient to explain human behaviour. In the case of the American soldiers, there are obvious alternative explanations for the observed delirium. They were participating in a war: at any moment they might have been forced to kill others, and were continually at risk of being seriously disabled or losing their lives. They also saw their fellow soldiers maimed and slaughtered. Relatives and friends who might have been a source of psychological support in this extremely trying situation were half-way around the globe. In other words, these soldiers were in an extremely difficult and demoralizing setting.

Delirium in war was a well-known phenomenon long before fighting men had access to narcotics. But because these soldiers in Vietnam had smoked cannabis before showing symptoms of delirium, even such a drastic setting as a war is ignored, while the effects of the drug are given all-pervading significance.

As an alternative to maintaining that the delirium observed in these soldiers was caused by 'hashish poisoning', it seems reasonable to seek causes in their war experiences. Then, to explain why some individuals, but not all, who participate in war show symptoms of delirium, it would be judicious to investigate the factors in people's sets that might make them more or less prone to react to the horrors of war with attacks of delirium.

If a researcher was particularly interested in the possible role of hashish in delirium, he would still have to look at set as many soldiers smoked hash, while relatively few showed these symptoms.

Cannabis Psychosis

In the 1980s the term *hashish psychosis* or *cannabis psychosis* became prevalent in the literature. However, the number of cases are few (ibid., p. 138) and it is difficult to pinpoint exactly what is meant by the term. In the left column below I present Nordegren and Tunving's description of cannabis psychosis; on the right I suggest an alternative explanation.

Nordegren and Tunving	*Alternative explanation*
1. An increase in hash consumption has often preceded the symptoms of illness. (Ibid., p. 138)	1. Some people with psychological problems have learned that hash can prevent latent symptoms from becoming manifest. An increase in consumption may therefore be an attempt to impede an impending psychosis. If this fails, the psychosis has not been caused by the drug. At most, hashish may be one factor in the equation. Why label a problem by one of many contributory causes?
2. The patient did not have a history of being oversensitive, timid, or vulnerable. There is no history of mental illness among his relatives. (Ibid.)	2. It is difficult to understand how a physician can make such statements with any degree of certainty. Even if he had had fairly good contact with the patient before the symptoms became apparent, and/or the patient's file did not mention these symptoms, a doctor would have little

basis for expressing himself so unconditionally. Can it really be true that there never had been any situations in these patients' lives where they had been oversensitive, timid, or vulnerable? I would be alarmed if I met such a person.

It is also difficult to understand how a physician can say anything at all about the psychological state of each and every relative of the patient.

3. The development of the disease follows a characteristic pattern. The patient's mood changes rapidly, but he is often in good spirits, and has delusions of grandeur. At the same time, he has difficulty concentrating and feels confused. Often he believes that he is being observed and persecuted. Visual and auditory hallucinations are common.

Aggressive behaviour is also usual. (Ibid.)

3. All of these 'symptoms of cannabis psychosis', with the exception of aggressive behaviour, are very common reactions to hashish, especially when it is taken in large doses. It is usually called getting high, being paranoid, etc. Why equate this with psychosis?

A significant per cent of the population of the industrialized world has tried cannabis. For instance about two-thirds of the young adults in the US have taken marijuana at least once (Shedler and Block, p. 613). Except for those who didn't feel anything, almost all of these people have experienced some of the 'symptoms of cannabis psychosis' mentioned above. To say that so many people have been in a psychotic state dilutes the meaning of the concept.

4. The psychosis usually abates without treatment. In most cases, the patient is completely normal within a few weeks, but occasionally it can take as long as a year. (Ibid.)

4. When the drugs are broken down by the body the effects wear off and the 'symptoms' disappear. If they don't, i.e. they last more than a month, the American Psychiatric Association (p. 314) does not consider them substance induced, but rather an underlying psychotic disorder.

5. Relapse (*recidivism*) is common with continued (cannabis) abuse. But many of those who have had a cannabis psychosis find the experience so unpleasant that they refrain from further use of hashish. (Ibid.)

5. If a person continues to consume hash he will have similar experiences in the future; which everyone who has taken cannabis on several occasions understands. If someone doesn't wish to expose himself to this he will stop taking the drug. What does this have to do with psychosis?

If these five points explain what is meant by cannabis psychosis, the concept is more confusing than illuminating. However, by saying this I do not mean to imply that cannabis never has anything to do with psychosis. But drugs are only a small part of an individual's total life experiences. Recognizing this, the American Psychiatric Association (pp. 310–15) does not use the term cannabis psychosis but rather speaks of substance-induced psychotic disorders. Even this term gives drugs an inordinate role, but is clearly better than narcotic psychosis. Once again, drugs should be seen as one of many links in a long chain, not the single or even primary cause. In their extensive review of the literature on cannabis, Hall et al. (p. 179) conclude:

> There is little support for the hypothesis that cannabis use can cause a chronic psychosis which persists beyond the period of intoxication. Such a possibility is difficult to study because of the likely rarity of such psychoses, and the near impossibility of distinguishing them from individuals with schizophrenia and manic depressive psychoses who also abuse cannabis.

In conclusion, it is important to emphasize that neither the explanations proposed by Nordegren and Tunving nor my own are scientific facts. By including and/or accentuating other aspects than those presented here, new images appear. As there are no objective measures, different conceptualizations must be compared, and their explanatory merits weighed.

4 Why Do People Take Drugs?

ALCOHOL

Why Do We Drink Alcohol?

As alcohol is the most commonly used psychoactive drug in the industrialized world, I will begin my discussion of why people take drugs by presenting some reasons for drinking. Both legal and illegal drugs can be used to achieve the same goals, and problematic consumers of narcotics often drink alcohol as a substitute for, and supplement to, their favourite substance.

Bo Löfgren (p. 192), a physician and alcohol therapist, divides the reasons for using alcohol into three main theoretical categories. People drink in order to:

1. deal with a difficult psychological situation;
2. re-create an earlier relationship (usually from childhood);
3. influence relationships with others.

He exemplifies these main groups with 18 different reasons for drinking (ibid., p. 192ff) but I shall limit my discussion to only a few of them.

Included in the first category is utilizing alcohol to *reduce anxiety*. The most common use of alcohol is to abate temporary tension. People who suffer from long-term serious anxiety may drink on a daily basis in an attempt to subdue it (ibid., p. 192f).

Another reason for drinking in Löfgren's first category is what he calls '*disguise, camouflage, alibi*'. Needs that are difficult to satisfy without breaching societal norms are often camouflaged. Problematic consumers, for instance, 'disguise their need to remain passive and dependent on others by getting drunk. If people were allowed to express these needs without being intoxicated, they would not drink to the same extent' (ibid., p. 193).

In the second category, Löfgren mentions alcohol as *a means of regressing to earlier stages in life*. In situations where worry and conflicts weigh heavily, it is not unusual for people to resort to immature patterns of behaviour such as eating, sleeping, procrastinating, avoidance, letting someone else deal with the problem, etc. But in some cultures it is difficult for adults to behave in this fashion as neither the individual himself nor others will accept it. If, however, the person is inebriated, his intoxication can be interpreted as an extenuating circumstance (ibid., p. 194).

Alcohol can be used *to confirm what the individual believes to be true about life*. Many problem drinkers have learned early in life that others reject them and/or try to dominate them. 'An easy way to corroborate this "fact of life", is for instance to come to a treatment center drunk and behave uncooperatively, thereby provoking physicians and social workers to respond in an authoritarian and rejecting manner ("come back when you're sober")' (ibid., p. 195f).

Problematic consumers often base their behaviour on at least two incorrect suppositions:

1. They assume that because their earlier experiences have followed a certain pattern, all future relationships must necessarily do likewise.
2. They see themselves as objects; denying that they have any part in what has taken place. They clearly see/feel that others have rejected them, but they don't allow themselves to comprehend what they have done to provoke this reaction. Thus they are able to continue believing that rejection is a necessary part of all relationships and there is nothing they can do about it.

A reason for drinking which falls into Löfgren's third category is to *test the loyalty and devotion of others*. 'Individuals with psychological problems, especially alcohol abusers, distrust others, but also have an enormous need of affection and attention. Intoxication is often used to test the limits of other's consideration and friendship. "Testing" is necessary because their lack of basic trust is so great' (ibid., p. 205). For instance, they can get so drunk at a party that they can't make it home on their own: to see if their friends/spouse care enough to help them.

An aspect of Löfgren's list of reasons for drinking, worthy of special notice, is that he shows that alcohol can be used to achieve diametrically opposed effects; i.e. *to show or conceal emotions*. 'Many people have been taught at an early age that it is bad manners, wrong, or dangerous to show their emotions' (ibid., p. 200). However, in some cultures it is permissible to be emotional when inebriated. Under the influence of alcohol people may laugh heartily, joke, sing, show appreciation, and help create a congenial atmosphere. 'But most often, intoxication serves as an "alibi" or excuse for otherwise unacceptable behaviour. Above all many become aggressive, probably the most forbidden emotion of our time... [in Sweden]' (ibid., p. 200f).

On the other hand, alcohol can also help people hide emotions that are potentially dangerous or socially not accepted (ibid., p. 201). In a drunken stupor; rage, sorrow, sexuality, and other feelings can fade into somnolence.

People have motives when they take drugs. Löfgren's list gives examples of different kinds of needs that people in general, not only problem drinkers, attempt to satisfy with the help of alcohol. Neither the devil nor sensuality are in the bottle; they are in the individual. Alcohol is used in an attempt to deal with human needs, but alcohol is not the root of these needs.

The list of motives for drinking presented here is far from complete, and I am convinced that readers can quickly add many more reasons. All one has to do is think of what people do when they drink that they find difficult to do when they're sober.

The Influence of Social Norms on the Effects of Alcohol

By permitting, forbidding, or requiring certain behaviour, social norms set the stage for how alcohol may be used in that particular society. With the help of anthropological studies Craig MacAndrew and Robert B. Edgerton show that alcohol can evoke a multitude of different types of behaviour depending upon the cultural setting in which it is used. They argue that 'while there is indeed an abundance of solid evidence to confirm alcohol's causal role in the production of changes in at least certain sensorimotor capabilities, there is no corresponding body of hard documented evidence for the notion that alcohol plays a similar causal role in the production of changes in man's comportment' (MacAndrew and Edgerton, p. 84), '. . . however great the difference may be between persons' sober and drunken comportment – and there can be no doubt that these differences are often very great, indeed – it is evident that both states are characterized by a healthy respect for certain socially sanctioned limits' (ibid., p. 85). '*Over the course of socialization, people learn about drunkenness what their society "knows" about drunkenness; and, accepting and acting upon the understandings thus imparted to them, they become the living confirmation of their society's teachings*' (ibid., p. 88) (emphasis in original).

MacAndrew and Edgerton use a term we recognize from the world of sport – *time-out*. They argue that it is unreasonable to demand that people be responsible for everything they do under all circumstances. Every society creates some kind of 'safety valve' which permits forms of expression that are normally deemed unacceptable. The implications of time-out can be summarized as follows: 'if people have been brought up to believe that one is "not really oneself" when drunk, then it becomes possible for them to construe their drunken changes-for-the-worse as purely episodic happenings rather than as intended acts issuing from their moral character. So construed, not only can the drinker explain away his drunken misbehaviour to himself ("I never would have done it if I were sober"), those around him too can decide, or can be made to see, that his drunken transgressions ought not – or at least, *need* not – be taken in full seriousness ("After all, he was drunk"). ... Time-out affords people the opportunity to "get it out of their systems" with a minimum of adverse consequences' (ibid., p. 169). But once again, that which people must get out of their systems while intoxicated is dependent upon what society permits, forbids and demands while they are sober.

That alcohol is used in so many cultures in conjunction with time-out behaviour is due to it being easy and inexpensive to produce from grains that are accessible almost everywhere. Intoxication is also easily recognizable, thereby sending a clear signal to others that the consumer has called time-out.

WHY DO PEOPLE TAKE NARCOTICS?

All of the reasons for using psychoactive substances mentioned above have been gleaned by studying alcohol, but they can also be relevant for narcotics. I shall now present a number of motives for taking drugs ascertained from studies of narcotics consumption. These objectives may also apply to drinking.

Probably the most common explanation for why people use drugs is that they are addicted; i.e. they have lost control of their own actions and are 'chemically dependent'. However, this does not help us understand why anyone starts to use illegal drugs, and cannot explain many known facts. We shall return to chemical dependency shortly.

Another explanation is based on the assumed euphoric effects of narcotics. In the previous chapter I discussed why euphoria is neither the cause nor necessarily the result of narcotics consumption. However, there are people who take illegal drugs to experience something that they themselves consider desirable. In the masterful words of Aldous Huxley (p. 49):

> That humanity at large will ever be able to dispense with Artificial Paradises seems very unlikely. Most men and women lead lives at the worst so painful, at the best so monotonous, poor and limited that the urge to escape, the longing to transcend themselves if only for a few moments, is and always has been one of the principal appetites of the soul. Art and religion, carnivals and saturnalia, dancing and listening to oratory – all these have served, in H. G. Wells' phrase, as Doors in the Wall. And for private, for everyday use there have always been chemical intoxicants. All the vegetable sedatives and narcotics, all the euphorics that grow on trees, the hallucinogens that ripen in the berries or can be squeezed from roots – all, without exception, have been known and systematically used by human beings from time immemorial.

In the narcotics debate in some countries there has been an unwillingness to as much as mention these kinds of motives. Based on theories of chemical dependence, it is assumed that the only course to pursue is to frighten people from as much as trying narcotics, as a person never knows how long it will take before he becomes dependent (loses control). Therefore, descriptions such as Huxley's have been labelled 'drug romanticism', 'lunacy', 'attempts to excuse one's own drug habits', and so on.

Regardless of one's opinions of these tactics, the fact remains that there are people who consider drugs 'a door in the wall'. Their main objective for using psychoactive substances is to experience something different and/or gain insight.

Weil (p. 20) assumes that there is 'an innate human drive to experience periodic episodes of nonordinary consciousness'. Behaviour that can be interpreted as an effort to attain such states of mind can be witnessed among youngsters in all cultures.

> Anyone who watches very young children without revealing his presence will find them regularly practicing techniques that induce striking changes in mental states. Three- and four-year-olds, for example, commonly whirl themselves into vertiginous stupors. They hyperventilate and have other children squeeze them around the chest until they faint. They also choke each other to produce loss of consciousness. (Ibid., p. 25)

Certain drugs give the user a temporary increase in energy. Cocaine and amphetamines can dampen fatigue and make it easier to concentrate on a task. For instance some American college students use central stimulants to be able to cram for several days and nights before exams, and members of the Norwegian underground in World War II used amphetamines so that they could go out on raids at night and be able to work the next day.

It is sometimes claimed that narcotics such as cannabis or LSD enhance creativity; and some people use them for this reason. However, the relationship between psychoactive substances and creativity is complex. While it is certainly not true that taking these drugs automatically makes people creative, narcotics can influence expression. Some consumers may be able to use experiences of the kind Huxley describes, to help them get in touch with that which they bear within; thereby providing material for creative activity. But there is no more creativity in the narcotics themselves than there is a devil in a bottle of alcohol. Possibly, the placebo effect might play a role. If a person is convinced that a substance enhances creativity, it might decrease some of his fears and/or inhibitions, thereby instilling the courage to delve deeper into his psyche and/or more daringly express himself.

Drugs have been a part of religious rituals for thousands of years. Wine is used in both Christian and Jewish ceremonies and some drugs now classified as narcotics have served a similar function in many cultures. The effects of hallucinogens are often described as profoundly spiritual.

These examples indicate that some consumers see narcotics as a means to personal development. Objections to this kind of consumption have been raised on two grounds:

1. *Questioning the ends*: Some consider the objectives themselves as undesirable; or even a threat to the foundation of our society. For instance, no

one can be certain as to what the effects on the workforce would be if people were to: develop new capabilities, experience new sensations, come in contact with their subconscious, see themselves as creative beings, become more spiritual, etc. Different observers have different visions of what such changes imply, and draw different conclusions as to whether or not the foreseen scenario would be an improvement or a catastrophe.

2. *Questioning the means*: If the means of achieving these ends were something other than illegal drugs, more people might deem it positive that their fellow citizens attempt to develop themselves in the ways mentioned above. In this case, it is not the ends, but the means which are found objectionable.

Regardless of one's opinion, there are individuals who take psychoactive substances in the hope of developing themselves in some way. But far from all consumers have this as a major objective. For some the destructive effects of drugs are an essential motive for taking them.

In an autobiography, writer and former problematic consumer of amphetamines, Birgitta Stenberg, describes some of her experiences:

> We saw and experienced the city through the change of perspective caused by the high, with a clarity shining inwards, and rapture and anticipation quivering in our guts. ... The amphetamine somehow imbued us with the gestalt of the moment, and impressions flowed freely through all our senses. (Stenberg, p. 5)

> The low tree outside our window rustles against the panes, and my heart pounds. It's happened, they've come, and while a few of them are silently picking the lock of the door in the lobby, a couple of them have slipped into position outside the window to cut off that escape route. That's the way it is. ... Panic is a part of the deal when you buy capsules or bags. (Ibid., p. 8)

> The first orgasm shakes my body before he's on top of me, before he's even touched me. ... he can keep it up hour after hour, and his touch sets my skin aflame. At the same time, we listen. ... A car silently passes. ... Is it going to stop? (Ibid., p. 12)

> Stenberg's boyfriend, Baku, tells her point blank: 'If you write something the cops can use, I'll kill you.' (Ibid., p. 14)

> I got him! It hit so hard he couldn't hide it. Then both of us lay there with our pain; until the amphetamines swept it away. (Ibid., p. 18)

> '... a chick's gotta help out sometimes. We need the bread. ... You've already sold some of your things.'
> 'Just stuff I don't need.' (Ibid., p. 19)

'Well I'm not going to start selling my ass. Not me! Not me.' (Ibid.)

Morality is clear-cut and primitive on the scene: he calls the shots and she obeys, because he's physically stronger and both of them know it. (Ibid., p. 20)

Never sad, never glad. Just don't think in those terms. Either the stuff is good, and then everything is great. Or you freak. That's it! (Ibid., p. 21)

A fix to sleep on. Go home, hit up, and feel good in a cold world. (Ibid., p. 24)

The fear paralyzes you...just listening for hours on end. (Ibid., p. 24f)

And when I think: would I want others to experience what I've gone through with amphetamines, the answer is obviously no. But the junkie, who is also me, would like people to have those fantastic first experiences. But that's also a lie. Speed freaks couldn't care less about what anybody else experiences. (Ibid., p. 29)

Anything can happen to me; editors can refuse my work, Baku can kick the shit out of me, I may never finish the job I got an advance for. Nothing matters! (Ibid., p. 48)

But what kind of life do I want to live with him? Wage-slave Baku – home at four-thirty. Cooking. Dishes. Routines. Hell no! But then again...The other life isn't much better. Actually it's much worse. The phone ringing all night. People coming and going. Paranoid about the cops. Hoarse whores. (Ibid., p. 66)

I can talk to irrelevant people, meet their glances in stores and in traffic. But it's getting harder, and nowadays I always wear dark glasses. (Ibid., p. 115)

The girl I invited over split. She couldn't put up with my ego-tripped, one-track speed-freak babbling. I can't stand it much longer myself. (Ibid., p. 135)

Feel the stench from that goddamned speed. Think about your blackish-brown urine. Look at your gutted apartment; where are the books you had, what happened to the furniture? When are you going to scrape the blood off the floor, or the milky-white stains of spilled solution? (Ibid., p. 151)

At about five o'clock, I started coming out of it and the bed was full of blood. Nauseated, I staggered toward the bathroom, but stopped when I saw myself in the bedroom mirror. I perceived the outline of a death's-head starting to take shape in my drawn, emaciated face. Blood-covered thighs and lacerated arms. A black and blue mark on my arm where

> I'd hit a nerve. Paranoia flickering in my hungry eyes. There was a destitute speed-freak, staring at her identityless image, standing in front of a soiled mirror, in an old and dirty room, longing to die. (Ibid., p. 141)

What was Stenberg trying to accomplish by taking drugs? Because her description contains both experiences she found of value, and extremely self-destructive elements, there is leeway for alternative interpretations. And this is at the heart of part of the controversy in the narcotics debate. Some believe that 'those fantastic first experiences', i.e. the change of perspective, impressions freely flowing through the senses, orgasms, etc., are the principal reasons for consuming drugs. From this point of view, the hope of re-experiencing all of this explains why junkies are willing to bear all the negative consequences. However, a considerable amount of data point to a very different conclusion. As has already been mentioned, there are problematic consumers who have never had 'fantastic experiences' – not even in the very beginning. Furthermore, as Stenberg's text indicates, even when the effects of drugs were at their very best, life was tarnished by paranoia and fear.

Others believe that by the time substantial consumers become aware of the negative aspects of life on the drug scene, it's too late. This is most often seen as being due to chemical dependence. I shall return to this shortly.

All of these explanations are based on the assumption that problematic consumers are attempting to create a good life for themselves. This was also my assumption when I started my fieldwork, and it took a long time before I abandoned it. As I had always attempted to make my own life as positive as possible, I assumed that everybody else did the same. However, as long as I clung to this supposition, much of what I observed couldn't be explained. In order to have any explanation at all I found myself thinking things like: 'they really don't understand what they are doing', although I could clearly see that my research subjects were far from feebleminded. In the course of my discussions with them, and by reading their poetry and other things they had written, the depth of their self-contempt revealed itself time and again. Self-contempt evokes much of the self-destructive behaviour I had so often observed. In other words, the negative aspects of life on the drug scene are not unintended side-effects of attempts to reach some other goal (i.e. euphoria), but rather, *self-destruction is a primary objective for problematic consumers of narcotics.*

I believe that to understand problematic consumption we must change assumptions. Instead of seeing the substantial consumer as a person who lacks control over his acts, he should be thought of as a subject with motives for what he is doing. Using this assumption, we can observe what he actually does, and use this to ascertain his objectives.

What did Birgitta Stenberg's life as a problematic consumer of narcotics consist of? One way to gain insight is to examine the ideas and concepts that dominate her autobiography. From the quotations above we see, on the one hand, she enjoyed a short period with new perspectives, impressions freely flowing through her senses and orgasms; and on the other hand, a long period of paranoia, terror, threats, eradicated feelings, prostitution, violence, apathy, indifference, inability to meet elementary social demands, stench, bodily decay, a gutted apartment, filth, lack of identity and longing for death.

THE ESSENTIAL NATURE OF PROBLEMATIC CONSUMPTION OF NARCOTICS

There are many theories of the 'essential nature' of substantial consumption of narcotics. Lack of space limits my discussion, but I shall briefly present three models before introducing the theoretical basis of this book.

Scientists from all fields agree that narcotics initiate biochemical processes in the organism. It is generally accepted that drugs either damage cells in the central nervous system and/or disrupt the functioning of at least some transmitter substance (i.e. dopamine, GABA, serotonin, etc.). But there is a lack of consensus as to how this relates to behaviour. As opposed to psychosocially orientated researchers, biochemical theoreticians consider these physiological changes to be of central importance. However, even among the biochemically inclined there are differences of opinion. Some emphasize *negative reinforcement*; i.e. that drug taking is an attempt to avoid distress, most notably abstinence. Since the significance of withdrawal was put into question in the previous chapter, I shall not repeat the arguments here. Instead I will turn my attention to *positive reinforcement,* where drug consumption is seen as pleasure-seeking behaviour.

The Chemically Controlled Drug Abuser – Positive Reinforcement

Nils Bejerot states:

> from the standpoint of biology and the psychology of learning, there is no basic difference between caffeinism, nicotinism, drug dependency, alcoholism, and narcotics addiction. They are all very closely related states, originating from conditioning to different substances; all of which having in common that through different mechanisms they affect structures in the central nervous system, and thus, the individual's sense of pleasure and well-being. (Bejerot, 1979, p. 37f)

'That the individual has become chemically controlled and has serious deficiencies or completely lost self-control vis-a-vis intoxicants is the essential nature of narcotics addiction' (ibid., p. 90). 'The dependent individual is... steered by his instincts' (ibid., p. 95).

For Bejerot, drug dependency is caused by biological and chemical changes in the organism. He calls the period from the initial drug intake until one becomes dependent, the *voluntary phase*. 'Characteristic of the voluntary phase is that the individual's will can override the effects of the drug; the individual is in control of his behaviour' (ibid., p. 29). But eventually the biochemical effects of narcotics take command and the individual enters the *dependency phase*.

Bejerot's argument is based on the assumption that an individual who is dependent on drugs is controlled by instincts. He does not clarify exactly what these instincts are, but the following quotations give some indication: 'Dependency [is]... a state in itself, independent of what led to experimentation with drugs and the initial abuse' (ibid., p. 119). 'Once dependency has been established, it becomes biologically deviant to discontinue consumption. Instead, it is normal to concentrate all efforts on maintaining the instinct, which becomes stronger than the sexual drive' (ibid., p. 160). '[I]t is easiest to understand narcotics addiction... as a "short circuit" in the pleasure/pain-principle, and dependence as an artificial drive resulting from this' (ibid., p. 166). '[T]he addict does not generally suffer from his disease, he enjoys it. ... the drug effects take on the strength of libidinal desire and outweigh all mental, physical, social, and economic complications arising from the abuse' (Bejerot, 1970, p. xvii).

In other words, Bejerot sees drug abusers as being steered by their instincts, and by dependency caused by the chemical properties of the drugs they take. The addict has lost control over himself and seeks pleasurable sensations. Underlying structures in his personality, the reasons why he started taking drugs, and all the negative experiences he acquires in conjunction with problematic consumption, are not of central importance for explaining his behaviour.

The Chemically Controlled Drug Abuser – Sensitization

Recognizing the shortcomings of both negative and positive reinforcement theories two biochemically oriented researchers, Terry E. Robinson and Kent C. Berridge present an alternative explanation for the way chemicals control behaviour. They ask: 'What is the relationship between "wanting" drugs and "liking" drugs and does this relationship change during addiction?' (Robinson and Berridge, p. 249). Starting from the well-known fact that 'as craving for drugs increases the pleasure derived from drugs often decreases' (ibid.) they present *The Incentive-Sensitization Theory of Addiction* which posits that 'addictive behaviour is due largely to progressive and persistent neuroadaptations caused by repeated drug use' (ibid.). Based on the concepts of *sensitization* (a progressive increase in drug effect with repeated intake), and *incentive salience* (the attractiveness of external stimuli), they propose that '*the defining characteristics of addiction (craving and relapse) are due directly to drug-induced changes in those functions normally subserved by a neural system that undergoes sensitization-related neuroadaptations*' (ibid.) (emphasis in original).

> Sensitization of this neural system by drugs results in a pathological enhancement in the incentive salience that the nervous system attributes to the act of drug taking. ... Thus with repeated drug use the act of drug taking and drug-associated stimuli, gradually become more and more attractive. ... the neural system that mediates 'wanting' becomes progressively sensitized. 'Wanting' evolves into obsessive craving. ... But 'wanting' is not 'liking'. The neural system responsible for 'wanting' incentives is proposed to be separable from those responsible for 'liking' incentives (i.e. for mediating pleasure) and repeated drug use only sensitizes the neural system responsible for 'wanting'. (Ibid.)

In other words once the body has been sensitized to drugs, 'wanting' is seen as biochemically determined. By giving biochemical changes in the 'wanting system' precedence, R and B believe they have found a biochemical explanation for why drug taking behaviour continues even though the drugs are not liked. 'In colloquial language, it is usually assumed that addicts "want" drugs because they "like" drugs and the more they "like" them the more they should "want" them. ... we propose the progressive increase in drug "wanting" is not accompanied by an increase in the pleasure derived from drugs' (ibid., p. 249f).

This theory can be seen as a biochemical explanation of what I will explain psychosocially. To understand the differences between R and B and myself we must look at basic assumptions. Although not explicitly stated, it seems clear that R and B's theory is based on the assumption that people strive to have as good a life as possible. Yet R and B clearly see that addicts destroy themselves with narcotics without so much as getting pleasure from the drugs they take (ibid., p. 253). R and B reconcile the contradiction between their assumption and the observed behaviour by turning the individual into an object. They posit that neurochemical changes rather than human motives determine behaviour.

For the biochemically oriented it doesn't seem to matter whether the effect of drug taking is pain reduction, euphoria or self-destruction; any and all reactions are explained by neurochemical processes which override the individual's will. But what biochemical theories cannot explain is why:

a. some (very few) choose to take drugs to the point where they become dependent/sensitized;
b. even after many years of taking narcotics any given individual's consumption will vary at different times and in different places;

c. many of those who have become dependent/sensitized manage to stop taking drugs (become non-dependent/unsensitized).

The Psychosocially Disturbed Addict

Jan Ramström, a physician with long experience as a drug therapist, has a theoretical model vastly different from biochemical explanations. Ramström believes that underlying structures in the consumer's personality are of vital importance for substantial consumption. Put concisely, he describes three main phases of psychosocial development leading to addiction (Ramström, 1983, p. 84).

1. An early established personality disorder
2. Rejection
3. Adopting an addict identity

The first phase builds upon psychoanalytic developmental psychology. In short, an early established personality disorder is: 'one of the psychopathological states which are caused by disturbances in early object relationships' (ibid.). Ramström sees two parallel processes. The first consists of disturbed relations early in life between the individual and his parents. This in turn causes disorders in another process: the individual's psychological development.

According to Ramström, deficiencies in the parent–child relationship can have two origins, although usually consist of elements from both. *Primary resource deficiency* occurs when parents are 'unsure of their own identity, have weak egos, and have an inability to form intimate relationships and give of themselves' (ibid., p. 86). This is due to problems they bear with them from their own childhood.

Secondary resource deficiency refers to disturbances in family relationships originating in external circumstances such as economic and social problems. For instance, to earn a living the parents may have to work two jobs or commute long distances, giving them little time and energy for their children. As a result of primary and/or secondary resource deficiency in his family the future addict has learned that the world is 'insecure, without love, and not to be trusted' (ibid.).

The second stage in Ramström's model is rejection.

> Due to his early established personality disorder, and the thereby inhibited ego development, the future addict's object relationships are characterized, on the one hand, by the oral dependence personality's endless demands, and on the other hand... impulsiveness, and an inability to tolerate frustration and emotion. The child acts out his basic depression in the form of so-called depressive equivalents, such as restlessness, inabil-

ity to concentrate and irritability. Others see him as troublesome, and he is often rejected by people outside his family. (Ibid., p. 86f)

Ramström's third phase is the development of an addict identity. All adolescents must separate from their parents and develop their own identity, but due to his early established personality disorder and having been rejected, the prospective addict is not as well equipped for this task as his contemporaries. He finds it difficult to hold his own in social situations that would give him a chance to create a positive identity, and therefore 'chooses a negative identity rather than no identity at all' (ibid., p. 88).

Ramström's perspective has much in common with my own. Both are based on stages through which the individual must pass before becoming a problematic consumer. Both of us maintain that narcotics must be understood on three main levels – the macrolevel (structural level), the mesolevel (interpersonal processes) and the microlevel (intrapsychic processes). For instance, Ramström writes: 'it is just as important to ask – *What is the state of the society in which the young person seeks a foothold for his social identity...?* as it is to look at the *personal resources* the adolescent has to help him form a positive identity' (ibid., p. 89) (emphasis in original).

The principal difference between Ramström and myself is that we emphasize different things. Ramström is a psychoanalyst whose main objective is to create a theoretical framework that can used as a basis for *treatment*. In his own words: 'those seeking a theoretical model for *prevention* must look at abuse from a different angle' (ibid., p. 84). One of the principal aims of this book is to present a conceptual basis for preventative measures.

As Ramström's ideas are based on psychoanalytic developmental psychology, I will state my position in relation to that theoretical school. Ramström (ibid., p. 88) writes: 'The basis for constructing an identity is laid while growing up and continues through the crucial period of development which takes place during adolescence.' Essentially I agree with this statement, but from my point of view psychoanalytic developmental psychology overemphasizes the first years of life and does not attach sufficient significance to experiences gained later on. I also think it necessary to place greater emphasis on relationships established outside the home. In modern society, parents (mothers) no longer play an all-pervading role in the lives of their offspring. Many children attend a daycare centre or have a nanny from the time they are very small and spend a great deal of time away from their parents. I shall therefore emphasize both the activities of people outside the family, and macrolevel factors (as these determine both the functions people have in society and the resources available to them to fulfil their obligations).

I am aware that my own approach also has limitations. For instance, the intrapsychic processes that take place during an individual's first years are undoubtedly extremely important, and I am unable to give them the attention they deserve. Psychoanalysis is a better tool than participant observation for the in-depth study of early development.

That I emphasize the experiences substantial consumers of drugs have later in life, is partially because this is the information I have greatest access to, but also because I believe that important pieces of the puzzle as to what constitutes the essential nature of narcotics can be found by studying what problematic consumers actually do while on the drug scene, and by looking at the reactions this behaviour evokes from others. In other words, I emphasize current acts and experiences, even though I am aware that to explain what takes place in the present we must take into consideration experiences from the past.

The Self-Destructive Problematic Consumer

Early in my fieldwork one of my research subjects gave me the following advice: 'Don't feel sorry for anybody kicking cold turkey [going through abstinence]: junkies are masochists who want to suffer and die.' As previously mentioned, at the time I assumed that everybody strove to have as good a life as possible. Furthermore the literature I had read had convinced me that the main reason for taking narcotics was euphoria. For these reasons I found my informant's advice absurd.

After many months and much confusion, I understood that he in fact had given me an important key to unravelling much of what I was observing in the field. But at the time the thought was so far from my pre-understanding (the ideas I had with me when I first went out into the field) that it took a long time before I was able to incorporate it into my thinking.

Most researchers agree that problematic consumers run a great risk of dying prematurely. For instance, the European Monitoring Centre for Drugs and Drug Addiction (EMCDDA, 1996, p. 1:14) reports:

> Studies which have tracked groups of addicts (mainly regular heroin injectors) over several years suggest that out of every 100 on average one or two die each year from overdoses, accidents, suicides, or drug related diseases. Where HIV infection is rife among drug injectors, the risk of death may increase to three or four per cent a year.

Ruining your health, being scorned by others, having no friends you can depend upon, breaking the law every day, being paranoid, freaking out, etc. are other well-known negative aspects of problematic consumption. Why would anyone subject himself to all of this?

The most common answers are variations on Bejerot's theory. Consumers have lost their self-control! The euphoria experienced outweighs the negative aspects!

But upon closer examination these explanations are lacking. While it is true that drugs can give rise to pleasurable sensations, substantial consumers must spend considerable amounts of time on the drug scene to have a chance of getting drugs regularly. This means that *problematic consumers are not merely purchasing drugs, they are buying a way of life*. The lifestyle on the scene is such that anyone who takes drugs regularly soon has one negative experience after the other. The proportions between pleasure and pain tilt increasingly toward the latter the longer and more frequently one uses drugs (see Stenberg, above).

Even those who argue that drug abusers seek euphoria accept that this is the case. However, they usually defend their viewpoint by referring to one or both of the following arguments:

1. The euphoria of the initial drug consumption was so overwhelming that substantial consumers continue to take narcotics in the hope of experiencing it again.
2. By the time problematic consumers discover the negative sides of drugs, it is too late; as they are chemically dependent and can no longer control their actions.

I shall now examine these two arguments.

Initially I will remind my readers that some problematic consumers have never become euphoric from narcotics, not even early on. Therefore their objective for taking narcotics cannot possibly be to re-experience something they have never known. But as there are many substantial consumers who have had some positive experiences with drugs, we must delve further into the matter.

Some problematic consumers nurture a dream of euphoria, but this is hardly an explanation for why they continue to take drugs. Perhaps the role of euphoria for problematic consumers can be understood by comparing it to wishful thinking: many a John Doe buys a lottery ticket and lets his thoughts wander to what he's going to do with the millions he's about to win. The fantasy of hitting the jackpot, that one big event which in the turn of a hand sweeps away all troubles and grants happiness, is nurtured by a great many people. Dreams make it a little easier to bear the burdens of life, but not many substantial consumers or John Does really believe they're going to come true.

If we leave the realm of fantasy and examine more closely what the lives of problematic consumers actually consist of, euphoria is hardly the first word that comes to mind. On the contrary, the general direction of problematic consumers' pattern of life is inflicting themselves with pain. By saying this, I do not mean to imply that everything substantial consumers do is directly and mainly focused on hurting themselves. But the long-term effects of their lifestyle and their actions point in that direction.

Let me supplement Birgitta Stenberg's description of her life by presenting a little of what I observed in the field. Some problematic consumers are called *needle freaks* because they are preoccupied with hypodermic needles. For instance, needle freaks can take a needle and tap it against something hard (such as a table) until the point is blunted. This makes it both difficult and painful to penetrate the skin. The obtuse (and non-sterile) needle is then forced into a vein, rotated, pushed further in, removed from the blood vessel, reinserted, and so on. The process can be repeated time after time – even though there is no syringe attached to the needle.

Certain unhealthy aspects of life on the drug scene are well known, but I am not convinced that most people understand how drastic some of the self-destructiveness can be. For instance problematic consumers can rinse a syringe in the toilet bowl of a public lavatory instead of using water from the sink standing next to it; or borrow the 'works' of others, in spite of the risk of hepatitis and HIV/AIDS; or ask others to smuggle alcohol (instead of a drug that is more gentle on the liver) into the hospital while being treated for hepatitis; or find a pill in the street and swallow it without having any idea of what it contains.

Aside from these more drastic events, everyday life is decidedly unhealthy, due to improper diet, lack of sleep, physical abuse, prison sentences, sexual abuse, venereal diseases, prostitution, paranoia, dental problems, bodily decay, bleeding sores, poverty, etc., etc., etc. Or, in the words of an American problematic consumer:

> Every day I risk my health, and my life for that matter, when I shoot up. Every time I go out to cop [buy drugs] I risk getting cut [stabbed] or even killed. Every time I'm strolling [walking the streets soliciting clients] at night, there are all kinds of crazies, geeks, thugs, and death freaks out there just waiting to carve up my ass. Now they say that if I use some dirty needle I can get sick, even die in a few years. So I care? I'm probably already dead. Why should I care? (Inciardi, p. 194)

According to Bejerot problematic consumers put up with all of this because they are chemically dependent. He writes: 'addictive drugs give rise to pleasurable sensations which he eventually is unwilling to be without, in spite of all the complications which arise. This is what it means to be dependent' (Bejerot, 1979, p. 119). By now it should be apparent that Bejerot's ideas do not explain what problematic consumers actually do and experience. Neither narcotics nor anything else in their lives is particularly pleasant.

Another way to try to get around the obvious self-destructiveness of problematic consumers is to simply state that these people do not understand what they are doing. The argument usually follows one or more of the following trains of thought – substantial consumers:

1. are intellectually lacking;
2. cannot think clearly because they are under the influence of drugs;
3. deceive themselves.

None of these statements helps us understand the behaviour I observed in the field. It is true that it can be difficult to think clearly when under the influence of drugs. It is self-evident that many people (including substantial consumers) sometimes resort to self-deception, and problematic consumers often hold straight people at bay by saying foolish things. However, when I got to know them it became clear that taken as a group there was no reason to believe that their intelligence differs widely from the population at large. And on the whole, they understand as well as the rest of us where their lifestyle is leading them. Still, they continue to take narcotics.

A short poem from one of my research subjects:

Things get worse from day to day,
But what does it matter anyway?

The substantial consumers in my study clearly saw that they themselves and everyone around them were destroying their lives; yet they continued to use drugs. Therefore there must be a powerful self-destructive side to their personalities.[1] As least as far as the population I studied is concerned, it is reasonable to conclude that *people who do not have strong self-destructive tendencies do not become problematic consumers of narcotics.* However, the extent to which this can be generalized can only be ascertained through research on different populations of substantial consumers.

Seeing self-destructiveness as a major element in the essential nature of substantial consumption of narcotics helps us to understand an important difference between recreational and problematic consumers. Recreational consumers seek certain experiences, i.e. an altered state of mind, sexuality, spirituality, new sensations, etc., and they are willing to pay a price to achieve their goals. But they are not willing to sacrifice everything. When the economic, social, psychological and/or physiological costs get too high, they either desist altogether or limit their consumption. Most people do not want to destroy their lives and this may explain why only a very small percent of those who try psychoactive substances use them frequently for an extended period of time.

For people with strong self-destructive tendencies, the negative effects of the lifestyle on the drug scene can be an important reason to continue consuming drugs. Problematic consumption of narcotics may be seen as a major element in their self-destructive life-project.

Prospective problematic consumers may initially believe that something positive can stem from taking drugs. They hope that narcotics will help replace

[1] I shall discuss how they have developed this self-destructiveness in Part II.

the negative feelings and thoughts that dominate their conscious state with something positive; or at least make it possible to escape from or still their terrifying thoughts and emotions. But my research subjects bear within a deep well full of negative experiences. If they manage to bypass their defence mechanisms with the help of drugs, they do not discover a new and positive conscious state. Instead, they are haunted by hoards of demons which pop up out of the depths of their long repressed past. These despairing experiences, feelings and thoughts originate in negative relations to others. To be able to feel better, they must establish and maintain positive social relationships. This is why their attempts to create a positive conscious state by taking drugs is doomed to failure. Each monster aroused from the dark corners of their subconscious mind serves as further confirmation of their inferiority as human beings. The hope of finding something better, or at least finding a way to escape, soon dissolves and is replaced by a reinforced conviction that they deserve to be destroyed. Problematic consumption is a means to that end.

SPONTANEOUS REMISSION

But how can this be reconciled with *spontaneous remission*: that many older substantial consumers stop using narcotics without medical care or other formal treatment? For example, Mossberg and Änggård (p. 16) report in their study of literature on narcotics careers that 'approximately 2/3 of all intravenous abusers are able to break their habit on their own, i.e., they "mature out" of abuse'. I do not claim to have a comprehensive explanation for spontaneous remission, but the following discussion may provide some clarification.

I have already briefly mentioned one way to get off narcotics. If a substantial consumer manages to retain a new and more positive network of significant others – i.e. people who react to him in a way that helps him improve his self-image – then he has laid a foundation which can help him feel better about himself and eventually get off drugs. Finding a new partner to live with who does not use drugs, joining a narcotics anonymous organization, going through a religious conversion with the resulting social contacts in the congregation, etc. are examples of how this can be done. But the question is, why should anything like this happen right now; why hasn't it happened earlier? To explain this, we must take a short detour.

Just about all of the substantial consumers in my study had two ways of looking at their lives. They sometimes saw themselves as subjects, i.e. the actions they take affect their future. But at the same time they have a strong fatalistic vein. When they put on their 'fatalistic glasses', they do not see themselves as masters of their destiny, but rather that fate steers their lives. They see themselves as objects.

When a somewhat older problematic drug consumer looks back on his life, what has fate held in store for him? Obviously he was not 'destined' to die young – as he previously believed. The fact that many of those he has known over the years have met that fate – but not he – raises the question, why am I still alive? The older substantial consumer still believes that he does not deserve to live, but he cannot deny that he is still here. If he can convince himself that an early departure from this life was not in his stars, he no longer has to continue being his own executioner.

But this revelation is still a far cry from considering himself to be just like anybody else. It is impossible for him to simply forget what he has done over the years and begin to live like the rest of us. As one of my research subjects put it: 'After everything I've been through, I just can't live straight.'

Although the older problematic consumer doesn't really understand why, he has now come to the realization that he apparently has the right to exist. The problem is finding a way to do it. A common first step in this direction is to gradually switch from illegal to legal drugs, such as alcohol, methadone and/or psychoactive medicine. In this way he reduces much of the self-destructiveness that is an integral part of life on the drug scene, and diminishes the number of negative reactions he gets from others. This in turn makes it possible for him to start to change his self-image.

Eventually he can take further steps which augment the process. For example, he can take a part-time job, start a family, establish a permanent residence, etc. But all of this takes time. Using substantial quantities of legal drugs may be a way to position himself somewhere between the straight world and those whose fate it is to destroy themselves with narcotics. But at the same time, these small changes make it easier for him to establish better relations with others – thereby creating a more positive social network.

CONCLUSION

Substantial consumers were not born self-destructive. It is therefore important to understand their personality structures, and the environments that have created them. I shall begin by examining their psychosocial backgrounds.

5 The Psychosocial Background of Problematic Consumers

INTRODUCTION

It is often claimed that anyone can become a narcotics abuser during adolescence; whatever his background or previous social experiences may have been. Under the heading, 'An external enemy', the father of a problematic consumer relates:

> When drugs came into our home, it felt as if our son had become another person. The lack of contact between us was worse than a normal puberty crisis. It's not enough to just wonder about red eyes and morning fatigue. To discover if your child is using drugs you have to really know him. *The worst part is the betrayal.* A family is normally built on mutual trust. Drugs destroy the family bonds. When the ties are broken they're replaced by lies. Initially we believed them. What else could we do? But then the atmosphere rapidly deteriorates. Small bills aren't where you left them. Inherited keepsakes disappear and your child gets into crime. The worst part is the betrayal. Not the loss of odds and ends, but betraying the family. Things can go pretty far before you see what's happening. For a long time we thought there was something basically wrong with the family that caused all this to happen. It was hard for us to fathom that it was an external enemy.
>
> (from Nordegren and Tunving, p. 235) (emphasis in original)

This interpretation is not unique. It is not merely a last straw desperately grasped by a parent in despair, but reflects the more or less official interpretation of a number of organizations, e.g. Parents Against Drugs (FMN) in Sweden.

What are the assumptions behind this kind of explanation? The fundamental idea is that a basically problem-free family can suddenly find that their completely normal teenager has become changed beyond recognition overnight by an external enemy (narcotics). The implication is that relations between family members had always been good until narcotics came into the picture. First then is the closeness, the mutual trust, and the parents' deep understanding of their child destroyed. Deceit begins with drugs; then the atmosphere in the family turns bad. It is not the parents who have betrayed their child, but it is the child (due to the chemical effects of narcotics) who has betrayed them. There have never been any major problems in the family – the current situation has been caused solely by drugs – an external enemy. The underlying idea is that there is nothing unusual in the problematic consumer's background; any family with teenagers can be 'stricken' by narcotics. Narcotics alone are to blame!

That an organization such as FMN holds this view is understandable. Most of their members are parents of problematic consumers, and one of the main goals of the organization is to help these people come to terms with their grief. Defining the situation in this way may help to ease the burden that many of FMN's members bear. I understand and sympathize with this objective. But the methods they use, i.e. reducing the causes of drug consumption to the chemical effects of narcotics and ignoring the individual's past experiences (set), deprives us of the possibility of learning from previous mistakes and makes it difficult to find effective preventive measures.

This 'external-enemy perspective' has another major disadvantage; it increases fear in other parents as they are given the impression that there is nothing they can do to protect their children. If drugs smite blindly, then nobody is safe. Neither current nor future parents have anything to gain by this frightening and pacifying interpretation. A more useful approach is to convey information which can help parents understand what they can do to reduce the chances of their children becoming substantial consumers. This is one of the objectives of this book.

A multitude of studies on different populations all over the industrialized world clearly show that the vast majority of problematic consumers of narcotics are recruited among individuals who have extremely negative childhood environments. However, this does not imply that there is a list of background variables that makes it possible to predict exactly which individuals will become substantial consumers. But we do know that certain kinds of experiences in childhood and adolescence are more common among problematic consumers than in the population as a whole. In this chapter I shall present some of these research results.

However, before examining family relationships, I will mention a macro-level variable. While it is true that people from all social classes become problematic consumers, it is incorrect to claim that social class is irrelevant. A number of studies have shown a marked overrepresentation of substantial consumers from the lowest social stratum. Social class is not a sufficient explanation of who will become a problematic consumer, but it is an important variable in this context. A good economy doesn't guarantee that a child will not become an addict, but money can be used to partially offset unsatisfactory social relationships within the family, by for instance hiring help or sending the child to boarding school. However, not even this always helps when family ties are extremely bad.

THE FAMILIES OF PROBLEMATIC CONSUMERS

As early as the 1960s, Chein et al. (1964) showed that social background plays an important role in heroin consumption. In a demographic study, they found that: 'The areas of high incidence of drug use are characterized by the high incidence of impoverished families, great concentration of the most discriminated against and least urbanized ethnic groups, and high incidence of disrupted families and other forms of human misery' (ibid., p. 10). 'Even before they started using drugs regularly, most users have had friends who had been in jail, reformatory, or on probation' (ibid., p. 13).

> Their home life is conducive to the development of disturbed personalities, which they display in abundant measure. Relations between parents are far from ideal, as evidenced by separation, divorce, overt hostility, or lack of warmth. In almost half of the cases, there was no father and no other adult male in the household during a significant portion of the boys' early childhood. As children they tended to be over-indulged or harshly frustrated. The parents were often unclear about the standards of behavior they wanted their sons to adhere to and tended to be inconsistent in their application of disciplinary measures. Their ambitions for their sons were typically unrealistically low, but in other instances they were unrealistically high. Although we had hoped to do some special studies of deviant cases – that is, of addicts coming from psychologically adequate homes and of non-delinquent nonusers coming from psychologically deficient homes – we were frustrated because we did not find such cases. (Ibid., p. 13f)

Similar results have been found in a great number of studies. For instance, Australian physician Chaim Rosenberg (p. 72) writes:

> As a group the addicts had grown up in adverse circumstances. The low socioeconomic status of their families was due mainly to the ineffectiveness, temporarily or permanently, of the father as a breadwinner as a result of alcoholism, mental illness, chronic physical illness, imprisonment, desertion, separation, divorce or death. The resulting domestic instability and lack of adequate parental control could account for some of the personality and sexual disturbances shown by most of these subjects.

American psychiatrist Leon Wurmser (p. 80), who has had extensive experience treating problematic consumers of narcotics, writes:

> By no stretch of the imagination can we postulate these people to be considered healthy, were it not for their one problem of drug use. No one who knows them well and has learned the rudiments of psychiatry

> would declare them well even if the drug problem was magically wiped out. Theoretically I allow for exceptions: perhaps there are some compulsive drug users who have not shown any other symptoms of severe psychopathology. They have eluded me however.

Since the studies cited are from the US and Australia one can question if they are relevant in the context of other nations. Social processes in many countries increase the risk that a portion of the population will grow up with the kinds of destructive life experiences described above. Among these factors are:

- labour market conditions which make it difficult for those with least education and/or work experience to find gainful employment;
- unequally distributed educational opportunities;
- segregated housing;
- hostility to foreigners;
- refugees/immigrants who bear with them extremely negative experiences from their home countries;
- discrimination towards minority groups.

SOCIAL HEREDITY

Concurrent with Chein et al., researchers in other countries were arriving at similar results. A Swedish physician, Gustav Jonsson (1969, 1973), presented a theory he called 'social heredity'. By studying the families of adolescents at a treatment centre for troubled youth in the 1950s and 1960s, he found poverty, mental illness, alcohol abuse, poor emotional relations between parents and children, etc. to be a recurrent theme going back three generations. Similar results were reported in the 1980s by Professor of Social Work Sven Hessle, who sees the following development for substantial consumers: 'Unwanted as a child → failure in school → never admitted to the labor market → *rejected as an adult citizen in society*' (emphasis in original) (Hessle, 1987, p. 16).

However, it is important to note that social heredity is not an automatic process; a given social background does not necessarily mean that an individual will inevitably become a deviant. What we can say is that compared to others, individuals from such environments run a far greater risk of pursuing a deviant career due to their family's position in society.

Professor of Criminology Jerzy Sarnecki (p. 28) writes:

> stating that everyone, regardless of social background, runs the same risk of becoming a drug abuser, is obviously false. Young people who come from socially difficult circumstances, and who have begun to have social

> problems (i.e. juvenile delinquency, truancy, alcohol abuse, etc.) run a much greater risk of becoming intravenous narcotics addicts than adolescents who have not shown these signs.

He also states:

> The problem of narcotics does not seem to be an 'exceptional' kind of deviant behavior, as some claim. It is the same youths who run the risk of having various kinds of social problems as adults who risk becoming intravenous narcotics abusers. (Ibid.)

Professor of Criminal Statistics Hanns von Hofer, and Professor of Criminology Henrik Tham (p. 341) conclude:

> Narcotics abusers are most likely to be found in the same groups that were previously distinguished by criminality and serious alcohol consumption. Socially disadvantaged groups have switched from crime and alcohol, to alcohol and narcotics and even more crime.

In another article, Tham (1992, p. 87) writes: '[narcotics] abuse appears to have been primarily established in groups consisting of criminals and other deviants. Its potential expansion is limited by the size of these groups.'

An international comparison under the auspices of the Council of Europe, compiled by criminologist Leif Lenke, shows the same tendency in six European countries. Lenke (p. 18) concludes: 'A statement to the effect that injection use of drugs (during the last decade) is a phenomenon concentrated in the lower and even lowest strata of the populations, stands on safe ground.'

In summary, the evidence points to the conclusion that problematic consumers of narcotics are recruited from the same marginalized groups that have always produced deviant behaviour of one kind or other. In the words of physicians Claes Sundelin and Göran Kjellberg (p. 6):

> a number of important publications clearly show that serious health problems . . . are closely correlated with the social situation in which people live. Almost any area investigated shows that those who were most deprived died earlier and were more unhealthy than people belonging to groups that were better off.

GENDER AND BACKGROUND

Until the 1980s few narcotics researchers discussed distinctions between male and female problematic consumers. Little was said about diversities in their paths to narcotics, gender-related experiences in conjunction with drugs and disparate treatment needs. However, gender is now being given more attention.

In her doctoral dissertation in medicine Maj-Britt Holmberg (p. 23) found that males who later became problematic consumers had a previous history of officially recorded crime. This was not the case for females, who were primarily reported for truancy and nervous disorders.

Sociologist Marie Torstensson (p. 188) found that as opposed to males, there is no clear correlation between registered deviance in early adolescence and later drug abuse among females. Her interpretation is that deviant behaviour in adolescent girls usually takes the form of running away from home, truancy, misbehaviour in school, etc., while boys commit crimes such as theft, vandalism and assault. This helps to explain why young girls do not appear in official records as often as boys. Another possible explanation is that the authorities are less inclined to register the wrongdoing of adolescent females.

Based on a number of studies from the US, Menicucci and Wermuth (p. 137) conclude that accessible data indicate that 'parental substance abuse, family tragedy and loss, and sexual and physical abuse are more highly associated with later drug abuse in women than in men (even when controlling for the greater degree of sexual abuse of girls than of boys)'. Furthermore they have found that female abusers have fewer years of formal education and less success on the labour market than both male abusers and women in the normal population (ibid.).

Concerning the girls who have become heroin addicts, Chein et al. (p. 319), write:

> Their families resembled the families of male adolescent addicts, in terms both of their life-long family situations and their current familial environments, the notable exceptions being that indexes of unrealistic aspirations for the children and distrust of major social institutions were found to be lower for the families of the girl than of the boy addicts. There is thus reason to believe that the female adolescent opiate addict developed her difficulties in social adaptation and her psychopathology ... in a malignant familial environment.

Women's paths to problematic consumption most surely contain life experiences which differ somewhat from their male counterparts. Modern gender research convincingly shows that during childhood and adolescence girls are treated differently than boys in a number of ways; i.e. the demands made upon them, the amount of time devoted to them, responses given to them in school, etc. Therefore their expectations of life and their patterns of behaviour differ in important ways from males. This should be taken into consideration when, for instance, planning treatment programmes. But for my purposes here, to describe the psychosocial background of problematic consumers at large, it is most likely that the greater part of the research results presented are applicable to both sexes.

We shall now take a closer look at two Swedish studies, supplemented by references to other research. Each of the main surveys has a longitudinal design, following their populations for many years. Both are stringently executed (i.e. they follow accepted methodological rules) and are based on large populations.

A STUDY OF HIGH SCHOOL STUDENTS

Holmberg asked 15 year olds in Gothenburg to fill in a questionnaire concerning their drug habits. She then followed these youths for eleven years with questionnaires, interviews, and by studying public records.

> Compared to others, those who stated that they used narcotics, came from broken homes, did not get along well with their parents, spent fewer evenings during the week at home, resided in smaller living quarters, spoke less often about their problems with their guardians, had siblings and friends whom they thought used drugs, were more often truant, and had less ambition to continue their education. They frequented youth centers and dances, and they met their friends in town and at cafés more often than others, and had better knowledge of drug-related slang. They also acknowledged having previous and present nervous disorders, to a greater extent than those who didn't use narcotics.
>
> (Holmberg, p. 12)

Other important variables were 'coming from a multiple-problem family, child-psychiatric care, placement in remedial classes, early contact with social welfare services, and dropping out of school' (ibid., p. 23).

Holmberg (p. 30) concludes:

> The findings indicate that those in a given age group who have the earliest and most serious disturbances are those who were most likely to become addicts. They were more frequently known to the social authorities, but the measures taken were not sufficient to change the course of their lives. During the eleven-year follow-up, their social and medical problems became aggravated still further.
>
> Large groups lacking early social problems had a brief, usually hidden, period of drug abuse without tangible social or medical consequences for these individuals.[1]

[1] Holmberg uses the concept drug abuse here. In my terminology she is referring to recreational consumers.

A STUDY OF MILITARY CONSCRIPTS

Research on the drug habits of Swedish military conscripts has been carried out almost annually since the 1960s. One of these studies, comprising more than 50 000 inductees was transferred to magnetic tape in a way that made it possible to follow the conscripts in other databases covering a 20-year period. Artur Solarz, a researcher at the Swedish National Council for Crime Prevention (BRÅ), made use of this possibility to gather data on the backgrounds of substantial consumers. Solarz calls individuals who have either used narcotics more than 50 times or inject drugs *abusers*; while those who have used drugs less than 50 times and who do not inject, are *sometime users*.[2] These categories resemble my concepts problematic and recreational consumers.

Solarz investigates a number of variables to see if there is anything that distinguishes the home environments of abusers from those of sometime users and abstainers. He describes the worst home conditions as having several of the following characteristics: low socioeconomic standard, alcohol abuse, corporal punishment, conflicts, at least one biological parent not present or a father who lacks interest in the family. The best homes had a high economic standard, father and son have common interests, the frequency of contact between child and parents is high, and the parents give the child a chance to make decisions and maintain his independence (Solarz, p. 44). He concludes that sometime users are recruited among adolescents with many different home backgrounds. But approximately 30 times as many abusers came from the worst home backgrounds than the best (ibid., p. 45).

THE CHILDHOOD ENVIRONMENTS OF PROBLEMATIC CONSUMERS

With the help of Solarz's study we shall now take a look at the childhood environment of future problematic consumers, placing special emphasis on their parents and conditions in the home (the page numbers in parentheses refer to Solarz's book). I will also refer to some other studies that have come to similar conclusions: Berit Andersson's doctoral dissertation in sociology in which she uses data from intake interviews with newly-admitted patients to treatment centres in Malmö, a report by sociologist Börje Olsson from the SWEDATE project which analysed and compared different treatment centres, and finally an interview study of patients admitted to the

[2] Solarz divides *sometime user* into four sub-categories, and presents statistics for each. As this in no way changes the conclusions presented, I will only use the main categories abuser/sometime user. For the results for each sub-category see Solarz, pp. 45–93.

narcotics treatment clinic at Långbro Hospital in Stockholm by Jan Ramström and Staffan Lindberg.

- Abusers, more often than non-abusers, come from homes where the parents suffer from serious illness (p. 48) (see also Olsson, p. 23 and Ramström, 1983, p. 128f).
- The father's alcohol habits show covariance with the son's narcotics habits. The correlation is more pronounced the more the father drinks (p. 48f) (see also Andersson, 1991, p. 95, Olsson, p. 22 and Ramström, 1983, p. 128).
- Extremely strict upbringing is strongly correlated to the use of narcotics. Extremely lenient upbringing is more strongly correlated to narcotics consumption than 'neither lenient nor strict upbringing' (p. 49f).
- Corporal punishment is strongly correlated to narcotics consumption. Children who have been frequently beaten become abusers more often than those who have sometimes, very occasionally, or never been struck. Those who had been hit on rare occasions have the lowest incidence of narcotics use (p. 50f).
- Almost all abusers have run away from home, most often on several occasions (p. 51f).
- Those who lived with their mother, or other than their biological parents, became abusers three times as often as those who were raised by both biological parents (p. 52) (see also Andersson, p. 95, Olsson, p. 20 and Ramström, 1983, p. 128f).
- There was no correlation between family economy and sometime use of narcotics. However, families with poor economies are overrepresented among abusers. Similar correlations were found for overcrowded living conditions (p. 53f) (see also Olsson, p. 22).
- The risk of becoming an abuser was ten times greater for those who were unhappy in their childhood home compared to those who got along well with their families (p. 54) (see also Ramström, 1983, p. 129).
- While growing up, certain symptoms such as headaches, insomnia, depression, stomach troubles and nervousness were more common among those who became abusers than among the others (p. 127).

In conclusion Solarz states:

> The chance that an individual will try narcotics at some time is the same regardless of whether he comes from a home with a low socioeconomic standard, alcohol abuse, beatings, conflict, divorce, one or both parents deceased and where there is no father who shows an interest in the family; or from a home with good family relations and a good socioeconomic standard. But among narcotics abusers, the difference between those who had more favorable and less favorable family conditions is very clear. *Of*

those belonging to the category 'most frequent narcotics abusers', 30 times as many came from 'bad' homes as from 'good' ones.

(Solatz, p. 55) (my italics)

INDIVIDUAL CHARACTERISTICS OF PROBLEMATIC CONSUMERS

I agree with Bakalar and Grinspoon (p. 43) when they write: 'it is not true that only and all people who have some special characteristics identifiable in advance will use or misuse drugs'. There is no automatic connection between, on the one hand, a certain social background and/or personal attributes, and on the other hand the way a person consumes drugs. However, we can say that certain individual characteristics are extremely common among problematic consumers; differentiating them as a group from both recreational consumers and abstainers.

Some research reports show no essential differences between recreational consumers and abstainers. For example, Weil and Zinberg compared recreational consumers of marijuana with abstainers. No identifiable differences in their personalities were found (Weil, p. 12). As we have already seen, Solarz reached a similar conclusion.

However, two researchers at Berkeley, Jonathan Shedler and Jack Block, found clear and important differences. A sample of 130 children were recruited at age three and followed in a longitudinal study until they were 18. The subjects were tested at different times and in different ways. For instance at age five they participated in a joint assessment session with their mothers and a separate joint assessment session with their fathers. Parent and child were left alone to perform given tasks, and were observed through a one-way mirror and videotaped. Two separate trained observers assessed their interaction using a 49–item Q-sort.

At ages four, 11 and 18 the subjects were given intelligence tests. When they were seven the children were given the 100-item California Child Q-sort which measures personality characteristics. At age 11 a 63–item abridged version of this Q-sort was administered, and at 18 the 100-item California Adult Q-sort was used. Furthermore, a four-hour videotaped individual interview covering such topics as schoolwork, dating experience, peer relations, family dynamics, personal interest and drug consumption was conducted with the 101 18 year olds (49 males and 52 females) still remaining in the study.

Based on the information collected at age 18 the subjects were divided into three groups; abstainers who had never tried any narcotic (29 subjects), experimenters who had used marijuana a few times and who had tried no more than one other narcotic (36 subjects), and frequent users who reported having used marijuana once a week or more and who had tried at least one other drug (20 subjects). Sixteen subjects 'fell between the cracks'.

The groups were compared as to socioeconomic status, and on the basis of the three administrations of intelligence tests; 'no associations approaching significance were observed' (Shedler and Block, p. 615). Then, based on the three Q-sorts, the personality characteristics of each group were compared. To summarize the results, the personalities characteristic of each group *antecedent* to drug consumption were:

> the frequent users appear to be relatively maladjusted as children. As early as age 7, the picture that emerges is of a child unable to form good relationships, who is insecure, and who shows numerous signs of emotional distress. These data indicate that the relative social and psychological maladjustment of the frequent users predates adolescence, and predates initiation of drug use. (Ibid., p. 618)

At the same age abstainers were described as:

> a child who is relatively over-controlled, timid, fearful, and morose. While the characterizations of these children as 'anxious', 'inhibited', and 'immobilized under stress' are telling, more telling, perhaps, may be the descriptions of what these children are not; relative to the reference group of experimenters, they are not warm and responsive, not curious and open to new experience, not active, not vital and not cheerful. (Ibid., p. 619f)

Personality characteristics of the three groups at age 18 were summarized as follows:

> Relative to experimenters, frequent users are described as not dependable or responsible, not productive or able to get things done, guileful and deceitful, opportunistic, unpredictable and changeable in attitudes and behavior, unable to delay gratification, rebellious and non-conforming, prone to push and stretch limits, self-indulgent, not ethically consistent, not having high aspirations, and prone to express hostile feelings directly.
>
> Relative to experimenters, frequent users are described as critical, unforgiving, not sympathetic or considerate, not liked or accepted by others, not having warmth or the capacity for close relationships, having hostility towards others, prone to avoid close relationships, distrustful of people, not gregarious, not personally charming, and not socially at ease.
>
> Finally, frequent users are described as relatively over-reactive to minor frustrations, likely to think and associate to ideas in unusual ways, having brittle ego-defense systems, self-defeating, concerned about the adequacy of their bodily functioning, concerned about their adequacy as persons, prone to project their feelings and motives onto others, feeling cheated and victimized by life, and having fluctuating moods. (Ibid., p. 617)

Concerning the personalities of abstainers Shedler and Block conclude:

> Relative to experimenters, abstainers are described as fastidious, conservative, proud of being 'objective' and rational, over-controlled and prone to delay gratification unnecessarily, not liked or accepted by people, moralistic, inexpressive, prone to avoid close interpersonal relationships, predictable in attitudes and behavior, not gregarious, not able to enjoy sensuous experiences, basically anxious, not straightforward and forthright with others, not physically attractive, not personally charming, and not socially at ease. (Ibid., p. 618)

It is interesting to note that the abstainers and the experimenters achieve identical high school grade point averages (3.0 in both cases) while frequent users show significantly poorer results (2.3 on average) (ibid., p. 617f).

Based on the joint assessment sessions at age five, Shedler and Block compare the *quality of parenting* experienced by the three groups. Compared to the mothers of the experimenters:

> *the mothers of the frequent users are perceived as relatively cold, unresponsive, and under-protective. They appear to give their children little encouragement, while, conjointly, they are pressuring and overly interested in their children's 'performance'. The apparent effect of this double-bind is that they turn a potentially enjoyable interaction into a grim and unpleasant one.* Few items discriminated between the fathers of frequent users and the fathers of experimenters.[3] (Ibid., p. 621) (emphasis in original)

Concerning the mothers of the abstainers Shedler and Block conclude:

> *Like the mothers of the frequent users, these mothers are perceived as relatively cold and unresponsive. They give their children little encouragement, while, conjointly, they are pressuring and overly interested in their children's performance. Again, the apparent net effect is that they make the interaction grim and unenjoyable.* (Ibid.) (emphasis in original)

Compared to the fathers of the experimenters, the fathers of abstainers are characterized in the following way:

> *The picture that emerges is of an authoritarian and domineering father who squelches spontaneity and creativity and who demands that things be done his way. He does not appear to enjoy being with his child, and he ensures that his child does not enjoy being with him.* (Ibid., p. 622) (emphasis in original)

The research of Shedler and Block implies that regardless of the age of the subjects at the time of measurement, or the methods of data collection, those

[3] In most studies, including the ones cited earlier in this chapter, the fathers of frequent users are either physically absent or play a very negative role in the family.

who became frequent users were found to be significantly more disturbed than the other two groups. Furthermore the experimenters are found to be psychologically healthier than either abstainers or frequent users (ibid., p. 625). However, these findings must be understood in their cultural setting. Among Californian youth marijuana is widely accepted and easily accessible (ibid.). Therefore, Shedler and Block conclude:

> it is not surprising that by age 18, psychologically healthy, sociable, and reasonably inquisitive individuals would have been tempted to try marijuana. We would not expect these essentially normal and certainly normative adolescents to abuse the drug (and it is crucial to distinguish between experimentation and abuse) because they would have little need for drugs as an outlet for emotional distress or as a means of compensating for lack of meaningful human relationships – but we should not be surprised if they try it. Indeed, not to do so may reflect a degree of inhibition and social isolation in an 18-year-old.

While this may be true in the current California setting, it is not necessarily true in another cultural climate, i.e. where there is a more restrictive attitude to drugs.

MORE INDIVIDUAL CHARACTERISTICS OF PROBLEMATIC CONSUMERS

Chein et al. (p. 14) write of teenage addicts: 'They are not able to enter prolonged, close, friendly relations with either peers or adults; they have difficulties in assuming a masculine role; they are frequently overcome by a sense of futility, expectations of failure, and general depression; they are easily frustrated and made anxious, and they find both frustration and anxiety intolerable.' 'They participated in a smaller range of leisure activities than did their peers; they showed little interest in extracurricular programs, in any aspects of the political situation, or indeed in anything outside their immediate lives' (ibid., p. 198). They tend to avoid disappointment (ibid., p. 200), avoid personal growth (ibid., p. 202), they feel weak, inferior, have a negative self-image (ibid., p. 207) and they also feel insecure and undeserving, in spite of the fact that they often try to hide it behind a façade of self-confidence and arrogance (ibid., p. 208). Problematic consumers have 'an extraordinary lack of capacity to feel happy' (ibid., p. 246).

These are the characteristics Chein et al. found in the heroin addicts they studied, and I can confirm that in my fieldwork I never met a single problematic consumer of narcotics who did not show signs of several of these personality traits. However, the critical reader may object by pointing out that both Chein et al. and I have studied individuals who were already substantial consumers of narcotics, and therefore it might be the drugs themselves that created these traits. Chein et al. (ibid., p. 208) write: 'The adolescent addicts we have studied had little sense of accomplishment and, indeed, they had accomplished little. They had adjusted poorly *prior to drug use*. They had given up schooling and were involved in overt misbehavior or deviant behavior. Their work history was also unsatisfactory' (my italics).

> The 'preaddict', if we may use this term, has been notoriously unsuccessful in his educational, occupational, sexual, or familial life. For those few exceptions who were able to manage without conspicuous failures in one or several of these areas, there are quite evident anxieties or psychiatric symptoms which contaminated, blunted, or negated whatever else was satisfactory in their lives. (Ibid., p. 244)

'... we have reason to believe that, by virtue of their functioning prior to and apart from their first use of opiates, their lives would have entered other maladaptive paths, ranging from serious behavior disturbances to neurotic character disorders to psychoses' (ibid., p. 365).

Another possible objection to Chein et al.'s description of the personality traits of problematic consumers is that these are very common characteristics in the environment of poverty and destitution studied. But Chein et al. have also studied non-deviants who grew up in the same environment. The researchers found that:

> These boys are not as yet at odds with the major institutions; they do not drop out of school, and many manage to hold a job. Their general orientation at sixteen was reasonably realistic in that they had some sort of definite plan for the immediate future, and they did not wish for things they knew they could not possibly get. Their relation to their environment was positive in the sense that they were interested in and able to utilize available opportunities, such as extracurricular activities, to their enjoyment and benefit. (Ibid., p. 143)

In all of these respects they clearly differ from their peers who already were, or who were on their way to becoming problematic consumers of narcotics.

Another important difference is that those who didn't use narcotics:

> indicated in a variety of ways, a determined effort to stay away from those 'others', who might 'get them into trouble'. Nearly half the users, on the other hand, expressed neutral or even friendly feelings toward the 'others', and few expressed distinctly negative feelings. (Ibid., p. 147)

A final objection to Chein et al. is that their list includes so many characteristics that a great number of people display at least some of them. There is an important point in this observation. Problematic consumers do not belong to a different species than the rest of humanity. We should not consider the problems of substantial consumers as distinctly different from those of many other individuals. Instead, it is the number and intensity of their psychosocial problems which differentiates problematic consumers from others.

SCHOOL, EMPLOYMENT, LEISURE

Solarz investigated the significance of achievements in school, in the workplace and leisure time activities as background variables for substance abuse. I shall summarize some of the variables that show correlations with problematic consumption of narcotics (the numbers in parentheses refer to Solarz). As I have done previously, I will refer to other studies which collaborate these conclusions. Problematic consumers of narcotics:

- were poor achievers in school. For every abuser who did well in school, there were 28 who didn't (p. 59) (see also Andersson, 1991, p. 95f and Olsson, p. 23f);
- felt themselves unjustly treated in school (p. 60);
- were truants (p. 60) (see also Andersson, 1991, p. 95);
- received bad grades in conduct (p. 60);
- were often absent from school because of overexertion (p. 60);
- were left back or placed in a remedial class (p. 61) (see also Andersson, 1991, p. 96);
- were maladjusted on the job (p. 63) (see also Olsson, p. 24f);
- have never held a job for more than three consecutive months after leaving school (p. 64);
- felt themselves unjustly treated at work and quit (p. 64);
- have been fired several times (p. 64f);
- come into conflict with superiors (p. 65f);
- disliked many of their coworkers (p. 65f);
- have not participated in organized activities during their leisure time (pp. 67ff).

CRIMINALITY AND CONSUMPTION OF OTHER DRUGS PRIOR TO NARCOTICS DEBUT

Solarz found that drug abuse is closely correlated with:

- heavy tobacco consumption in adolescence (p. 73f);
- frequent intoxication, hangovers, and need of a pick-me-up during adolescence (pp. 74ff) (see also Ramström, 1983, p. 129);
- having sniffed organic solvents more than ten times (p. 77f) (see also Ramström, 1983, p. 129);

- repeated shoplifting during adolescence (p. 79f);
- being known to the authorities. For every abuser who has never had contact with the police or the Child Welfare Board in his youth, there are 22 abusers who have had several such contacts (p. 80) (see also Ramström, 1983, p. 129).

PSYCHOLOGICAL STATUS

Solarz gives an account of the results of psychological evaluations based on medical and psychological studies conducted on the conscripts. The results show that problematic consumers of narcotics, to a greater extent than others:

- have psychosomatic symptoms (p. 88);
- exhibit low stress tolerance (p. 88);
- are anxiety prone (p. 88);
- have difficulties controlling nervousness and/or channelling aggression (p. 89);
- are dependent on others (p. 89);
- find it difficult to make contact with others (p. 89);
- are irresponsible (p. 89);
- lack initiative, and give up in the face of difficulty (p. 90f).

SUMMARY

In this chapter I have presented research results showing correlations between problematic narcotics consumption and:

1. conditions in the home
2. achievements in school
3. employment
4. leisure time activities
5. consumption of other drugs
6. crime
7. psychological traits

In summary, the picture which emerges shows that substantial consumers of narcotics are primarily recruited among individuals with many of the following factors in their background:

- poverty
- at least for one parent with excessive alcohol consumption
- physical abuse

- serious conflicts in the family
- not raised by both biological parents
- if the father was physically present, he showed little or no interest in the family
- received little encouragement
- spoiled or severely frustrated
- subjected to diffuse demands
- subjected to inconsistent use of punishment
- chronic physical and/or mental disorders in the family
- sexual abuse
- overcrowded living conditions
- multiproblem families
- dissatisfaction with the home environment
- ran away on multiple occasions
- subjected to discrimination

Furthermore, the prospective substantial consumer usually has several of the following psychosomatic symptoms:

- depression
- headaches
- stomach troubles
- insomnia
- low stress tolerance
- anxiety
- nervousness
- aggressiveness
- projection
- brittle ego-defence

His childhood and adolescence are characterized by:

- inability to form positive social relations
- insecurity
- emotional distress
- distrust of others
- hostility
- difficulties in taking initiatives
- giving up in the face of difficulty
- poor adjustment in school
- feeling unjustly treated in school
- low grades
- left back or placed in a remedial class
- truancy
- poor grades in conduct

- heavy smoking habits
- sniffing organic solvents
- extensive experience with alcohol, hangovers and pick-me-ups
- criminal behaviour, such as shoplifting, violence, theft, vandalism, etc.
- many contacts with the police and/or child welfare authorities
- feelings of inferiority
- a negative self-image

All of these research results speak against the idea that just anyone can become a problematic consumer of narcotics when he reaches his teens. But at the same time, we cannot say that all individuals whose psychosocial background coincides well with the picture presented above will become a substantial consumer. Even if these factors play an important role, there is no simple correlation between them and problematic consumption. It is impossible to predict who will become a problematic consumer, but with the help of the factors mentioned in this chapter, we can identify those who are at great risk, and those who are all but immune.

Chein et al. (p. 366) conclude that they 'have come to regard addiction ... as another complex expression of human suffering and human attempts to cope with it and as another manifestation of widespread need for therapeutic and preventive efforts'.

Part II
Deviant Careers

6 The Deviant Career: a Model

LABELLING THEORY

The roots of labelling theory can be traced to Charles H. Cooley (p. 277f), who wrote in 1902:

> If a man appears to be about to do something brutal or dishonest, we may either encounter him on his present low plane of life by knocking him down or calling a policeman, or we may try to work upon his higher consciousness by giving him to understand that we feel sure a person of his self-respect and good repute will not degrade himself ... [and evoke] the disappointment and contempt of those who before thought well of him. In other words, we threaten, as courteously as possible, his social self.

Cooley's understanding of deviance (he uses *degeneracy*, but in modern terminology *deviance* is more appropriate) is clear, although explaining it was not his primary objective.

> [Deviance] is altogether a social matter at bottom; that is to say, degeneracy exists only in a certain relation between a person and the rest of a group. In so far as any mental or physical traits constitute it they do so because they involve unfitness for a normal social career ... The criminal, largely because his abnormality is of so obvious and troublesome a kind that something in particular has to be done about it ... becomes definitely and formally stigmatized by the organs of social judgment. (Ibid., p. 406f)

Cooley uses two central concepts in labelling theory, *career* and *stigma*.

Modern labelling theory started to take form in the US in the 1960s. Being a relatively new perspective it has not as yet developed a clear and generally accepted core of concepts and assumptions. At present, the school contains a number of variations that are not entirely consistent with each other. Various authors have used the same concepts in dissimilar ways and emphasized different theoretical aspects, causing confusion and leading to criticism.

In his critical examination of the school, criminologist Johannes Knutsson (p. 52f) states: 'Because the perspective is so full of contradictions, any description of it and the discussion following thereof, is dependent on what evidence you choose.'[1]

[1] Knutsson's ideas have been confronted by several labelling theorists, and he in turn has responded to them. Interested readers are referred to *Brå apropå*, pp. 35–60.

I agree with much of the criticism Knutsson directs at individual authors. However, while he believes that his arguments are devastating for the approach in its entirety, I shall show how labelling theory helps us understand problematic narcotics consumption.

Before I present my model, I will introduce some of the ideas generally accepted by labelling theorists.

1. *Sequential (process) model* – it is important to think and analyse in terms of processes that begin in the past and continue beyond the present into the future. This as opposed to *simultaneous models* which assume that all of the factors which operate to produce a phenomenon operate concurrently. In such models we lose sight of the history of both the individual and the society in which he lives. An example of simultaneous thinking is the desperate parent who laments: 'My son was a wonderful kid until he fell in with the wrong crowd and was enticed into smoking a joint; which led to his downfall.'

   In this explanation all previous life experiences are deemed irrelevant. To my way of thinking it is unreasonable to believe that one event, however traumatic or euphoric it may have been, can obliterate everything a person has previously learned. *Behavioural patterns are not established overnight;* they develop throughout our lifetime. Labelling theoreticians try to trace the different stages in an individual's life; both those which initially led him away from society, and those which maintain deviant activities once they have been established.

2. *Career* is a concept used to describe this process. In a manner similar to the way in which a professional athlete begins in a sand lot, goes on to play in junior leagues, and works his way up through higher divisions before becoming a professional, also those whose behaviour is considered deviant go through various stages where earlier experiences build the framework upon which latter stages are built.

3. There are no objective criteria for determining what is deviant behaviour; no act is deviant in itself.

   > The same behaviour may be an infraction of the rules at one time and not at another; may be an infraction when committed by one person, but not when committed by another; some rules are broken with impunity, others are not. In short, whether a given act is deviant or not depends in part on the nature of the act (that is whether or not it violates some rule) and in part on what other people do about it. (Becker, p. 14)

4. Labelling can be evoked, not only by acts (what you do), but also by 'what you are'. In other words, labelling reactions can be elicited by skin colour, ethnic background, religion, physical or mental disabilities, economic status, social status, etc.

5. Groups create the rules that define which people and what kinds of behaviour are acceptable. 'Differences in the ability to make rules and apply them to other people are essentially power differentials (either legal or extralegal). Those groups whose social position gives them weapons and power are best able to enforce their rules' (ibid., p. 17f).

   Power is a central concept in labelling theoreticians' explanations of deviance:

   > Elites, ruling classes, bosses, adults, men, Caucasians – superordinate groups generally – maintain their power as much by controlling how people define the world, its components, and its possibilities, as by the use of more primitive forms of control. They may use more primitive means to establish hegemony. But control based on the manipulation of definitions and labels works more smoothly and costs less; superordinates prefer it. The attack on hierarchy begins with an attack on definitions, labels, and conventional conceptions of who's who and what's what. (Ibid., p. 204f)

   I shall discuss *ideology*, a concept often used to describe this type of power, in Chapter 12.

6. 'One of the most crucial steps in the process of building a stable pattern of deviant behaviour is likely to be the experience of being caught and publicly labeled as a deviant' (ibid., p. 31). This leads to serious consequences for both the individual's future possibilities and his self-image.

   For instance, in many countries teenagers convicted of criminal offences are sentenced to reformatories, and even sent to prison. By reacting in this manner we eliminate any prospect of their having experiences similar to contemporaries on the outside. Incarcerated adolescents are denied a normal education, and don't even have a theoretical chance of forming vital social ties with non-delinquent peers and adults. Instead, they are forced into an environment that reinforces their feelings of being deviant. At the same time they gain important knowledge and make contacts that prepare them for a future outside society. In the long run reform schools and prisons are more likely to lead to further criminality than to behaviour consistent with societal norms.

   This is not to imply that these teenagers would have automatically terminated their deviant careers, had they been able to continue their education in a normal school. It is likely that most of them would have chosen to continue to associate with other outsiders and proceed with their deviant careers. However, in correctional institutions they are forced to exclusively associate with others stigmatized as deviants. Thereby they become all the more convinced of who they are and where they (don't) belong.

This doesn't mean that I believe that laissez-faire is an adequate way of responding to adolescent deviance. Knutsson (p. 5) claims that labelling theory 'implies laissez-faire, that is, society should refrain from doing anything as any action merely makes the situation worse'. There is no logical connection between labelling theory and laissez-faire policies. In fact, labelling theory calls for exactly the opposite; it explains why others must react when someone does not comply with societal norms. But it also helps us understand why certain reactions are preferable to others: some constitute labelling, others do not. Naturally it is the latter type which labelling theoreticians advocate.

Unfortunately, labelling reactions are very common in society, for instance in penal institutions and treatment centres. When those who think in labelling terms point this out, representatives of these institutions often reply by claiming that we must choose between doing nothing at all or accepting the methods currently being used. As opposed to this *either/or thinking*, I maintain that we almost always have more than two alternatives: i.e. we can choose to react, but in a way which does not stigmatize. As we shall see in the course of this book either/or thinking is a recurrent element in the narcotics debate.

An example of a non-labelling reaction from society is when a city government decided that methods other than police coercion were necessary to stop inebriated adolescents from creating a public nuisance by cruising around the centre of town in automobiles. Funds were allocated to establish an automotive centre where young people whose main interests is cars could gather. Social workers were assigned to the project to help start a club, which would encourage responsible behaviour from these youths by giving them responsibility for the centre. The club achieved the intended effects.[2]

7. All human behaviour whether classified as normal or deviant has a collective component. In the case of deviance, we must consider the actions of both the perpetrator and those who feel it their duty to 'defend morality' by detecting wrongdoing and applying sanctions. All are involved in a complex interaction and it is not possible to understand any of the participants without relating his actions to what the others are doing/have done.
8. Everyone has at some time committed deviant acts. Why only a few pursue deviant careers can be explained with the help of labelling theory.

[2] I expound upon this and some other non-labelling reactions from society in Goldberg, 1990, pp. 62–76.

A LABELLING MODEL

Introduction

The model presented here is based on my participant observation studies of problematic consumers in Stockholm. When doing fieldwork a researcher meets many people with different characteristics, personalities, strengths, weaknesses, etc. The wealth of data is so great that it is easy to drown in a sea of details. The main objective of this model is to look beyond individual differences and present what I believe is a major underlying pattern common to those who made narcotics the central element in their lives.

However, as drug consumption is a complex phenomenon regulated by cultural norms and definitions, place, time, age, gender, etc., I am unable to determine the extent to which my model can be generalized. Hopefully readers will feel inspired to test its applicability on other populations.

Some Concepts

The *self-image* is an individual's conception of himself in relation to the ideals of his culture. But people aren't free to choose their self-image; it is established and modified through relations to others. A person who plays an important role in the creation, maintenance or reassessment of an individual's self-image is a *significant other*. A child's parents (those who raise him) are his first and usually most important significant others. It is through the parents that the child begins to establish his identity. As the individual grows older and comes into contact with society outside his home, some of the people he meets will become significant others and influence his self-image. However, its basis has already been established by that time. The initial labelling comes from the parents. Societal labelling is the second stage.

A person with a *negative self-image* has learned through interaction with significant others that there is a low degree of correspondence between himself and cultural ideals. *Labelling* is a course of events consisting of repeated negative reactions from significant others, which taken as a whole cause the individual to redefine his self-image in a negative direction. It is an ongoing process during an extended period of time, and even if the individual can identify dramatic events, these do not constitute a sufficient explanation. The self-image develops from the sum of many seemingly insignificant experiences and reactions during the entire lifetime of the individual, and therefore once it is well established it takes a long time to change its essential content; even if adjustments can be achieved in a shorter time frame.

With the help of these concepts, we can understand the four stages that constitute my deviant career model. I will briefly present the stages here, and then devote a separate chapter to each of them.

THE MODEL'S FOUR STAGES

> My mother loves me.
>   I feel good.
> I feel good because she loves me.
> I am good because I feel good
> I feel good because I am good
> My mother loves me because I am good.
> My mother does not love me.
>   I feel bad.
> I feel bad because she does not love me
>   I am bad because I feel bad
> I feel bad because I am bad
> I am bad because she does not love me
> She does not love me because I am bad.
>
> (R. D. Laing)

Parental Labelling

My basic assumption is that humans are born without a self-image. This means that I do not agree with those labelling theoreticians who assume that marginalized individuals were born with a positive self-image that was later transformed into a negative one as a result of labelling. At birth babies cannot distinguish between their own bodies and their surroundings. As infants don't even know that they have hands and feet, how could they possibly understand something as complex as what kind of human beings they are?

Primary deviance consists of acts which do not comply with societal norms, but which are not committed with malice aforethought. They are the result of a lack of understanding of the plausible consequences of one's actions. Cultural anthropologist Ralph Linton quipped: 'the newborn child is a barbarian invader from another planet'. That is, infants know nothing of the rules regulating the culture in which they will grow up. In order to learn societal norms (right from wrong), children must be given reactions to their spontaneous behaviour. This is one of the reasons why laissez-faire is contrary to the basic principles of labelling theory.

While everyone begins their lives with primary deviance, only some are given labelling reactions from their significant others. Somewhat oversimplified we can say that some children learn that they themselves are good, even if what they are doing for the moment is unacceptable. Others learn, after a sufficient number of unsuitable reactions, that it is not merely current activities that are unsatisfactory, but rather they themselves are bad. This is *parental labelling*, the *first stage* in my deviant career model.

Some parents appear to be unable to help their children develop a positive self-image: the question is why. Where answers are sought depends upon one's assumptions regarding the relative importance of nature and nurture. I shall briefly describe three types of explanation.

Those who assume that human behaviour is primarily of biochemical origin see deviance as being the result of some combination of faulty genetic constitution, metabolic disturbance or malfunction in vital organs such as the brain, glands or nervous system. For instance Robinson and Berridge (1993, p. 249) assume that 'addictive behaviour is due largely to progressive and persistent neuroadaptations caused by repeated drug use'. *Biochemical perspectives* imply that the root of deviance lies within the individual and/or the drugs themselves, and that the causes of the problem have little or nothing to do with either his social experiences or other people. Solutions are sought by attempting to find substances which will maintain a normal chemical balance within the individual, surgery, sterilization, trying to prevent access to narcotics, etc.

By defining deviance as a problem lying within the individual and/or the drugs themselves, the biochemical perspective is of major political significance. The implication is that deviant behaviour is not an indication of a need for social change.

Although no serious researcher disputes that some people have biological abnormalities, most social scientists reject this type of *biological reductionism*. Criminologist Albert K. Cohen (p. 54) writes: 'the linkages of biology to the various forms of deviance will be as various, indirect and remote as its linkages to the varieties of conforming behavior'. I would add that even if biologically inclined researchers at some future date are able to establish that such correlations do exist, it would still be impossible to rule out the possibility that some disorders of the body can be caused by social factors such as stressful living conditions, pollution, improper diet, etc. It is, therefore, insufficient to limit ourselves to biochemical factors when analysing deviant behaviour.

Psychological explanations are sought by looking for traits in the individual, such as his personality, temperament, subconscious needs, etc. The researcher asks: how did this person become such as he is? Answers are primarily sought on the microlevel; for example, in the individual's family, and other groups he currently belongs to and/or belonged to in childhood.

Sociological explanations originate in social structures and examine what creates possibilities/problems for individuals depending upon their position in society. Social institutions, culture, power, history, etc. are focal points for this perspective.

There is no fundamental antagonism between psychological and sociological models; they complement each other. Although psychologists usually emphasize the micro and mesolevels, while sociologists place emphasis on societal aspects, good social science includes elements from both perspectives.

The basic assumption common to both is that humans are social beings; that is, their behaviour is primarily governed by social relations. Researchers within these fields do not deny that individuals differ in terms of genetics and biology, but these differences are given subordinate roles. This book is based on the assumption that biology should be seen as a framework, setting maximal limits for what an individual can achieve. Social factors determine the extent to which the different elements in an individual's biological framework will be developed. This implies that an individual's behaviour cannot be analysed by looking solely at the individual. We must also consider processes and decisions on the macrolevel and in his microenvironment which create possibilities/obstacles for him. In other words the individual should be seen as bearing the problems of his family, while the family bears the problems of society. Therefore it is necessary to include a political dimension when analysing an individual's behaviour.

To return to the question of why some parents label their children, I emphasize both psychological and societal variables. Sociological explanations are important as they reveal the societal pressures people in different socioeconomic groups are subjected to and thereby the increased probability of certain types of behaviour. Statistically, such factors as belonging to a minority group, having poorly educated parents, living in a slum, etc. significantly reduce one's choices in life. But societal pressure is only a framework, not an inescapable force coercing people to act (or not act) in a particular way. Indeed all people in similar social situations do not behave in the same manner. Why Smith but not his neighbour Jones succumbs to societal pressure and labels his child cannot be explained sociologically. We must therefore also look at psychological variables, and examine what actually takes place in families that label their children. We must also ask, what can be done to help parents better fulfil their roles? My point of departure is that it is reasonable to assume that if we can reduce the negative societal pressure people are submitted to, we will decrease the number of people who have difficulty dealing with their life situation, and thereby reduce the number of parents who label their children.

Societal Labelling

As a child grows up it spends an increasing amount of time outside of the home, thereby coming into contact with society; represented by neighbours, daycare personnel, teachers, etc. An increasing number of people now become significant others. During this period children continue to learn social norms through reactions to their behaviour.

In their initial contacts with society the activities of children are principally characterized by primary deviance, but as they grow older and gain more social experience, their actions become increasingly influenced by societal norms. All children exhibit primary deviance in their initial contacts with society; the most important element is not the behaviour but the reactions from significant others. Once again most will learn that they are OK even if certain things they do are not. A few will learn that the problem lies not in their activities for the moment, but with themselves. This is *societal labelling*, the *second stage* in my deviant career model.

Which children will be labelled in their contacts with society is not merely a matter of chance. A child who has been labelled by his parents runs a far greater risk of being subjected to similar reactions in his contacts with society. To explain why, I must introduce the concept behavioural incongruity. *Behavioural incongruity* arises when an individual's activities aren't in harmony with his self-image. He will react by trying to diminish the incongruity by either changing his behaviour or his self-image. Figure 6.1 illustrates the concept.

However, there are several problems with the picture conveyed by this figure. First, it gives the impression that people are static, when in reality

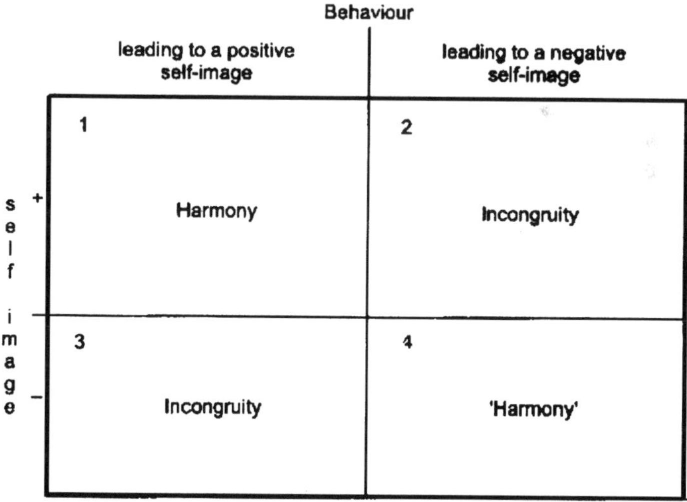

Figure 6.1 Behavioural incongruity

they change. Some of the more important factors influencing changes in my research subjects will be discussed shortly.

Secondly, there are degrees of positive and negative self-images. We can conceptualize the matter as a continuum between those who look upon themselves as one step under the deity, and those who see themselves as Satan reincarnated. Depending upon where a person stands on this continuum, a certain range of behaviour will be acceptable to him; that is his behaviour will not cause incongruity as long as he keeps himself within this domain. If he leaves this range in either direction; i.e. either acts more positively or more negatively than his self-image will allow for, he will experience incongruity. He must then either discontinue these activities or change his self-image to one which allows for such behaviour. Figure 6.2 presents a somewhat oversimplified model of these relationships.

An individual with a self-image at position C can behave between points 3 and 6 on the behaviour scale without causing incongruity. If he should start acting according to point 2 he will either have to change his self-image in a positive direction at least as far as point B, or desist from such actions. If he should start behaving according to point 7 he will either have to change his self-image in a negative direction at least as far as point D, or refrain from such activity. Note that the behaviour ranges for neighbouring points on the self-image scale overlap. This is because people don't change their entire behavioural pattern at once, but rather a little at a time.

Individuals with a negative self-image tend to behave so as to provoke others to confirm what they 'know' about themselves rather than cause incongruity by

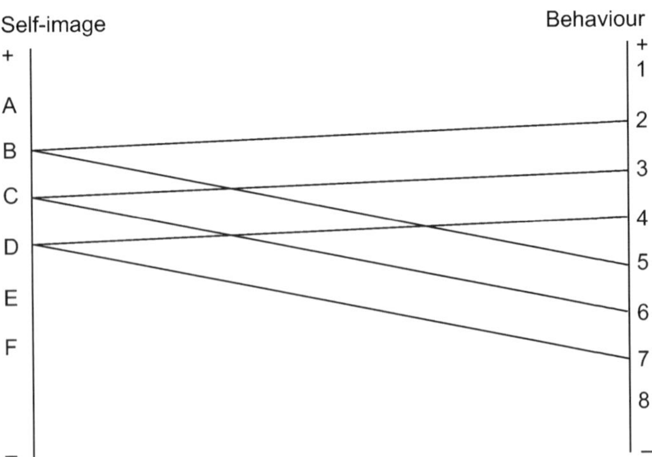

Figure 6.2 The relation between self-image and behaviour

acting in a way which would impute a more positive self-image. For this reason, the early-established self-image is difficult to change. Negative reactions from significant others tend to modify the behaviour of those who basically have a positive self-image, because these reactions are incongruous. For those who already have a negative self-image, reproach is usually interpreted as a confirmation of what they've already accepted as true. This is why castigation usually doesn't lead to behaviour more in line with societal norms in individuals with a negative self-image.

The self-images of the problematic consumers of narcotics in my study did not originate in negative reactions from society, but societal reactions did have two primary effects:

1. Labelling – reinforcement of the previously established negative self-image.
2. Guidepost – by condemning certain behaviour we frighten off people with a positive self-image, but also show those with a negative self-image how to evoke responses which confirm it.

Another complication with Figure 6.1 involves the nature of the harmony in cell 1, as compared with the 'harmony' in cell 4. In spite of their negative self-images my research subjects grew up under the influence of mainstream society and have internalized societal norms. Although some authors believe that problematic consumers of narcotics belong to a subculture (Svensson), I am of the opinion that this concept has little explanatory value for what takes place on the narcotics scene in Stockholm. Subculture might possibly be relevant when discussing immigrant groups which bring with them habits, values and attitudes towards certain drugs which are at variance with those dominant in the new country. For instance some East-Africans may continue to chew khat while living in Europe, or some Iranians might continue to smoke opiates after emigrating. However, this kind of culturally regulated consumption has little resemblance to the way drugs are consumed on the narcotics scene. When an immigrant becomes a problematic consumer, i.e. an Iranian starts smoking heroin several times a day, he is no longer acting within the framework of his culture, and his countrymen find his behaviour unacceptable.

For a deviant subculture to arise and remain in existence, its members would have to neutralize societal norms. Although Sykes and Matza (pp. 667ff) describe five different ways to accomplish this, I was unable to distinguish any significant degree of neutralization in my research subjects. When 'straight' people talk to substantial consumers they are often given the impression that those who take drugs reject society. However, if one penetrates behind the façade shown to strangers the picture changes drastically. Not only do problematic consumers accept societal norms, they actually have very traditional values.[3] As former problematic consumer Birgitta Stenberg (p. 20) writes: '[substantial consumers] are unbelievably moral, even sentimental. Their eyes tear when they hear Christmas carols.'

To the long list of tragedies in the lives of substantial consumers of narcotics it must be added that they regularly break rules they themselves feel they should be following. Consequently their actions cause self-reproach which reinforces the negative reactions they get from others, the result being that the threat of having to devalue one's self-image is ever present. Deviance, therefore, contains a certain degree of incongruence. I have indicated this by placing quotes around the word 'harmony' in cell 4 (Figure 6.1). There is a great deal of pressure towards compliance with societal norms, and almost everybody I met while in the field took tentative steps in that direction, i.e. attempting to find a job. If this initial step is well received it may initiate a re-evaluation of the self-image. If the endeavour is met negatively, it can become more difficult to try again.

In their early contacts with society children who have been labelled by their parents exhibit rudiments of the provocative behavioural patterns recognized by everyone who has worked with marginalized people. Although the child's self-image is not firmly established, he can consciously break rules he is aware of and in doing so provoke negative reactions, which serve as a confirmation of what he has started to believe about himself. The more frequently a child receives confirmation of his developing negative self-image, the more strongly established it becomes. It is therefore of primary importance that adults who interact with these children have a clear theoretical and/or emotional understanding of what the child is trying to convey with his behaviour, so that the reactions given do not confirm what the child suspects (that there is something wrong with him) or even worse, become a part of the labelling process (teach the child that he is even worse than he previously believed). The goal is to convey norms without labelling the child: to react to his activities of the moment, but not against the youth himself.

It is important to try to compensate for parental labelling as early as possible, as the longer the labelling process continues, the more difficult it will be to counteract it. German psychoanalyst Wolfgang Schmidbauer (p. 94f) writes:

> there is a tendency for deviants to abuse their helpers. They are so used to being met by hate and inconsideration that they react with contempt to the friendly, obliging helper, who is anxious to establish a positive relationship. Aichorn is of the opinion that behind this disdain is the fear of experiencing the painful feelings that are a part of the repressed need to be loved. Disturbed adolescents try to provoke the helper, maltreat him, and expect

[3] There may be exceptions, but I have not encountered them.

> that in the long run he will use his power and start to tyrannize them; a situation these adolescents have experienced before and have learned to deal with.
>
> Many helpers who have worked with this kind of client can most certainly agree with what I've written thus far. But Aichorn's promise that the provocations will cease, that the thus far disdainful, rejecting youth will suddenly release his repressed tender feelings for the helper and thereafter become a new person – this promise of a happy ending, for which the helper patiently tolerates so much vexation, usually does not come to pass. The blame lies with the helper. He didn't have enough patience, couldn't endure the provocations long enough.

In other words, it is extremely difficult and time-consuming to try to help a person who is convinced that all relationships sooner or later turn sour. Attempts to remedy the situation will be easier, and the prospects of success greater, if they are made early on. The longer we wait before mobilizing resources to counteract labelling, the more firmly established the negative self-image becomes. Thereby we increase the probability that Schmidbauer's frightful scenario, rather than Aichorn's hopeful prophecy, will become reality.

Secondary Deviance

When a child has matured to the point where he has a reasonable understanding of social norms, and established a self-image based on a significant number of life experiences, he can enter the *third stage* of the deviant career, *secondary deviance*. The age at which this ensues varies depending upon such factors as the amount and the severity of labelling in the earlier stages. For most of my research subjects the stage was established in the early teens, but in extreme cases even earlier.

Secondary deviance is characterized by acts contrary to societal norms of which the individual is cognizant. Secondary deviance is a product of a relatively well-established negative self-image and is a means of attempting to deal with manifest and/or latent problems arising from labelling. The adolescent has a relatively clear comprehension of right and wrong, and his behaviour is now greatly influenced by his negative self-image.

When an individual has accepted that he does not meet cultural standards, normal social controls cease to function. People with a positive self-image can be influenced to refrain from doing certain things as the negative reactions of others threaten both their self-image and their continued membership in the group. But a person with a negative self-image already knows that he is different, unacceptable and an outsider. He doesn't interpret negative reactions as a guide that will help integrate him in the social community, as his earlier life experiences have taught him that he is incapable/unworthy of such acceptance. Instead, negative reactions are taken as further confirmation of his inferiority.

When a person has a deep-seated negative self-image, other people can no longer exercise control over him by threatening to withdraw social support. Bob Dylan expressed this idea concisely: 'When you ain't got nothin', you got nothin' to lose.'

By defining certain acts as commendable and others as reprehensible society shows its citizens how to maintain their self-images. For instance, the consumption of certain chemicals is called narcotics abuse (that is deplorable). Those who have negative self-images know that people like them do unacceptable things. They are therefore attracted to these chemicals. For people with more positive self-images, on the other hand, it becomes difficult to consume narcotics without experiencing behavioural incongruity. If these people choose to attempt to deal with their social situation by using chemicals, they will go to a doctor to get a prescription for legal drugs. They can do this without causing behavioural incongruity because it is legitimate to take medicine (even if the prescribed substances should happen to have similar chemical effects to illegal drugs). If we were to remove current social and legal stigmas on narcotics, the pattern of consumption would change. New groups would be able to take them as it would no longer be experienced as incongruent, while people with strong negative self-images would be obliged to find new ways to confirm their status as outsiders.

Problematic consumers of illegal psychoactive substances have at least some, and most often all, of the following objectives when they take narcotics:

1. confirmation of a deep-seated negative self-image;
2. escape from their own and other people's expectations;
3. self-destruction;
4. revenge.

Due to labelling problematic consumers of narcotics have drastically negative self-images, initiated prior to their starting to take drugs. Others have judged them unworthy and they have accepted the ruling. They try to flee, for instance with the help of psychoactive substances, but they have already internalized the condemnation, and no one can escape from what they bear within. Due to all the negative experiences problematic consumers endure as an integral part of the life they lead on the narcotics scene, they confirm for themselves that they deserve to be severely punished; after all, they destroy for others and have devastated their own lives. As time passes and the quantity and magnitude of negative life experiences escalates, they become all the more convinced that they do not deserve to exist. Their life pattern increasingly becomes a process of ensuring that justice is done. Others have condemned them, they have accepted the verdict, and they become their own executioners. But at the same time, by stealing from them, frightening them, giving them a bad conscience, etc., problematic consumers wreak revenge on those who have passed judgement.

People establish their self-image via others, and they must have help from others to change it. The more negative the self-image, the more a person deviates from the norms of society. If we want an individual to change his ways, we must be willing to take the role of significant other, and not only refuse to confirm the negative self-image but also give responses necessary to help him embark upon and endure the long process which leads to change. But this is easier said than done when the labelling process has proceeded to the point where an individual expects negative responses. When such a person is given positive reactions the world becomes incomprehensible. If for instance a social worker or some other significant other does not react as expected, he is looked upon as either being ignorant or simply not having understood what a terrible person he is dealing with. This calls for extremely provocative behaviour to bring forth the 'correct' responses. If others understand that they are being provoked, and manage to react in a way that does not label the individual, this can initiate a re-evaluation of the negative self-image. But if the provocations are 'successful', which sooner or later they usually are, it leads to more labelling and little by little the marginalized individual embarks upon the fourth stage in the deviant career.

The Deviance Spiral

The *fourth stage, the deviance spiral*, consists of the elements shown in Figure 6.3. Labelling creates a negative self-image, inducing secondary deviance, which is a failure according to cultural definitions, and therefore gives rise to more labelling, etc. Each deterioration is partially the result of earlier failures, and contributes to future setbacks. In this stage the individual's behaviour is usually secondary deviant in several different areas, i.e. narcotics, theft, drug trafficking, prostitution, unemployment, living on the streets, etc. He is therefore subject to labelling reactions from many different sources.

The deviance spiral is a deterioration of the third stage. The individual is now caught in the vortex of a vicious spiral, drawing him downwards. When failures and negative reactions accumulate it becomes all the more difficult to maintain the self-image at the same (low) level; the risk of having to devalue the self-image still further is ever present.

Only people with extremely negative self-images allow themselves to follow the deviance spiral into oblivion. Almost everybody has a point where they have had enough. Some reach this point quickly and leave the scene almost immediately. Others have to go a lot further before they attempt to pull out. If they stay on the scene long enough problematic consumers hit

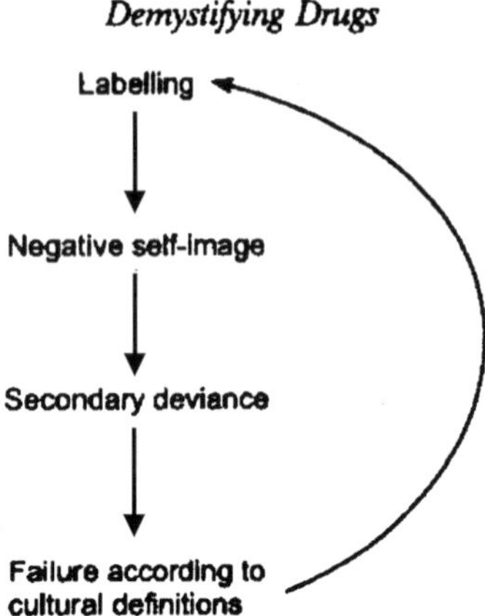

Figure 6.3 The deviance spiral

'rock bottom', where only two choices remain: either commit suicide (i.e. by taking an overdose or by 'burning' a murderer), or more actively attempting to get off drugs. In his autobiography, former problematic consumer Lasse Carlsson (p. 169) exemplifies this point:

> New Year's Eve. I'm alone in my room in a fleabag hotel. It's almost midnight and I've filled my works with a massive mixture of amphetamines, Ritalin, and Palfium [dextromoramide, an opiate]. Normally, this would have been a deadly dose, it could kill an ox, but since I'm neither normal nor an ox, I probably have a fifty percent chance of surviving.... I empty the witches brew into a vein and close my eyes; I feel no fear, only emptiness, and resolution as I sink down into my bed.
>
> I survived! Fate has decided that I shall continue living – or start living. Now, it's all up to me. But can I pull it off? (Ibid., p. 171)

With his back to the wall the side of the problematic consumer which wants to join society but which has been held back, is given higher priority. But if he fails now, all that remains is death. It is therefore not advisable to let the deviance spiral go this far. By not confirming the problematic consumer's negative self-image (for instance by understanding his provocations and finding non-labelling responses to them) we can help him break the negative spiral much earlier; preferably before it even starts.

As it is probably difficult to understand how it is practically feasible to do this, an example may be illuminating. A. S. Neill (p. 119), former headmaster of Summerhill, a school in England which had many 'problem children' among its pupils and which used very unusual pedagogical methods, writes:

> If I should be painting a door and Robert came along and threw mud on my fresh paint, I would swear at him heartily, because he has been one of us for a long time and what I say to him does not matter. But suppose Robert had just come from a hateful school and his mud slinging was his attempt to fight authority, I would join with him in his mud slinging because his salvation is more important than the door. I know that I must stay on his side while he lives out his hate in order for him to become social.

I will summarize my career model by comparing *two extreme careers*. Both begin with primary deviance, but the reactions received make the careers go in diametrically different directions.

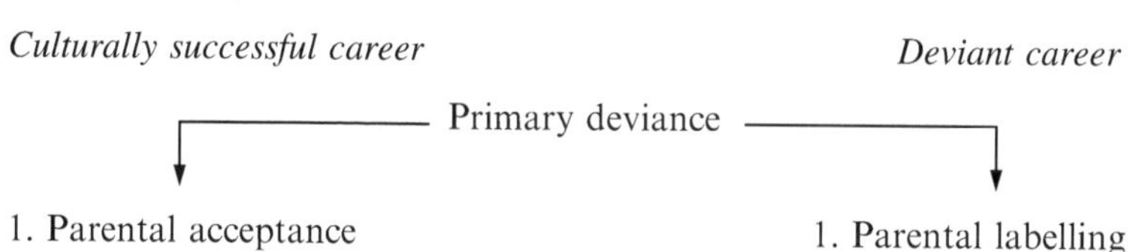

Culturally successful career	*Deviant career*
1. Parental acceptance	1. Parental labelling
2. Societal acceptance	2. Societal labelling
3. Normative behaviour	3. Secondary deviance
4. Personality reinforcement	4. Deviance spiral

The stages in the careers should not be considered as being mutually exclusive. They can be in progress concurrently and either reinforce or counteract one other. For instance parental labelling begins before societal labelling, but continues for years after the child has made many contacts outside the home. It is also not necessarily so that an individual will receive the same kinds of reaction from both parents and society, as is the case in the two careers outlined above. Labelling reactions from certain significant others can be counteracted by acceptance from others, in which case the emerging self-image will neither be decidedly positive nor negative (see Figure 6.2). In other words the number of possible careers far exceed the two mentioned here.

7 Parental Labelling

INTRODUCTION

Sociologist Mats Hilte (1990, p. 57) found that 57 per cent of the problematic consumers at the treatment centres he studied had 'not grown up with their biological parents. Most of them were raised by one parent, usually the mother (sometimes with a step parent). By the age of 16, approximately 14 per cent of those interviewed, had been placed in foster homes or institutions.' These results are similar to those found in other major studies, i.e. UNO-79 (a nationwide study of problematic consumption in Sweden) and BAK/SWEDATE (the most comprehensive evaluation of Swedish treatment centres thus far).

During my fieldwork I gathered data about the childhood family situation of my research subjects. The ideal in society is for children to be raised by both biological parents and have a trusting and loving relationship with them. None of my subjects reported that they were brought up in such an environment. This extremely high figure is due to the breadth of my concept, and my methods of data collection. Participant observation allows the researcher to be in contact with his subjects over a long period of time. If a relationship based on mutual trust can be established, the information offered changes; touching on more intimate subjects, which can be discussed further and developed as time passes. For example, some of my research subjects, early in our relationship, did in fact answer my questions about their childhood families with comments such as: 'it was OK' or 'nothing unusual'. However, the picture changed as we got to know each other better.

What I found remarkable was that there were no deviant cases; in the long run no one maintained that they had had a good relationship to both parents. As we have noted in Chapter 5 Chein et al. didn't find any deviant cases either and Wurmser can be interpreted in the same way. It is possible that these results mirror methodological deficiencies and are therefore exaggerated. But even if this should be the case there is an abundance of evidence showing that on the whole everything was not as it should have been in the childhood homes of problematic consumers.

In that which follows it is not my intention to question the motives of the parents of problematic consumers. My basic assumption is that almost all parents try to do what they can for their children. I do not believe that parental labelling is due to malevolence, but most likely to one or more of the following factors:

1. Primary resource deficiency – The parents lack the personal resources needed to succeed in their role; i.e. they bear 'scars' from their own childhood.
2. Secondary resource deficiency – The family lives in a social situation which makes it difficult to be parents, or, at least, does not support the parental role.
3. Misunderstanding parenthood – The parents make use of (believe in) unsuitable methods of childrearing.

In other words, parents do not have to be malicious to label their children. In putting the spotlight on parental labelling I am not passing judgement; but rather trying to learn from past mistakes.

As children spend the first part of their lives with their parents, parental labelling is the first stage in my deviant career model. Most adults consider it self-evident that the way parents fulfil their role is of vital importance for the well-being of children: otherwise they wouldn't invest so much time, energy and resources to give their offspring a good start in life. Based on this supposition the question arises – what becomes of children whose parents do not give what children need?

PERPETRATOR OR VICTIM?

Most people become indignant when they hear that a child is maltreated by his parents. It arouses negative feelings not only towards the parents, but against everyone thought to have had a part in the ill-treatment, i.e. 'negligent' relatives, neighbours, or social workers. It also arouses protective feelings toward the child who has been abused. We can clearly see all of this in *the Mikael case* which was given a lot of attention in the media in Sweden.

Mikael was a four-year-old who had been subjected to physical abuse by his mother and stepfather for his entire life. During a camping trip they beat him so severely that he died. With good reason, people in Sweden were incensed. Accusations were hurled at the social authorities who had not observed the boy's predicament and done something to help him in time. The Parliamentary Ombudsman (JO) started an investigation, which eventually led to the prosecution of the department head of the social welfare authority in the town where the family lived. She was found guilty of negligence by the District Court and sentenced to a heavy fine.

The Swedish National Union of Local Government Officers (SKTF) felt that the verdict was 'a slap in the face' of an entire profession, and questioned why the local politicians had not been put on trial. SKTF argued that working conditions were such that the convicted social worker had been putting in 20 to 30 hours of overtime every week and still could not satisfactorily deal with her case load. Rhetorically the union asked: who is responsible for this? Their answer is: 'It is the responsibility of the City Council and the Social Welfare Board to ensure that municipal employees have the resources needed to do their jobs; the District Court... should have looked into this' (see *Dagens Nyheter*, 1991, p. A5). In other words, there is a difference of opinion as to the extent to which the sentenced employee should be considered as a subject who bears the responsibility for her actions (or lack thereof); or as an object, a 'victim' of political decisions beyond her control.

Public opinion was voiced in countless letters to the editor in every major newspaper. One recurrent theme was chastising the neighbours who knew about the beatings, yet did nothing more than report the matter to the social authorities, and then stand by and let the child abuse continue without further intervention. Another theme was demanding that Mikael's parents be severely punished. To my knowledge, nobody considered Mikael himself to be anything other than a victim. No one publicly expressed that he deserved all the suffering he had endured during his short life.

I have asked myself what would have become of Mikael if the abuse had continued and he lived to become an adolescent? How would he have behaved as a teenager? Obviously we can't say for sure, but for the sake of argument, let's say that he had become 'troublesome'. I wonder how many people would still consider him a victim? At least some would view him as a perpetrator and demand that he be punished, in the same way many demanded that his mother and stepfather (both of whom had been abused as children) should be sentenced severely.

It is important that people react when laws and norms are broken. But when we react, we must remember that today's perpetrators may well have been yesterday's victims. Through my own and the research of others, much evidence has been gathered pointing to this conclusion. Therefore, we must learn to recognize the circumstances in society which increase the risk that children will become victims.

LABELLING IS MORE THAN PHYSICAL VIOLENCE

As this chapter begins with the Mikael case, some readers may have been led to believe that parental labelling is primarily a result of domestic violence, or maybe even continuous physical abuse. While it is true that many problematic consumers have been subjected to corporal punishment, many have not. It would be a gross simplification if we were to limit parental labelling to physical violence in the home. Of primary importance are the psychological signals transmitted: some children are led to believe that there is something basically wrong with them. Obviously this message can be conveyed by physical abuse, but we will better understand the labelling process if we consider beatings as a tangible external confirmation of an even more serious process, primarily conveyed by other, more subtle, means. *The essence of parental labelling is that the child is taught that he is not an independent being with the right to physical and psychological integrity, to a will of his own, to his own ideas and to satisfaction of his needs. Instead he learns that if he has any right to exist at all, it is to satisfy the needs of others.* Parents can get this message across without resorting to physical violence.

Chein et al. (p. 257f) present some ideas concerning the family's influence on the potential problematic consumer's personality:

1. The experience of being accepted by others and being worthy of their love is needed for self-acceptance.
2. The receiving of overwhelming love, affection and indulgence impairs the ability to defer gratification in light of the requirements of reality.
3. Overanxious parental reactions and concern with illness interfere with … the development of a sense of competence by facilitating a view of the world as filled with overwhelming dangers which cannot be coped with.
4. Marked social or cultural disparities among parental and with peer identification models interfere with the development of a clear-cut sense of identity and group membership.
5. Parental expectations that are markedly higher or lower than the ability of the child may lead to an unrealistic sense of competence or to feelings of incompetence.

In a comprehensive survey of the literature concerning the family situation of problematic consumers, illustrated by a number of case studies from his own practice as a psychoanalyst, Leon Wurmser (p. 277f) concludes that problematic drug consumption

> is a derivative of the whole family's attitude of inconsistency, self-centeredness, and, most importantly, of inner and outer dishonesty. The deceptiveness and wiliness of many drug abusers is a reflection of their parents' denial or deviousness and power-hungry manipulations, or it is a frantic escape from disillusionment and anger about the unavailability of their parents as persons during the crises of growing up. The hierarchical structure and authority within the family is split up, broken, blurred, subverted and overthrown. All the limits and boundaries shift, are unreliable, get blurred, are transgressed.

A MULTIGENERATIONAL PERSPECTIVE

Professor of Social Work Sven Hessle (1988, p. 220) found five patterns of interaction between parents whose children were taken into custody by the social authorities and their children:

1. *Symbiotic relationship* – The parent is dependent for his own 'survival' on the child.
2. *Rejection* – The parent does not accept the child, and spurns him in different ways. All of the parents in Hessle's study who were problematic consumers had felt unwanted as children (ibid., p. 215). As parents, they subject their own children to similar experiences.
3. *Preoccupied* – The parent is negligent in his parental role. The relation to the child may be warm and loving, but the parent is so preoccupied by his own problems, for instance drug or alcohol abuse, that he doesn't function consistently.
4. *Ambivalence* – The parent has a conflicting and contradictory relationship with his child, which can include both symbiosis and rejection. For example young, immature mothers who have difficulty in accepting their roles as parents often fall into this category.
5. *Varied relationship* – The parent has good and loving relations with the child.

Hessle observed the patterns of interaction between parents and children twice, with a two-year interval. In both studies only two of the 35 adults were judged as having a varied relationship to their children. Those remaining were placed in one of the other four categories; with a clear majority for rejection and ambivalence (ibid., p. 223).

> When a parent rejects or is ambivalent to his child, it may be a desperate cry for help and support *for himself.* The message of parental rejection... 'you are worthless, you are not loved', was interpreted as *a transfer of the parent's own negative self-image onto the child.* Our analysis indicates the necessity of a multigenerational perspective.
>
> (Ibid., p. 225) (emphasis in original)

A multigenerational perspective can also be used to explain how extremely traumatic experiences in one generation affect the following generation(s). The *survival syndrome* is relevant in modern narcotics research because there are an increasing number of refugees who have endured traumatic experiences in their homelands, i.e. war, torture, extensive prison terms served in inhuman conditions, etc. Such experiences may have had extremely negative effects on the psyches and self-images of these individuals. The survival syndrome can be described as:

> repeated anxiety characterized by fear of annihilation, disorientation, chronic depression and feelings of guilt because one has survived, social isolation, symptoms bordering on psychosis, change of self-image: 'I am someone else', or, 'I'm nobody', psychosomatic symptoms, psychological stagnation, etc.... People with 'survival syndrome' have difficulty in their parental role. Because of their extremely negative self-images, and inability to enjoy life, these parents isolate themselves from their surroundings. Because they are preoccupied with earlier experiences, they find it difficult to be accessible for their children in an adequate manner. They become extremely overprotective, fearing that something will happen to their children. Or, they transfer their unbearable memories and guilt to their children who must bear their parents' trauma, freeing the parents from some of their anxiety. The children serve as substitutes for relatives who have been murdered or died – they bear someone else's identity.
>
> (Ibid., p. 226)

> The child identifies himself with, and successively assumes the extreme insecurity and negative self-image that the parent has internalized through his own experiences. (Ibid., p. 228)

RELATIONS BETWEEN PROBLEMATIC CONSUMERS AND THEIR PARENTS

It isn't possible to give a complete picture of the relationships problematic consumers have had with their parents. This subject has been discussed in hundreds of scientific publications (see Stanton, p. 408) yet much is left to be said. Within the confines of this book, I cannot as much as relate what my research subjects have told me. Another problem is that I have access to only one side of the story. Having met but a few of the parents of 'my' problematic consumers, I know almost nothing about how they experienced their children's upbringing. This one-sidedness is a weakness of participant observation as a method of data collection.

Yet another problem with the following presentation is that I cannot give a more detailed description of the intrapsychic processes that have taken place in those who have been subjected to parental labelling. Unfortunately I do not have the necessary theoretical training to make such an analysis.

In this chapter I will present a number of elements which can be a part of the parental labelling process. I shall not attempt to paint a comprehensive picture; only to give examples of some of the ways in which parental labelling is manifested. But before proceeding, I will once again emphasize that labelling is a process, not a few isolated acts. The parent who occasionally says or does something inappropriate need not be anxious. It is the patterns in a child's upbringing – the themes repeated time and again over the years, which are vital.

THE ENTANGLED FAMILY

> In the *entangled family*, members are so deeply involved in each other that there is uncertainty concerning both role differentiation and boundaries between individuals.... One of the parents and the drug abusing adolescent are often entangled in each other. They have a low degree of autonomy and attempts to break free from this pattern are counteracted.
>
> (Ramström, 1983, p. 185) (my italics)

Chein et al. (p. 212) write: 'A prominent feature of the family situation of the adolescent opiate addict... is the peculiarly close relationship between the addict and his mother. It is not a closeness of warmth or mutual regard so much as it is a clinging and feeling of being bound together.' The mothers of problematic consumers are often described as 'domineering persons who limited their sons' self-assertion, used them unfairly for their own emotional and physical needs, and gave them little in return' (ibid., p. 213f).

> Though the mothers are unable to encourage or enhance the development of their sons toward independence or maturity, many have great difficulty in refusing things. They tend to be indulgent in material things, unable to discipline the boy, and inconsistent in their expectations and in the setting of limits. Some of the mothers are, however, repressive and non-giving even of material things. (Ibid., p. 214)

It is almost uncanny to read Chein et al.'s examples, as so many of them so closely resemble my own observations. For instance, they describe a situation in which a substantial consumer was given leave from a hospital to spend some time with his mother. Before he was released, the staff made an agreement with the mother that she was not to give him any money. In spite of this she gave her son some cash: exactly the amount needed to buy a bag of heroin (ibid., p. 214f). While working in a treatment centre I made an agreement with a mother that she could have her son at home for a weekend. When he didn't show up on Monday, I called her. She told me that because he had been so good and stayed off drugs for several weeks she felt that he should be rewarded, so she had given him some money. When I asked her how much, the sum was exactly the going price of a capsule of amphetamine.

Another example (ibid., p. 278f) concerns a boy who slept in his grandmother's bed until he was 15. I have also had contact with a male problematic consumer who shared a bed with the adult woman who reared him (in this case, his mother) until he was 15. This is an example of what Chein et al.

mean when they say that the relationship between mother and son was too close, and that the sons were used unfairly for the mothers' emotional and physical needs (ibid., p. 213).

PARENTIFICATION: BEING A PARENT TO ONE'S PARENTS

Parentification means that the roles in the family are inverted; the child relinquishes his needs to satisfy the needs of the parents. Remarkably often the accounts of problematic consumers' childhood experiences related to me in intimate conversations, can be understood in this sense. For instance, I got to know a teenage girl who in many ways was a mother to her mother. Her family situation was as follows: her father, a successful businessman, felt that his main duty was to attend to his job, and was often away on business trips. He believed that raising children was the woman's responsibility, and neglecting his job to take care of kids was simply out of the question. But her mother had a career of her own, so she didn't really have time and energy for the children either. She also suffered from recurrent anxiety attacks. When she had one, she was unable to be alone in a room, even if others were somewhere else in the house. The daughter told me that from the time she was very young she regularly sat on the edge of her mother's bed all night long, trying to keep her mother's panic at bay.

DOMINANCE–SUBMISSION

Another common pattern in the accounts of substantial consumers can be called *dominance–submission*. For instance, a problematic consumer told me that his parents never listened when he tried to express his needs. When he was 17 they forced him to move to another country because they didn't think the girl he was dating was good enough for him. He told them that he did not want to go but they simply demanded that he do as he was told; which he did. However, a few years later when he was getting heavily into drugs and they told him to stop, it was he who wasn't listening.

People raised in families based on dominance and submission are not used to making their own decisions. This makes them insecure and irresolute in situations requiring choice. They also have difficulty in clearly expressing their needs. As a result they feel dissatisfied with themselves and bear feelings of hatred toward their parents, often expressed in terms of getting revenge. As previously noted, part of life on the scene can be interpreted as a means of wreaking revenge, especially on parents. 'In the course of addiction, the addict may begin to express hostility towards parental figures... through theft from the parental home; overt anger (becoming "evil and nasty"); or through the spiteful, wasteful, or destructive use of parental furnishings, money, decorations, or clothing' (ibid., p. 234). In the families of problematic consumers members punish themselves and each other. 'The mothers, on their parts, consciously suffered from the difficulties of their addicted sons. They felt that they were being martyred by what their sons were doing to themselves' (ibid., p. 214). In other words the substantial consumer is in pain, but so are his parents – which he is well aware of. This is a major reason behind problematic consumption – he wants his parents to hurt, just as he is tormented now and has suffered in the past.

The thought arises that it might also be the parents' intention to suffer; both as a punishment for the way they have treated their child, but also as a way to achieve martyrdom. From the examples above, where mothers give money to their sons on leave from treatment centres, we must ask if these parents aren't gaining something socially and/or psychologically, by having offspring who are problematic consumers. When the child has become a teenager, both he and his parents are involved in a relationship where all parties are both victims and perpetrators. This can be interpreted as a stalemate in an ongoing battle for domination.

Although problematic consumers most often have difficulty making decisions, they don't want to feel that others are telling them what to do. I also have noted that relatively few of my research subjects have successfully completed military service. They had either shown symptoms which disqualified them before they were inducted, or they were conscientious objectors. Of those who went into the military, most either got themselves discharged for disorderly conduct, or they deserted. They have taken more than enough orders in childhood.

PHYSICALLY PRESENT, BUT ABSENT

While some problematic consumers had parents who paid attention to them in an unsuitable way, others felt that their parents were not interested in them at all. This was particularly true of fathers. If the father were present at all, he usually did not take an active part in rearing his children. 'A father figure was absent from the household for some significant portion of the boy's early childhood in 48 per cent of the addict cases, as compared to 17 per cent of the controls' (ibid., p. 120). 'In terms of quantity of interaction between father and son, there was not much contact between them' (ibid., p. 273). Many of my research subjects never talked about their fathers unless I asked them. Then they would say something to the effect; 'he was just there', 'he didn't give a damn about me', 'he was a non-person', and so on.

That some fathers failed to take part in bringing up their children may to some extent be explained by an exaggerated interpretation of traditional gender roles. These fathers may have believed that child care is the sole responsibility of women. Another possible explanation is primary resource deficiency. For example, in Hilte's (1990, p. 59) study of institutionalized problematic consumers, '42 per cent stated that one or both parents were alcoholics when they grew up; usually the father. More than one tenth said that both of the parents had alcohol problems. Thirty per cent claimed that one of their parents was addicted to pills.'

BUY YOURSELF HAPPY

A problematic consumer I got to know was not rejected because his parents were addicted to alcohol or drugs, but money. His mother and father never had any time for him, but they did have lots of money. Both parents had grown up in poor families, but now that they had 'made it', their children were going to have all the (material) things they had lacked. When he went to his parents to seek support, they gave him money. Whatever the problem, the solution was always to go out and buy something – and then he was expected to both feel better and be grateful. They drowned him in cash. When he was 12, his allowance was five times as much as his classmates'. Instead of being grateful, he was disgusted. At times he set a bill on fire and used it to light a cigarette. Not even then did his parents understand that he needed something from them other than money. Instead they screamed at him that he was crazy.

ABANDONED

Many of my research subjects were not only emotionally abandoned by one or both parents, some were also physically abandoned: e.g. 'after my parents divorced, I never saw my father again', 'I was left to my older sister who became my mother', 'my parents didn't want me so I was sent to a boarding school', and so on. To take a specific example, a problematic consumer born in Germany in 1945, describes how his father moved in with his mother's sister after his mother died. When the boy was four, his father and aunt moved to Australia leaving him behind in an overcrowded orphanage. He told me he can never forgive them for leaving him, but in the same breath, added that they would never have done it if he hadn't been so bad. It may seem strange that a four-year-old would blame himself for what adults have done, and maybe even stranger that not even as an adult can he rid himself of his feelings of guilt. However, reacting this way appears to be the rule rather than the exception.

The extent of the damage inflicted on a child when he is abandoned depends on many factors, such as the child's age when the parents disappear, if he meets his lost parents later in life and comes to understand what happened, his relationship to his new guardians, etc. I cannot penetrate the subject here; interested readers are referred to Börjeson and Håkansson, Chapter 19, and Lindén.

What makes a parent abandon his offspring? I do not believe that such a drastic act can be adequately explained by malice toward the child; although these parents may have negative feelings which can be a contributory cause. But my assumption is that those who abandon their children do not do so out of malevolence, but because they do not have the resources to fulfil their obligations. In other words, we lose an important dimension if we merely consider parents as subjects; i.e. nothing hampers them from doing as they please. It is important to remember that parents have been, and to some extent still are, objects.

In the aforementioned example we see the parents as objects when we ask what they have experienced when they grew up in the poverty of the Weimar Republic and the madness of the Third Reich. We also ask: what alternatives did this boy's father and stepmother have in the chaotic situation in postwar Germany? What political decisions and societal processes made it difficult for them take care of a child?

Obviously the boy's parents were not responsible for the conditions in Germany while they were growing up, and after the war. But on the other hand, to regard them only as objects is just as incorrect as seeing them only as subjects. After all, many parents in Germany lived in similar conditions at that time, yet very few abandoned their children.

SCAPEGOAT

In families rife with internal tension, one way to ease the pressure is to 'appoint' a scapegoat; a family member who is considered responsible for all of the family's problems. Eventually the designated individual accepts this definition of the situation; starts seeing himself as the root of all evil, and acts accordingly. This in turn contributes to people outside the family, i.e. neighbours, teachers, social workers, etc., also regarding him as 'the problem'.

American psychiatrist M. Duncan Stanton (p. 405) describes some of the roles of the scapegoat:

1. He can protect the other family members from intrusion from external 'helpers' because all attention is directed toward him and 'his problems'.

2. Attempts to deal with the scapegoat's problems become the adhesive that binds some families together. If his symptoms were to disappear the family would fall apart.
3. But he can also be an obstacle for resolving problems; when other family members grow and improve he may try to restore the former order.

Another function the scapegoat may have is to free the others from feelings of responsibility, shame and guilt. If the father drinks, the mother is depressed, a sibling is doing poorly in school, another sibling has trouble making friends, etc. are all the fault of the scapegoat, and have nothing to do with the other family members.

Obviously a few isolated accusations do not make a scapegoat. It is the entire pattern of interaction in the family, developed in a gradual process over a period of time, which leads to the scapegoat embracing a sufficiently negative self-image to be able to live up to the abrogating expectations of the others.

The following example illustrates how a scapegoat can feel. When the boyfriend of a girl I knew was diagnosed as having cancer, she blamed herself for causing it. When I asked her how she could believe such a thing, she replied that she knew that she was not responsible for his tumour, but 'when you've always been the cause of everything that goes wrong, you feel that somehow it must be your fault anyway'.

Scapegoats can help us to understand how one child in a family can become a problematic consumer of narcotics while his siblings become solid citizens. Different family members are assigned and/or assume different roles.

TRIANGLE DRAMA

'It is possible to view the symptomatic person as being caught between the competing requirements of two people or subsystems which are important to him or her' (Stanton, p. 402). If, for instance, a child lives with a single parent who meets a new partner, a triangle drama may result. Especially in socially isolated families, the parent may see the new partner as his/her only chance not to be alone, while the child may see the new partner as a threat to the little security he has. The new partner and the child may in fact be competing with each other for the affection of the parent. If the child feels that his parent has chosen the new partner it can lead to a protracted trauma. If, on the other hand, the parent feels obligated to give up the new partner, it can lead to strong negative feelings toward the child. In both cases, a labelling process may result. In the example where the father and stepmother moved to Australia and left their son in Germany, the decision may at least partially have been the result of a triangle drama.

CULTURAL CONFLICT

Many immigrants find it difficult to integrate the norms and institutions in the new country with their native culture, giving rise to the feeling that they cannot/don't want to become a part of the new society. This can be reinforced when an immigrant finds it difficult to make social contacts with members of the majority culture. If he does not feel welcome in the new country, he may consider his stay a necessary evil to support his family, rather than a new home. This encourages idealization of the land of his birth and nourishment of the dream of returning to his roots. But the belief/dream that the family will soon return to the old country, thereby making adaptation to the new country unnecessary, can put the children in a difficult situation. The following example is taken from my fieldwork.

When I met her, she was 17. She had grown up with her biological parents who were immigrants from Turkey. Her mother, who had always been home with the children, had had almost no contact with Swedes, never learned to speak the language and knew very little about the new country. Her consolation was that the family would soon be returning 'home'. Hence, the only logical thing to do was to teach her daughter the norms of rural Turkey. Besides, what other knowledge and proficiencies did the mother have to convey?

Although her father had a job outside the home, and knew some Swedish, he did not feel that he was a part of Swedish society. He had no close contacts with Swedes, and found Swedish culture strange and frightening. He too dreamed of returning to Turkey.

The girl, on the other hand, had lived in Sweden since she was two and had attended Swedish schools. She spoke fluent Swedish without an accent and she did not feel at home when visiting her parents' homeland. That she had no desire to move to the old country, and felt that her future was in Sweden, was something her parents refused to accept. They also did not understand why she needed friends her own age. On the contrary, they saw Swedish teenagers as a threat to their daughter's future and their parental authority. Presumably their authority had already been sufficiently threatened by their being dependent upon their daughter as an interpreter in their contacts with teachers and other authorities. That she also might adopt foreign customs was unacceptable. They felt she was wasting time by going to school, when she could have been at home helping her mother and learning things a 'real woman' must know. However, as mandatory education was something her parents couldn't do anything about, they allowed her to attend school; but without support and encouragement.

What they could control, on the other hand, was how she spent the rest of her time. They forbade her to see her peers after school, insisting that she be given a meaningful education at home by her mother. She was also not permitted to dress like the other girls in her class. At that time the style was to wear jeans, and she, like most teenagers, wanted to look like her peers. But in her father's eyes, only prostitutes wore trousers, and he insisted that she wear dresses. But if she had done as he wished, she would have been made a laughing-stock. Once again we are reminded of how the parents of problematic consumers fail to take into consideration the desires of their children.

The girl was in a situation where she was forced to choose between being accepted by her parents, at the cost of not having friends her own age and alienating herself from Swedish society, or dissociating herself from her family to be able to have a future in Sweden. It is, of course, almost impossible for an adolescent to choose between these alternatives, and she tried to find a way to avoid having to do so. She stole jeans and other clothes from stores and kept them with classmates. Every morning she would leave home in a dress, but before going to school she stopped at a friend's apartment and changed clothes. After school she got back into her dress before she went home.

This solution worked for a while, but one day when she was 15 her father left work early and saw her in jeans. He beat her and threw her out of the house. She didn't dare to contact the social welfare authorities, and tried to deal with the situation by sleeping at different classmates' apartments, and continuing to go to school. But when their parents started asking questions, she gave up. Before long she was in the centre of Stockholm together with the outcasts of society. In that environment, a young girl need not remain homeless very long. But as the rock group 'The Eagles' put it: 'every form of refuge has its price'. When I met her, she had been on amphetamines for two years. She had also become what her father thought she was when he saw her in jeans.

Most certainly there are many immigrant children in similar situations. In part, it is the families themselves that are to blame, but even the host country has a responsibility for the way it integrates newcomers. By supporting immigrant groups trying to help their countrymen adapt to the new environment, and by showing an interest in the experiences, skills and knowledge of newcomers, a country can make it easier for settlers from abroad to make a reasonable adjustment.

SEXUAL ABUSE

By *sexual abuse of children* I mean an adult initiating sexual activities with a child or adolescent who is not mature enough to understand the implications of the act, and therefore cannot give well-informed consent. *Incest* is sexual abuse initiated by an adult upon whom the child or adolescent is emotionally and/or economically dependent.

During my fieldwork only a few problematic consumers disclosed that they had been sexually abused or subjected to incest in childhood, probably because it never occurred to me to ask. My blindness to this important question was due to:

1. the accounts I heard were few and spread out in time;
2. I hadn't seen any studies indicating that sexual abuse in childhood might be an important contributory factor in problematic narcotics consumption.

I therefore interpreted the accounts I was given as tragic, yet unusual, life experiences.

In spite of the lack of data from my own research, I will formulate the following hypothesis: *many problematic consumers of narcotics have been subjected to sexual abuse, especially incest, during childhood and/or adolescence*. What are the arguments?

I begin by posing the question – how can an adult sexually abuse a child, especially one who is emotionally dependent upon him/her? I can't give a comprehensive answer but it seems reasonable to assume that it would be impossible for an adult who is intent on satisfying the child's needs to commit such an act. To be able to abuse a child in this way a person would have to put his own needs foremost and/or see the child as an object, i.e. not consider the child as a human being with needs of his own, but rather as a thing to be used as seen fit. As we have already noted, this mind-set is common in the backgrounds of problematic consumers. That is, incest does not drastically differ from other behavioural patterns in these families. Instead, sexual abuse can be seen as yet another expression of a fundamental attitude that permeates these families: that the child is not his own person with his own needs is extended to also include his body. The theoretical framework presented in this book does in fact give a plausible explanation for the correlation in the hypothesis.

Research has been conducted on sexual abuse but comparisons are difficult as studies are based on limited samples, concepts are defined differently, control groups are often lacking, etc. However, certain conclusions recur in a number of studies.

Menicucci and Wermuth (p. 136) write:

> A history of child sexual abuse is more common among women than men drug addicts. Ellinwood and colleagues (1966) found sexual abuse by a father or male relative in 20% of their female cases, and Densen-Gerber and Benward (1975) found sexual abuse by a family member in 44% of the female cases. Additionally, Gutierres, Raymond and Rhoads (1979) found 16% of their sample of female drug abusers had been sexually abused as children, compared to none of the male drug abusers and 8% of a non-drug-abusing female comparison group.

Peggy Boström refers to several studies which suggest correlations between sexual abuse in childhood and contact with child psychiatry, running away from home, contact with adult psychiatry, being battered as an adult woman, repeated rape, prostitution, and drug abuse. Many of these experiences may be correlated to each other, but how they influence one another has yet to be explained. Furthermore, Boström (p. 12) writes: 'Two [American] researchers, independent of each other, found that as many as 40% of female drug abusers had been subjected to sexual abuse within their own families during childhood.'

Police inspector Monica Dahlström-Lannes (p. 64), who worked for many years with victims of sexual crimes, refers to two more American studies and writes: 'pronounced sexual disorders hardly exist in girls who have not been subjected to sexual abuse. Even depression, insomnia, criminality, and drug abuse are more common among sexually abused girls compared to others.'

A Norwegian psychologist, Jan Seidel (pp. 99–112) refers to still further American studies that come to similar conclusions. For instance, he refers to a study from California showing that '70 per cent of all teenage, problematic consumers had been subjected to sexual assault'. Referring to a Norwegian study by Sætre et al., with a sample of over a thousand people, Seidel concludes that 'the problems of the victims were so great that the study gives a clear picture of the long-term effects of sexual abuse. Both male and female victims mentioned sexual problems, insomnia, drug problems, and suicidal thoughts more often than people in the control group' (ibid., p. 111).

There are also a few Swedish studies which report similar findings. Social worker Gunhild Glingvall-Priftakis (p. 21) found that self-destructive behaviour such as anorexia, bulimia, attempted suicide, psychosomatic symptoms, prostitution, abuse of alcohol and narcotics, and criminality is common in girls who have been subjected to sexual abuse in childhood.

Social worker Britt-Louise Thorberg and physician Orsolya Hoffman (p. 132) found that 29 per cent of the 123 females treated at the women's drug clinic at Sabbatsberg Hospital in Stockholm during its first year of operation, 1994–5, had been subjected to incest, although none had ever filed a complaint with the police. Furthermore, the authors suspect that this figure is an underestimate as many of the women left the clinic before they could be properly interviewed.

In a study of a treatment centre in southern Sweden, physician and sexologist Boel E. Stjerna (p. 12) found that 75 per cent of all male LVM patients[1] treated during 1995 and 1996 had been subjected to

[1] LVM is the Act on Treatment of Alcoholics and Drug Misusers. Under certain conditions LVM requires that the authorities take substantial consumers of alcohol and narcotics into custody to motivate them for treatment; with or without their consent. Such measures are permitted only if the problematic consumer is in need of assistance to get off drugs, and there is no other way to get him into treatment. Furthermore, he must be seriously endangering his own or a relative's physical and mental health.

sexual abuse in childhood; 70 per cent of the perpetrators were males and 30 per cent females, while 45 per cent were relatives. Of the remaining 55 per cent most were professionals who work with children. As LVM is primarily applied to the most extreme cases, this may help to explain the exceptionally high incidence of sexual abuse Stjerna found among these males.

Another way to see the connection between childhood sexual abuse and problematic consumption is to examine the terms used to describe the two phenomena. When I started reading the literature on childhood sexual abuse I was taken aback by the similarities between the concepts used and the way problematic consumers describe their life experiences. The following terms have been taken from Boström and Dahlström-Lannes.

alcohol abuse
anger
anorexia
anxiety
belief that they are not entitled to their own bodies
betrayal
confusion
criminality
depression
desperation
difficulty in setting limits to the surrounding world
emotional stagnation
fear
feelings of worthlessness
focused on satisfying others
guilt feelings
helplessness
humiliation
introverted
lack of identity
lack of self-confidence
loneliness
loss of control
mental illness
nightmares
panic
passivity
powerlessness
promiscuity
prostitution
rage
regression
running away from home
self-contempt
shame
sorrow
stomach problems
suicidal
terror
truancy
victim of crime

The terms in this list are so strikingly similar to the concepts I use to illustrate problematic narcotics consumption that it is difficult to believe that it's purely coincidental.

CONCLUSION

The way parents treat their offspring is of major importance for the child's development. However, in modern, postindustrial societies, even very young children spend much of their time outside the family. Contacts with society play a vital role in the way we develop, and I shall now address this subject.

8 Societal Labelling

INTRODUCTION

As a child grows older his time is increasingly spent in the world outside his home. Both his contacts with society and his experiences at home are of vital importance for his development. We have already seen why children who have been labelled by their parents are at risk of being subjected to societal labelling. However, all is not lost as the self-image is far from well established. But now it is essential that those who become the child's significant others counteract the labelling responses he has been receiving at home. Others must react to the child's primary deviance; but without labelling him.

In this chapter I will limit myself to presenting examples of societal labelling from a few different arenas.

'TREATING' YOUNG OFFENDERS

Despite the fact that certain methods of treatment for young offenders have been used for generations, and there has never been any proof that those who received this kind of 'care' have changed their behaviour in a positive direction, we continue to implement the same old formula. With the help of an autobiography by former problematic consumer of narcotics, Lasse Carlsson I shall examine the labelling process.

Carlsson (p. 10) describes his 'crime career' until the age of eight:

> I had stolen in department stores, taken money from my mother's wallet, run away from home, played hooky, and had a big mouth. But there was one thing I had never done: gotten into a fight. Or, more correctly, started a fight. I was deathly afraid of physical violence. I felt sick at the very thought of it.

His fear of physical violence most likely came from the repeated beatings both he and his mother had been subjected to by his alcoholic father: abuse that continued even after his parents were divorced.

When his mother no longer felt she could take care of him, and after an unsuccessful placement in an orphanage, the eight-year-old boy was sent to an institution, Hammargården's School Home. How was this battered child, deathly afraid of violence, greeted upon arrival?

> The fight [with Pyret, another interned boy] was short, but intensive; after three blows, I was flat on the floor, ... I made it through the school's

welcome ceremony scared out of my wits, with one less front tooth, the taste of blood in my mouth, and a headache that lasted all day.

The next day, Pyret came up to me with a sly smile.

'Listen Billy, go pick a couple of litres of raspberries for me!'

'What the hell are you talking about???'

'Two litres of raspberries, or I'm going to work you over', he said clenching his right fist and shoving it in my face. (Ibid., p. 11)

There's a hierarchy at Hammargården. The smallest, that is the worst fighters, are at the bottom of the pyramid. The biggest, the physically strongest, are at the top. No one ever seriously questioned that rule. In reality, this meant that I had to pick two litres of raspberries a day for him during the raspberry season... Pyret then turns the raspberries over to a salesman... The salesman sells the raspberries on the main road.

Pyret keeps half the money and gives the rest to his bodyguard; a guy who has... fought himself into the position where he can protect his salesmen's turf, if anybody should try to muscle in on the action.

Highest in the pyramid, is Brain... His word is law.... None of the interns, and hardly any of the guards dare to mess with him.

(Ibid., pp. 11f)

Anyway, the raspberry business, and all the other businesses, help to make Hammargården a fairly nice place; for the guards.

The pyramid makes them almost unnecessary. They are free to attend to more fruitful activities: gardening, meditation, their wives, other people's wives.

What do I know?

In any event, they didn't give a damn about us. (Ibid., p. 14)

To say that the guards ignored the interns is not entirely true. The boys were used by some of the guards for sexual satisfaction (ibid., pp. 37, 103) or to give vent to their aggression. Assaults were committed by both the guards and the boys themselves.

Standard procedure for those caught attempting to escape was:

First, the headmaster: a little abuse, both physical and verbal... and then the other interns. The collective punishment isn't more lenient, only more ingenious. It usually starts with a gang beating. The runaway is shoved up against a wall. Then a myriad of fists scourge his body. The fists are exchanged for feet when the victim can no longer stand. The battering continues until Brain, by a gesture or a word, indicates that it's enough.... Then the runaway is locked in his room for the rest of the day to ponder his sins. Next day: the raspberry patch. The machinery can't be allowed to grind to a halt. Losses must be recovered. Two litres become four.

> Another kind of collective punishment is to run the gauntlet. The escapee has to run between two parallel lines of interns who kick him as he passes.
>
> A third variation is the tree: the captured runaway is bound hand and foot to a tree and sentenced to a certain number of lashes. After the flogging he is left bound to the tree for the rest of the day. That way you get out of being locked in your room all day. (Ibid., p. 17f)

In the quotations above, Carlsson uses *collective punishment* in an unusual way. More commonly this term denotes that an entire group is punished for something one or a few members have done. This is of course contrary to all legal tenets, but that doesn't prevent it from being used at institutions whose stated goal is to teach people to be law abiding citizens. For instance, when some jam disappeared from Hammargården and nobody admitted to 'the crime', none of the children were given any preserves for the entire winter and everyone had to go to bed an hour earlier for a month (ibid., p. 31). Another of Carlsson's examples, this time from Lövsta orphanage was placing all the kids in solitary confinement for two weeks because no one admitted knowing anything about a hacksaw blade found by one of the guards.

The basic rule of the system is the *thumbscrew method*: if a punishment doesn't have the desired effect, use an even more severe punishment, and if that doesn't work escalate still further. After a series of escapes from Hammargården, Carlsson is moved to Lövsta. Following an unsuccessful provisional discharge, he is handed over to 'Cool Carl', a guard:

> He is smiling, but there is a look of expectation in his eye. He starts beating me. When I don't make a sound and he hits me even harder.
>
> 'Trying to be tough are you?'
>
> After a while I'm screaming. Howling. Cool Carl keeps working me over. He's indifferent to my screams. The cell is soundproof. By the time he thinks I've had enough, I'm lying on the floor, almost unconscious. He departs with one last kick in the groin.
>
> . . . After a week in the cell, they let me out. Most of the bruises from my beating are gone, so Cool Carl never laid a hand on me. Not much point in complaining; no one would listen anyway. (Ibid., p. 46)

After another attempted escape, Carlsson is placed in a ward known as 'The Special'.

> The first thing that awaits you is a week's solitary confinement. You are locked in a cell two by three metres and not allowed to get out of your pyjamas. The bed and linens disappear in the morning and come back late at night. All there is to do all day is look out the barred window or stare at the naked walls of your cell. Smoking and reading are strictly prohibited.

> ...After the introductory week you're allowed to be with the other inmates on the ward during the day. At night, you are locked in.
>
> Treatment consists of hard work, beatings, and verbal abuse. Recreation consists of cards and pachisi. The minimum sentence here is three months. There is no maximum.
>
> ...In this manner we are taught to be useful members of society.
>
> (Ibid., p. 57f)

Similar descriptions of Carlsson's experiences at a number of different institutions fill the book. What has Carlsson learned from the care society has provided? Shortly before his release from prison, he decided to try to live straight, but a fellow prisoner was not impressed:

> 'Shit Billy, open your eyes. You're a loser! With your past there's no way you're ever gonna get straightened out. You've been had! Marked for life. The sooner you get wise, the better off you'll be.' (Ibid., p. 110)

When Carlsson replies that he can't keep on the way he's been going, he's told:

> 'You're dreaming! Who's gonna hire you? What papers are you gonna show 'em? There's a housing shortage; who's gonna rent you a place? Where are you gonna find a chick who's ready to help you? Do you really think you can hide your past? Think! Guys like you and me don't stand a chance. That's the way it is, one guy stomps on the next, and you and me are at the bottom of the shit pile: and we ain't goin' nowhere. Face facts; that way it doesn't hurt so bad.' (Ibid.)

Carlsson (p. 107) describes his experience of penal justice as,

> a succession of nervous breakdowns, and acting out after mental and physical torture from both guards and fellow inmates. In isolation, I hallucinate; am confronted by a dark world full of the most absurd monsters. In my desperation and terror, I freak out, pounding my fists to pulp on the walls and floor and smashing my head against the side of the bed in the hope that my brain will short-circuit and release me from the nightmare.
>
> On the outside, I feel hate, a hate that could kill, but inside, I'm a bottomless void. (Ibid., p. 147)

> Sure, life is for learning. Some are born to spend their lives behind bars. To be able to live with that, you hit the bottle. Alcohol anaesthetizes; keeps the darkness at bay, at least for the moment. Alcohol is salvation and hell.
>
> So: you get out of prison, buy a bottle, get drunk, puke, damn your hangover, get pissed again, and so on and so on for ever...or until something else happens to you.
>
> You're well adapted to your environment. (Ibid., p. 152)

While there is certainly no guarantee that more humane treatment would transform people like Lasse Carlsson into well-adjusted members of society, there are strong theoretical reasons to believe that civilized treatment would help to lessen their hatred, both of the world around them and of themselves. This would mitigate both aggression directed at others, and their self-destructive behavioural patterns.

I have devoted this section to some of the obvious societal labelling caused by institutions that base their 'treatment' on repression. But societal labelling is not always so apparent. I shall discuss some of its more subtle forms shortly, but first, a few words on social control.

FORMAL AND INFORMAL SOCIAL CONTROL

During preschool years, children's contacts with society are primarily with the staff of daycare centres, nannies, neighbours and relatives. That I put child-care personnel first is because an increasing number of people are living in conditions vastly different from traditional society. Families no longer live generation after generation in the same community, and relatives are no longer next door. Modern residential areas often lack deeply rooted social relations where the community is permeated by what sociologists call informal social control. Briefly, *informal social control* implies that people, because they have maintained social relationships for a long time and therefore are important for one another, regulate each other's behaviour by openly reacting to what others do. In doing so social norms are confirmed and maintained. Control is not the primary objective of social relationships, but it is a part of them. For instance, when a child does something improper, the neighbours know both the child and his family. When people feel they should do something, their reaction is a part of an extensive relationship, and is based on personal knowledge of the individual.

Informal social control has lost much of its social significance in modern cities and suburbs. There are many reasons for this, for instance, the great number of people who move in and out of an area. As a colleague put it: 'I don't try to make new friends anymore. It takes so long to really get to know someone, that I don't have the time. And even if I should manage to make a friend, either he or I will probably move and then he won't be nearby when I need him.' Admittedly this is a drastic point of view, but modern mobility is conducive to opinions of this nature. Many people are unwilling/unable to expend time, energy and emotional commitment on their neighbours.

Making new friends is not easy, even for those who would like to do so. During weekday working hours residential areas are fairly empty, and when people come home in the evening, they are tired, have their hands full with their own children and domestic chores and/or participate in other activities.

Furthermore a high material standard allows people to disappear from residential areas during leisure time. Christie and Bruun (pp. 217ff) feel that it is important to restore informal social control and suggest that working hours be changed to encourage us to spend more time in our neighbourhoods: that is by shortening not only the work day but also week-ends and vacations.

As informal social control decreases, we become more dependent on *formal social control*; authorities with control as a primary function. We hire police, security guards, social workers, etc. and charge them with keeping people on the straight and narrow. The less we know our neighbours, the less likely that we will personally intervene. It's far easier to go to a friend next door and ask him to turn down the volume on his stereo than it is to say the same thing to a stranger. If we don't know who is living next door and we don't have the time and/or energy to find out, we're more likely to anonymously report transgressions to the authorities, rather than dealing with the matter ourselves.

Formal social control is exercised by strangers who therefore cannot adapt their measures to the individual's needs and capabilities. Furthermore, the most important element in informal social control is missing; the threat of depriving the wrongdoer of friendship, support and/or love. When control is the principal reason for making contact, there is no friendship, support or love to withhold.

PRESCHOOL AGE

In modern society the responsibility for bringing up children has been increasingly transferred from the family to other social institutions. As the number of women working outside the home increases so do the number of children in daycare. In industrialized countries such as the US, which don't provide economic compensation for parents to stay home and care for their toddlers, many children are spending eight to ten hours a day in contact with society outside the family from as early as one month of age. This is why it is essential that there are efficient daycare services with well-educated personnel. Furthermore, it is important that working conditions are conducive to letting the staff put into practice what they have learned in their professional training. Moreover the environment must be sufficiently rewarding so the personnel will remain on the job and develop close, intimate and lasting relations with the toddlers left in their care. Under such conditions it is possible for staff members to at least partially compensate for the shortcomings in the homes of some of the children. This kind of intervention can be instrumental in retarding and maybe even preventing the development of a deviant career.

But is this really the responsibility of daycare? The answer is, what are the alternatives? As the urbanization process continues, and informal social control decreases, who else can compensate for eventual problems in a child's nuclear family?

The norms in industrialized societies are in flux. An increasing number of mothers with young children are working outside of the home. If we look at Sweden, which has probably gone furthest in this direction, preschools are considered one of many societal measures to support families. Other examples of social support are:

1. economic measures – i.e. child benefits, housing allowances, etc.
2. physical health measures – i.e. free maternal care before birth, free medical and dental care for infants and children, paid leaves of absence for parents to be home with a sick child, etc.
3. psychological measures – paid leave of absence from work for parents for 15 months after birth, extra leaves of absence reserved for the father, etc.
4. intellectual and socioemotional development – government supported daycare centres, schools, recreational centres etc.

What we are observing is increased societal support to families, supplementing, and sometimes taking over, roles which were previously the responsibility of parents. An obvious example, common to all industrialized nations, is schools. When we lived in a society where sons followed in their father's and daughters their mother's footsteps, parents had the necessary knowledge to prepare children for their future position in production. Today few people feel that they have both the time and the ability to give their offspring all the knowledge they need, and it is generally accepted that schools should play a major role in educating the next generation. Professor of Developmental Psychology, Bengt-Erik Andersson (p. 49) writes: 'But it is not merely a matter of [schools] giving children knowledge which their parents cannot provide.... it is also a question of... stimulating personal growth and social and emotional development in children.'

Furthermore, Andersson believes that these important processes should begin in daycare.

> Together with the parents, [the preschool] should promote the development of children in different ways by providing educational, social, and emotional stimulation. Preschool also has a special responsibility toward children who need extra support and stimulation. This might apply to children with various kinds of disabilities, immigrant children, and children who come from particularly deprived environments. (Ibid.)

The first question is whether daycare centres can even theoretically begin to meet such demands. Some research indicates that the answer may be yes. 'Concerning children in what may be called *high-risk groups,* because of their home environment, it seems that . . . daycare centres have been able to reduce the intellectual retardation often found among these children' (ibid., p. 61).

> The correlation between child care and social and emotional development is unequivocal . . . The pattern is clear for intellectual development as well . . . Children placed early in life in daycare and especially in daycare centres, are more extroverted, candid, secure, and independent compared to those who are admitted later, or those who never come in contact with these facilities. Daycare centre children also do better in school.
>
> (Ibid., p. 80)

Put concisely, preschool can play an important part in a child's development.

The next questions are whether preschools will be able to do so in the future, and if so, for how many children? These are, to some extent, political and ideological questions. The extent to which we build and maintain high quality daycare facilities, make them available to families in different socio-economic groups, staff them with sufficient numbers of well-educated people and equip them properly are all dependent upon how high daycare is placed on the political agenda.

If we once again look at Sweden, the conditions at many daycare centres were very good through the 1980s. However, ideological trends questioning high taxes and a large public sector have contributed to politicians cutting back on municipal spending in many areas, including child care. This tendency increased when the Conservative led coalition came into power in 1991 and reduced government subsidies to municipalities. Not even the return to power of the Social Democrats in 1994 changed the picture. Serious economic deficits in the national budget led to still further cutbacks.

This has meant that the building of new daycare facilities and the re-modelling of older ones has been drastically curtailed, the ratio of adults to children has been reduced, vacant positions were not filled, some daycare centres have been partially or entirely closed and staff members have been laid off or moved to other facilities. Furthermore, municipalities are trying to save money by minimizing pay increases and cutting back on benefits such as on-the-job supplementary education. Many highly qualified staff members have become dissatisfied and changed occupations. Some of those remaining are starting to question if what they are doing is meaningful. There is a danger that this will start a vicious circle where unfavourable working conditions lead to a greater turnover of staff members, further deteriorating working conditions, etc.

In this situation it is not only the staff members who suffer, but the children as well. If there is a large turnover of employees, the children soon learn that there is no point in establishing emotional ties to the personnel, as they are going to disappear anyway. And staff members neither get to know each child as an individual, nor establish relationships with the children's families. Furthermore it is hard to maintain educational objectives.

Another problem is that it becomes increasingly difficult for the staff to counteract and compensate for labelling in the home. Even if staff members know what should be done, they will have neither the time nor the energy to make use of what they have learned in their professional education. Children who react to their pain and sorrow by acting out must be silenced or the situation will become unbearable for the other children and the staff. Those who need help and react by withdrawing into themselves will not receive the attention they need to draw them out of their isolation. If the personnel consistently do not see and react to a child's needs they are in fact labelling him.

SCHOOL AGE

Changes in tax-financed schools parallel those in daycare centres. Many schools have been subjected to municipal cutbacks that impair their ability to function. Attempts to save money have often led to smaller schools being closed and replaced by larger units, which are believed to be more cost effective. In many districts the number of pupils in classes has been increased, while the number of non-teaching personnel, such as guidance counsellors, psychologists, nurses, recreational assistants, etc., has been cut back. By reducing staff in this manner schoolchildren have access to fewer adults who are potential significant others. Pupils have become increasingly dependent on each other for responses and support.

A consequence of having large classes is that teachers have less time to devote to children with special needs. It becomes extremely difficult (actually all but impossible) to have disorderly children, i.e. those who can't sit still, have minor learning disabilities, etc., in ordinary classes. In order for the well-behaved children to have an atmosphere conducive to learning, those with even moderate difficulties must be removed. Naturally there are advantages to putting children with difficulties in special classes but by doing so we are sending a crystal clear message to these youngsters that they are different from (and inferior to) others. Every day in school serves as a reminder of this fact. In doing so we help those who already have resources, but we also create a major source of labelling for those who can least afford this type of reaction. We may be saving money in the short term, but looking further down the road, some of those so labelled will surely come back to haunt us.

Grades are another labelling mechanism in school. I cannot give a detailed account of the pros and cons of giving grades here. But in short, pupils must be given feedback as to how they are doing in school, and institutions of higher education and future employers need information so they can choose among applicants. Grades serve these functions. However, from a labelling perspective giving grades has negative effects for some. Pupils compete for grades, and implicit in the word competition is that some win and others lose. The question is: what happens to the losers? Those who fairly consistently receive poor grades are thereby given very tangible proof of their (intellectual) inferiority. This is incorporated into their self-image, and will affect their behaviour later in life. The implication is that we must discuss how the functions currently filled by grades can be realized with a minimum of labelling.

Fortunately, there are also positive developments in the school systems in some municipalities, giving hope that societal labelling can be reduced. For instance, establishing closer ties between schools and recreational centres has made it possible for recreation centre personnel to be in the classroom. When this kind of cooperation has worked well there are several adults available, and pupils who need extra support can be given it without stigmatizing them by placing them in special classes.

My discussion of both preschools and schools has its roots in the ongoing discussion of how society's limited resources should be used. One such point of controversy concerns whether we should have an elite school where the seemingly talented are given higher priority, or mass education where resources are allocated fairly equally to all. Much of the difference of opinion stems from different assumptions. For instance, those who assume that human behaviour is primarily biological argue that we must develop the talent in those who are born gifted. Elite schools, its proponents tell us, lead to increased production and facilitate competition on the international market, thereby enhancing the economy and making it possible to improve conditions for the less gifted in the future. But the question arises, how do we know when the time has come to change strategy? After all, if we continue to support the elite, then according to the same argument, there would be even more resources further down the road, and if we wait still longer there will be even more resources, etc., etc., etc. So when do we have enough surplus to turn some of it over to those who weren't born with the same gifts as the elite?

Proponents of mass education feel that we have already come to this point; that modern industrial societies have access to the necessary resources. These people also usually start from the assumption that almost all of us are born gifted and that life experiences decide who will develop their innate resources. Mass education gives a better chance for more people to develop thereby increasing the nation's ability to compete internationally. Furthermore, they argue that by denying resources to some, we produce social problems which will require greater and greater expenditures the longer we wait to deal with them.

If we decide to give the elite high priority, we will do so at the cost of those who have difficulties now. By choosing to use society's resources in this way we are also deciding to further marginalize a part of the population. Labelling, and its future consequences – deviant careers – should be considered a minus in the cost/benefit calculations which precede political decisions on resource allocation.

The Swedish General Accounting Office (RRV, pp. 147ff) estimates that *public expenditure* for different types of drug careers ranges between $260 000 and $535 000. Two economists, Ingvar Nilsson and Anders Wadeskog found the *socioeconomic costs* of the drug career of a 'heavy addict' to be a minimum of $810 000 (all figures have been converted to 1998 currency). If we were to include these costs in our economic calculations, it might well prove to be profitable, even from a purely economic standpoint, to invest in all children. If ethical values are also taken into consideration, we find further justification for this course of action.

RECREATIONAL CENTRES

I conclude this chapter with a few comments on recreational centres. At least in Sweden, since the mid-1970s almost all politicians and staff are in agreement that recreational centres should be drug-free, i.e. only those who are not under the influence of any psychoactive drug are admitted to the premises. The primary argument in support of this policy is that it is difficult to carry on meaningful activities with inebriated, drugged or unruly adolescents who interfere with the activities of those who are well behaved.

While there may be some truth in this, we must realize that those who are not admitted to recreational centres are once again given proof that they are different (and worse) than the rest of us. In reality they are being told that they are not good enough to as much as associate with their peers. These adolescents, who presumably are those with the greatest need for establishing non-labelling contacts with adults, are barred from the very arena created for this purpose. Although some staff members try to reach these youths by spending time with them on the street, it is not difficult to understand how those who aren't allowed into recreational centres can draw the conclusion that they don't fit into society.

When we have taught a number of adolescents that they are not as good as the rest of us, and that we don't want to associate with them, it should not surprise us that they in later life find it difficult to live and work like other people, and to raise their children to follow the norms of society. Nor should it astonish us that they are attracted to people and activities looked down upon by law abiding citizens. This will be our next topic.

9 Secondary Deviance

INTRODUCTION

Children learn norms as they grow up, becoming increasingly aware of right and wrong as defined by their culture. This is usually accomplished by observing how others act and react in different situations, and by responses to their own behaviour from significant others. Belonging to the majority group in the country makes it easier to gain an adequate understanding of what is considered acceptable behaviour, but with the help of the mass media, obligatory schools, the local authorities, etc., minority group children are not far behind.

As the child grows into adolescence he becomes more certain of both what kind of person he is and the norms of society. His behaviour becomes increasingly regulated by his self-image. As previously noted: an individual with a negative self-image will tend to behave so as to provoke others to confirm this self-image rather than cause incongruity by behaving in a way which would impute a more positive self-image. Primary deviance gradually becomes secondary deviance, and the potential substantial consumer enters the third stage in his deviant career.

The places and events which constitute the everyday lives of problematic consumers is commonly called *the drug scene*, or simply *the scene*. Most of those who come into contact with the scene soon realize that they don't fit in, and withdraw shortly after arriving. For instance, while I was in the field I met quite a few adolescents who were tired of going to school, or were looking for something new and exciting. They turned up on the scene and tried it out. I have come to the conclusion that *it is not primarily the individual's experience with drugs that determines whether or not he remains on the scene. More important is whether or not the social experiences he has there fill the needs he brought with him. If he feels at home with the people and activities on the scene, he will return time and again, thereby increasingly coming into contact with narcotics.* As noted in Chapter 3 experiences with drugs are in part dependent on setting.

ON THE STEPPING STONE HYPOTHESIS

It is true that many problematic consumers make their debut with illegal drugs by smoking cannabis. However, this cannot be taken as support for *the stepping stone* or *gateway hypothesis* (that smoking cannabis leads to the abuse of hard drugs). To begin with, the stepping stone hypothesis is an example of simple causation, which has already been rejected as an oversimplification (see pp. 12ff). Furthermore, proponents of the stepping stone hypothesis make a fundamental logical mistake. It is not sufficient to maintain that one action causes another simply because the former precedes the latter in time. Following that logic we could assert that smoking cigarettes, or even drinking water, leads to the consumption of hard drugs.

If we are to consider the gateway hypothesis as valid, at the very least a high percentage of those who smoke cannabis would have to make the transition to hard drugs. Numerous studies in many countries have shown that this is not the case. For instance, UNO (a nationwide study of the prevalence of narcotics abuse in Sweden) found that while 15 per cent of 12–24 year olds had tried cannabis, only 2 per cent had ever tried central stimulants and 1 per cent had ever taken opiates (UNO, suppl. 2, p. 27). Five per cent of those who had tried amphetamines (0.1 per cent of 12–24 year olds in the country) admitted to having used them more than once in the preceding four weeks (ibid., p. 28). Put differently, for every 150 youths who admitted to having used cannabis, only one said he had taken central stimulants (the hard drugs most commonly used in Sweden) more than once in the preceding four-week period. (There are no data on opiates.)

In other words, having tried cannabis is a poor predictor of problematic consumption of hard drugs. Other indications appear to be better. Based on a study they did in New York, Kandel and Yamaguchi (p. 854) argue that early onset into legal drugs (alcohol and tobacco) is a crucial risk factor for progression to more serious forms of drug use. And Sifaneck and Kaplan (p. 503) quote another study from the US showing that problematic alcohol use preceded heroin use in 94 per cent of the study's population, compared with 30 per cent whose marijuana use was a precursor to heroin.

Sifaneck and Kaplan (p. 500) make another interesting point. In the Netherlands where cannabis can readily be purchased in coffee shops, some problematic consumers use it as a means of getting off heroin. In other words while cannabis sometimes is a prologue to hard drugs, it can also be an epilogue.

Although we must always be cautious when interpreting drug statistics it appears safe to conclude that only a very small percentage of those who use cannabis go on to become problematic consumers of hard drugs. It takes a lot more than testing cannabis before an individual should be considered a potential substantial consumer of hard drugs. The stepping stone hypothesis is misleading because it fails to take set into consideration.

DO PUSHERS ENTICE ADOLESCENTS INTO TRYING NARCOTICS?

A recurrent theme in drug war propaganda is that innocent children are enticed into drug abuse after being given free samples by pushers lurking near schoolyards. In reality dealers do not operate in this fashion. To consciously seek out and develop new markets it is essential to:

- make and execute long-term plans
- have initiative
- have assets to invest.

These are resources that small dealers lack. That wholesalers would take the risks involved in this kind of dealing is simply out of the question. First of all pushers know that there is no chance of soliciting customers in this way. And even if they thought it possible, they still wouldn't take the risk as those higher up in the drug hierarchy would be afraid to continue doing business with them. Anyone who wants to sell more than small quantities of narcotics must remain out of sight. Consequently there are no dope dealers lying in ambush near schools.

ESPAD, a study which compared drug consumption among 15–16 year olds in 26 European countries concludes: 'most of the students got their first drug from someone they knew very well' (Hibell et al., p. 85). My own study confirms this conclusion. I have never met a problematic consumer who claimed that an older person has lured or tried to entice him into using drugs. The initial contact with narcotics usually followed one of the following patterns:

1. Friends started using illegal drugs and by continuing to associate with them, the individual gained access to narcotics.
2. The individual himself actively sought out narcotics consumers.

At some point, the prospective problematic consumer either made a conscious choice to try drugs, or found himself in a situation where it was difficult to refuse. For instance, if he is at a party where a joint is passed around, he might take a drag to prove to himself and/or others that he's 'cool'. As most people don't experience anything noteworthy the first few times they smoke cannabis, it is hardly likely that he'll feel any great need for the drug afterwards. In other words, if he smoked hashish merely because he was in a situation where it was hard to say no, the chances are that in the future he'll see to it that he doesn't get himself into this kind of situation again. The easiest way to achieve this is to simply stay away from the scene: and this is precisely what most people who make contact with it soon decide to do. However, a small minority return time and again.

CONTAGION OR VOLITION?

Although it isn't scientifically accurate to do so, the term epidemic is generally associated with contagion. People in epidemics are seen as victims, not as individuals placing themselves in harm's way. The use of epidemic in conjunction with narcotics is deceptive as it can lead us to think of drug consumers as objects. But to procure and consume narcotics one must be active; a subject.

However, it is equally incorrect to see problematic consumers solely as subjects as it is to see them as objects. While it is true that they make many decisions, the alternatives they perceive are limited by their previous experiences: many of which have their origins in their childhood when they in many respects were objects exposed to both parental and societal labelling. We must therefore see substantial consumers as both subjects and objects.

If an individual seeks out the scene and finds that participation is incongruent with his self-image, he will withdraw. This is why only those with certain kinds of life experiences choose to remain for extended periods. While in the field, I met many who left for good after a mere glimpse, as well as those relatively few who thought they had found something they were looking for and decided to stay on for a considerable period of time. In either case, the decision was their own. No one was duped and/or forced to stay on the scene by a pusher or a problematic consumer. On the contrary, substantial consumers often warn novices to stay away from narcotics.

THE DRUG SCENE

What is life on the drug scene like? I shall not attempt to present a detailed picture of the scene in Stockholm as details change over time, and different people perceive and experience different things. Instead I will present a number of themes which I believe illustrate important aspects of the essential nature of problematic consumption. But first a few words of caution; the material presented does not convey 'the truth', but rather my interpretations. Another researcher might emphasize other aspects and interpret their experiences somewhat differently. Moreover the scene in other cities will obviously differ on many points. Further research is necessary to ascertain the extent to which the themes presented in this chapter are relevant elsewhere.

PERCEPTIONS OF TIME AND SELF

An aspect of the scene that was very foreign to me personally was the way time is perceived. In western cultures we are taught to divide time into rather precise units – from centuries down to fractions of seconds. In contrast, I have never met a problematic consumer who carried a calendar, and few wore watches. (Stolen watches are inexpensive and readily accessible if anyone should want one.)

The discipline of keeping track of time that most of us submit to, is all but nonexistent on the scene. Almost nothing has to be done at any particular moment. Yet problematic consumers do not enjoy their freedom. To do so they would have to rid themselves of societal norms demanding that adults earn a living, pull their own weight, contribute to society, etc. As previously noted problematic consumers have not neutralized societal norms. By acting as they do they breach norms they themselves accept, and subject themselves to both self-contempt and scorn from others.

There is another aspect of time as it is conceived on the scene which I found difficult. Everybody I knew before going into the field thought in terms of the past, present and future. For instance, when you make a new acquaintance you ask where he comes from, what he has done, what he is doing and what his plans are. In the process of questioning and answering we show who we are (or at least project an image, in the hope that others will accept and validate it).

Problematic consumers, on the other hand, try to ignore the dynamics of time, living as much as possible here and now. All that counts is what is happening at the moment. This enables them to be one person today and another tomorrow: no one demands that there be a continuity between the two. As one woman put it, 'on the scene I can be myself or anyone else I feel like being and nobody asks any questions'. This might sound nice, and may be so in the short term, but as we will soon see it creates difficulties in the long run.

It's not that problematic consumers are unaware of the past and the future; they just attempt to give these dimensions a different meaning. For instance, as all of those who remain on the scene for an extended period have an excessive number of negative experiences in the past which they usually don't want to be reminded of, no one demands that you reveal where you have come from. For those who haven't been to the finest schools, this is a relief. For some it's a necessary prerequisite to muster the courage to associate with other people at all.

Concerning the future, there is endless talk about one project or another. However, discussing one's plans does not imply any obligation to actually do something, and what is said is usually not taken seriously and immediately forgotten. For instance, when I published a book about the scene, a substantial consumer I had known for several years said: 'I didn't know you were writing a book.' I had spoken about the book many times (to explain why I was on the scene when I didn't use drugs), and when I reminded him of this, he said: 'Yeah – but you know how people talk.' I am aware that words and deeds often lead separate lives, but compared to other people I know, problematic consumers are at the far end of the continuum.

RELATIONS WITHOUT OBLIGATIONS

There are good reasons why substantial consumers perceive time as they do. It makes it possible for them to speak without arousing expectations they can't live up to, and they can change their presentation of self from one situation to the next without scaring everybody off. However, the price they pay is very high: it becomes all but impossible to establish intimate relationships. How can you trust the person you are with when he may well take on an entirely different identity the next time you see him?

As previously noted, problematic consumers have experienced a lack of reciprocity in their relations to parents and other adults. When prospective substantial consumers committed themselves the responses were negative, rejecting, oppressive, deceitful, brutal, etc. They now avoid subjecting themselves to this kind of pain. The result is that neither they themselves nor those they associate with really exist; that is, that which is here today is gone tomorrow. Nobody can depend on the people they meet and there is no solid substance upon which to develop stable relationships. The way people associate with others on the scene is a parody of human relations. Although problematic consumers are physically near people they call friends, there is no deeper contact and there is no one they can trust. They therefore don't grow and become stronger through their social relationships. On the contrary they feel all the more alone and weak; their humanity shrivels still further. In this way social relations on the scene reinforce the negative self-image.

However, it would be an exaggeration to claim that there are no mutual relations at all on the drug scene. For example, granting credit is the basis of doing business in all but the last stage in drug trafficking. The goods are paid for after they have been sold. But, the closer you get to problematic consumers, the less trust there is. Substantial consumers do not think in terms of the long-term consequences of their actions. Why bother when you have no idea whether you yourself or the other person will be around tomorrow? This way of thinking sooner or later leads to either burning someone else or getting burned yourself. Being a problematic consumer is more than a full-time job and it's all they can do to make it through the day. They have neither the energy nor the motivation to worry about what tomorrow may bring.

Understanding this gives us insight into the ongoing and controversial question of general prevention. *General prevention* denotes the idea that by punishing people who commit crimes, we are also preventing others from committing similar acts. Punishment is thought to both deter crime and strengthen moral codes. (For a comprehensive and critical examination of general crime deterrence, see Mathiesen, Chapter 3.) General prevention may have an effect on those who think about the long-term effects of what they are doing, but it is difficult to understand how it can work on those who live for the moment. As problematic consumers belong to the latter category, we have no reason to believe that general prevention helps to bring their activities more into line with the demands of society. On the contrary, in some situations, strict punishment may even inspire to still more crime. We shall return to this shortly.

In summary, those who stay on the scene can be characterized by their inability to clearly define the way they would like others to perceive them. As those they associate with do likewise it is difficult to have a clear conception of others. People neither have to behave in any particular way nor be consistent. This manifests itself through the absence of clearly defined norms on the scene, and in the language used, which consists of many slang expressions lacking precise meaning. Most often problematic consumers avoid voicing clear opinions which can't be withdrawn or immediately revised. On the scene it is common to change directions in mid-sentence, make contradictory statements, stop halfway through an idea, switch to another subject, etc.

A possible explanation for all this is that if a problematic consumer were to take a close look at himself, that is clearly define who he is and see this as relatively permanent, it would lead to drastic consequences, maybe even immediate suicide. Making everything ambiguous, and seeing his present self as a momentary construction, are survival strategies. They make it possible for him to hope that some day he may find a self-image, or have experiences, which will give him the desire/right to exist. Unfortunately, this strategy distances him from deeper social relationships; probably the most important prerequisite for bringing about such a change.

As time passes the situation becomes increasingly precarious. The longer he stays on the scene the worse things get, creating an almost desperate need to escape. Everyone tries to get away: they make promises to themselves, look for a job, move to another town or country, etc. If nothing else works, they commit flagrant crimes or irresolute attempts at suicide in the hope that someone else will bring about a change. And when nothing helps, when all efforts have failed, problematic consumers often try to convince themselves that they don't care what happens to them. When a person doesn't care about anyone, and no one cares about him, why should he care about himself? After all, he is already (socially) dead.

ESCAPE

Much of what I observed in the field can best be explained by the attempts of problematic consumers to escape – escape from the past, from the present, from society, from their feelings, from everything that passes through their heads, and from not having any future.

Before going into the field I had more or less expected that substantial consumers would feel that they do not belong in society and that they would not be concerned about what was going on in the country. But that so many would say that they didn't care what happened to themselves was beyond my imagination. In fact, the first few times I heard it, I simply didn't believe it. I tried to avoid having to deal with the implications of such statements by either rejecting them outright or by trying to convince myself that it might be pleasant not having to worry about a lot of obligations and responsibilities. For instance, I said to one of my research subjects: 'It must be nice not worrying about anything.' He answered: 'It's hard, damn hard.' Statements to this effect forced me to realize that behind their nonchalant façade there is emotional turmoil and deep tragedy.

Professor of Social Work Bengt Börjeson (1979, p. 83f) writes:

> When people make choices they do so on the basis of their conception of themselves and of the world around them. In this sense, people are prisoners of their own consciousness. This imprisonment may be more difficult to bear than any other, which explains why people repeatedly attempt to escape from their thoughts. [Drug] abuse is an attempt to escape; but it leads to even worse imprisonment.

That I most often was able to maintain good relationships with problematic consumers was probably because I accepted them as they were, while remaining 'real', in the sense that they could establish a reasonably clear and stable picture of me. This gave them a sense of security when interacting with me.

Many substantial consumers told me in serious conversations that they did not have the strength to go on. They were dissatisfied with the life they were leading, and they wanted to get away from themselves and everyone else. The dream of starting a new life, for instance in Bali or on a farm, helped many of them endure a little while longer.

Drugs are sometimes taken in the hope that there is a chemical escape route. At some point in their careers problematic consumers try just about any substance they can get their hands on, and when the same feelings and experiences remain, they increase the dose or create concoctions of different drugs. They take pills without knowing what they contain, eat seeds and smoke leaves. Who knows, something might happen!

At times problematic consumers feel like prisoners on the scene. They want out but don't know where to go. They make decisions, but can't effectuate them. Or, they make new decisions which effectively counteract the old ones. For instance, one of my research subjects was injecting morphine while he was a student (of sorts) at Stockholm University. He told me that he had decided to get off drugs for a while so he could study for an exam. But at the same time, he also decided to let another substantial consumer move in with him. The tacit understanding was that the tenant would be allowed to live in the apartment in exchange for sharing some of his morphine with his landlord. Our student knew he should be studying, but realized it wasn't going to work. So he created a situation where he got morphine without having to spend time looking for it, and where he could take it without making himself feel too guilty. After all he couldn't help it if his roommate was buying drugs and pressuring him into using them. But this was small consolation. By failing the exam he once again proved to himself that he was incapable of doing what he set out to do, and what he felt he should be doing; thereby increasing his self-contempt; and his need for escape.

BOREDOM

Before going into the field I thought life on the scene would be exciting, but I often found myself bored. The question is whether problematic consumers are also bored. On the one hand they have to get hold of a lot of money and then find drugs and a place to take them. For people on hard drugs this is more than a full-time job. So maybe they aren't bored. On the other hand, every day is pretty much the same; there are no weekdays or holidays on the scene. So in spite of everyone doing a lot of running around, the lack of variation may be boring.

There is also a lot of what might be called pseudoactivity. For instance speed freaks can spend hours taking an appliance apart and fiddling with its innards, or sweeping dust back and forth across the floor. While they are busy at it they are very much involved in what they are doing, and seem to find it worthwhile. However, the activity ceases to exist the second they stop. They've learned nothing they can use later on, and usually don't even remember what they had been doing. In other words, time has gone by and nothing of any value has been gained. Perhaps this is a good definition of boredom.

There are also periods which problematic consumers themselves find boring, i.e. waiting around for a dealer. At best, anticipation gives some meaning to the (in)activity.

Among problematic consumers of cannabis the boredom is more pronounced. They don't need as much money as people on hard drugs, and hash can be (and often is) replaced by alcohol. So they're not in the same rat race as people on hard drugs and they're not nearly as busy. In fact they have to find ways to kill time. For example, one day I was at a café with six problematic consumers; we just sat there staring at each other. Someone suggested that we go to a pub. Somebody asked what we were going to do when we got there. The answer was 'nothing', but it would take a little time to get there. After a while they got up and left while I stayed at the café. About an hour later I went to the pub and found the six of them sitting there, just as they had done in the café.

Of course, it was not always this boring, but a lot of time is spent waiting for something to happen. I am well aware that there are many people who lead a humdrum existence, but the scene can be pretty extreme.

Not even the many parties thrown by people on soft drugs dispersed the boredom. Very little differentiated a party from daily life. Everyone got high and waited for something else to happen. Once I brought a friend who was visiting me to one of these parties. A few hours after his first contact with the scene he noted: 'there's no joy here'.

TAKING RISKS

In Chapter 4 I wrote that self-destructiveness is an important part of the essential nature of problematic consumption, and described some of the physical and psychological risks substantial consumers take. I shall now portray risk taking in another light.

Case 1 – The post office robber. A substantial consumer who had been in some sort of custody almost all his life had been out of prison for a while and it looked like things were starting to work out for him. Amongst other things, he had a foster family who were doing everything in their power to help him.

One day he walked into a post office, placed himself in front of a security camera and without as much as a hat to disguise himself, he shot into the air with a rifle. He neither demanded money nor made any attempt to get away; he just stood there waiting for the police to arrive.

Case 2 – Travellers' cheques. A man who had stolen a large number of travellers' cheques made a deal with a problematic consumer to travel to several European cities, cash the cheques, and on his return to Stockholm he would be allowed to keep half of the money.

By using his own ID when he cashed the stolen travellers' cheques, he maximized the risk of being apprehended. Upon returning to Stockholm, he made no attempt to stay away from the scene, where he was known to the police.

Case 3 – Wanna buy some shit? A substantial consumer stood in a large park in Stockholm, waving about 1½ hectos of hash in the faces of passing strangers while asking them if they wanted to buy some shit. If the police, who were often in the park, had seen him, or if he had been reported, he almost certainly would have been sentenced to several years in prison.

Case 4 – Carrying drugs. Many problematic consumers make sure they have drugs on them almost every day, even when they are in places that are heavily patrolled by the police. At the same time, they dress and/or act in a way that attracts attention. A routine check is all it would take for them to be caught. Most of the time they're only carrying small amounts, but why run the risk?

Case 5 – The syringe. A substantial consumer sat at a café hangout where he knew the personnel collaborated with the police. Furthermore, the place was often raided. He was carrying enough opiates to get himself put away for several years. He placed the drugs and a syringe on the table and started playing with them. He then asked some strangers if they knew what he used the syringe for. They didn't, so he took it upon himself to inform them.

Case 6 – Check out the police. I was with a few problematic consumers in a square, well known as a place where drugs are sold. Suddenly the police started a major raid. One of my companions who was carrying a lot of narcotics left the crowd we were standing in, and sat down on the bumper of a car that two policemen were examining. Afterwards he told me that he was just 'checking out what the cops were doing'.

Case 7 – Security cameras. The police have mounted security cameras in some of the places where drugs commonly are sold. I have many times witnessed problematic consumers flash small amounts of drugs in front of these cameras, knowing full well that they were probably being observed by police who had monitors in a building nearby.

Case 8 – The smuggling trip. At a time when there was a shortage of hashish in town, a dealer, who was also a problematic consumer, decided to smuggle a major amount from Denmark. Before leaving he did a lot of unnecessary talking, and his plans were known to many people.

Initially I interpreted these kinds of acts as taking unnecessary risks. I did so because I couldn't come up with any reasonable explanation. This was because my thinking was trapped in the basic assumption that people who commit crimes want to avoid punishment, and do whatever they can to hide their illegal acts. While it certainly is true that problematic consumers often try to cover up their crimes, the examples above illustrate that such is not necessarily the case. How can we explain this behaviour?

WHY PROBLEMATIC CONSUMERS TAKE RISKS

A Desperate Attempt to Flee from One's Present Life-Situation

When problematic consumers feel they have lost control over their lives, they may become desperate and deliberately attempt to get themselves arrested. Case 1, The post office robber, illustrates this.

When things started going too well too fast for our post office robber he was literally scared out of his wits. The changes in his life went so rapidly that he didn't recognize himself in his new role as a 'useful member of society'.

He couldn't deal with the expectations of others, and the demands he made on himself. The life he was leading was incongruent with his still rather negative self-image and he felt that a person such as he did not deserve to have it so good. So he started shooting amphetamines again; but he couldn't deal with life on the scene either. The situation became increasingly desperate as he felt he could neither continue with drugs nor live a 'normal' life. He was so ashamed of his relapse that he felt he couldn't face his foster parents. So he sought out the only place he knew he could handle: prison.

In case 2, Travellers' cheques, our forger had been selling and smoking cannabis for about a year when the police caught him carrying drugs. Actually he was a small dealer but when he was arrested he happened to have a somewhat larger quantity than usual. He decided to stop dealing for a while, but as he didn't have a work permit in Sweden, he had no legal way to support himself and turned to theft. He said he did not want to be a thief and he went about it half-heartedly. After a while he started fighting with the guy he shared an apartment with, and generally seemed dejected. He had become introverted and successively more passive. The offer to cash the travellers' cheques came during this period.

Catharsis

Problematic consumers know that the longer they stay on the scene the more terrible things they will do. If they don't know how get themselves off the scene, and feel their self-contempt growing, then suicide is close at hand. Getting arrested and taking your punishment may seem to be a way out. The daily consumer hopes that serving time will act as a type of catharsis which will enable him to start a new life.

A few months before the incident described in Case 3, Wanna buy some shit?, I noticed that the protagonist was sliding downhill. His drug consumption increased drastically and he showed signs of unrest. He was shooting both amphetamines and opiates, and taking LSD almost every day.

A few months earlier he had deserted from the army. Before that he had gone AWOL several times and had served time in military prison. Now he started talking about returning to the army to take his punishment. But that plan (like so many others) was never executed. He told me that he was destroying himself in Stockholm and had to get out of the city, but he couldn't effectuate it. However, when plans were in the making for a smuggling run to Copenhagen, he offered to make the trip. He took money from several people, including two major pushers; and burned them all.

He had finally managed to get himself out of Stockholm, while at the same time seemingly cutting off any chance of returning to the scene there. So now there had to be a change. But he didn't feel any better in Malmö, where he had fled, and after a while, he was back in the capital city.

People who burn big pushers run the risk of being killed. His blatantly coming back to Stockholm probably indicates that at least one side of him wanted this to happen: it would have been a relief. But it didn't turn out that way – and this is when he started waving large quantities of narcotics in the faces of strangers.

I cannot say for certain what his motives were. That at least one side of him wanted to be arrested seems apparent. That I believe catharsis was a goal for him is because a recurrent theme in conversations I had with him during this period was 'taking his punishment'. However, his actions probably also contain an element of 'desperate attempt to escape his present, unbearable life-situation'.

Defying Authority

In the previous chapter, I described some of the difficulties problematic consumers have in relation to authority figures. It should therefore not come as a surprise that many substantial consumers act defiantly. It's like playing a game – you buck authority and if you get away with it you have proved that they are not as smart as they think. This pattern is well known and many who have had contact with problematic consumers have written about it. In Chapter 4, I mentioned a variation among alcoholics; passive defiance. In the cases, Carrying drugs, The syringe, Check out the police and Security cameras, we see examples of how this game can be played.

ON PUNISHMENT

The cases described in this chapter clearly show how complicated the question of punishment can be. On the one hand, substantial consumers have been repeatedly chastised in their lives, and have negative self-images as a result of it. On the other hand, some seem to seek punishment as a way out of their current unbearable life-situation.

Many of the measures currently taken to prevent drug consumption can be classified as punishment. The people I met on the scene have not been helped by being subjected to it. Castigation neither gave them new insight into their problems, nor the feeling that they had paid their debt to society and could now make a fresh start in life. Instead, chastisement either reconfirmed their negative self-images, or even worse, labelled them; damaging their self-image still further. Punishment does not help substantial consumers leave the scene, get off drugs, stop committing crimes or become less self-destructive. On the contrary, it drives them further into their deviant careers.

A possible hypothesis is that some people are helped by castigation, and (logically) these will not be found on the scene. This hypothesis cannot be tested with the methods I have used. On the other hand, it is the responsibility of those who maintain that punishment helps people avoid and/or leave deviant careers to prove that this is the case: something they hitherto have failed to do. To those who believe that punishment and coercion will reduce problematic consumption, I pose the following questions: How can you punish a person into believing he has the right to exist? And how can we force someone to like himself?

My empirical data do not lend support to the idea that punishment is a feasible way to help substantial consumers get off narcotics. However, I will remind my readers that problematic consumers do not profit from laissez-faire policies either. Everyone needs reactions to what they do; but nobody is helped by labelling.

CONCLUSION

I conclude this chapter with case 8, The smuggling trip, which reveals several motives for openly defying the police. This big dealer who had a myriad of contacts on the scene, had come to the point where he wanted out. But he knew that as long as he stayed in Stockholm, people would be making him offers and he wouldn't be able to stop dealing. Nobody would believe him if he said he had packed it up, and as is usually the case when substantial consumers make decisions, they themselves aren't sure if they really mean it. He felt trapped. It was in this context that he started to blab about his upcoming smuggling trip.

What was he attempting to accomplish by talking so much? He was well aware that he drastically increased the risk (possibility?) of getting caught by customs or the police. Afterwards he told me that he had hoped to be arrested – it would have meant a change. But although that didn't happen, he did get some satisfaction anyway. He told me he was playing a game with the police. Despite his uncool behaviour, they still couldn't catch him. He had defied them and got away with it. He won!

But among problematic consumers, there are no winners. Maybe they can emerge victorious from a few skirmishes, but in the long run they are doomed if they don't get off the scene, because sooner or later they will be drawn into the deviance spiral.

10 The Deviance Spiral

INTRODUCTION

The fourth stage in my deviant career model is *the deviance spiral.* It is a continuation and further degeneration of the third stage: originating in a dilemma caused by the substantial consumer's inability to neutralize societal norms. The problematic consumers in my study did not have a norm system significantly different from the rest of society. When I penetrated behind the façade they show to the straight world, I discovered that they believe that what they are doing is wrong, and it is they who need to change, not society. Most of them hold rather conservative values and long to be like everyone else. Yet day after day they break norms they accept. Consequently their behaviour not only provokes negative reactions from others but from them themselves as well. It is therefore difficult for them to maintain their self-images at the current (low) level. They are in constant danger of having to redefine their self-image in a negative direction, leading to a vicious spiral where the escalation of secondary deviance is taken as proof by everyone (including the substantial consumer himself) of his worthlessness. The self-image is 'devaluated' still further, leading to increasingly serious secondary deviance. He has entered into the vicious spiral described in Figure 6.3.

The deviance spiral can be observed in many areas of life. To illuminate the downward trend, I will present some examples.

SEXUALITY

Some teenage girls who long for something other than the life they're leading seek out the drug scene with its 'dangerous boys', who have crossed the line of socially acceptable behaviour. To associate with these people means taking risks and (therefore) excitement.

The most common scenario is that after these young women have had a taste of the wild side they decide that it isn't what they were looking for. I have met many such girls during my fieldwork, for instance Carina, a 15 year old, who started hanging out on the hash scene. She found it easy to make contact with boys, and she enjoyed the attention she was getting. However, she didn't really understand what she was getting herself into. One night, when her parents were away on vacation, she allowed a problematic consumer to stay at her house. He was homeless and unemployed and survived by letting women support him. Carina couldn't get rid of him. When her parents returned they threw him out, and Carina disappeared from the drug scene. As her 'instinct for self-preservation' was intact, and she had the support of her parents, she never got close to the point where a deviance spiral arises. But not all teenage girls have the support of their parents and (perhaps therefore) their instinct for self-preservation is deficient.

Some girls who seek out the drug scene have been labelled and are hurting psychologically. Their backgrounds include experiences such as serious conflicts in their homes, truancy, shoplifting, an early alcohol debut, sexual abuse, etc. Sometimes they are as young as 12 or 13 when they arrive on the scene. Instead of getting out when they start having negative experiences, they increase and intensify their deviant behaviour.

The transition from first contact with the scene to becoming a full fledged part of it often goes via experiences which initially do not differ radically from those other adolescent girls will have when they are a few years older. The potential problematic consumer meets a boy and 'falls in love'. It is important to emphasize that it is not merely bad luck that a young teenager falls in love with a substantial consumer of narcotics. These are girls who have learned through their earlier experiences that there is something wrong with them and therefore feel a certain kinship with social outcasts. In the company of problematic consumers they feel they are among peers.

Behind their tough façades they are frightened and insecure adolescents. They hope that love will be their salvation, but the 'love' they find on the scene is not likely to have this effect. Instead it will confirm what they already believe; they are not worth very much.

When their first relationship to a problematic consumer is over, these girls find someone else on the scene. That a teenage love affair ends and a new one begins is not unusual but soon even that relationship ends and the next and the next. She has become a 'mattress'. She feels that she has little more to offer than her body. Possibly her sexual behaviour is a way of confirming what she has already learned about herself from earlier experiences; i.e. by having been subjected to physical, psychological and/or sexual abuse.

Another aspect of the scenario is that her alcohol consumption increases and she starts smoking cannabis, and experimenting with other drugs. Her performance in school deteriorates still further, as does her relationship to her mother (and father, if he is still present in the family). She tries to keep up appearances and tells others she's fine, while in reality she is sliding downhill by staying on the scene. Still, she doesn't withdraw.

In extreme cases she takes her first injection. Contrary to common belief problematic consumers do not try to entice others into shooting up. Those who have been fixing for a long time usually warn novices not to start. But if a girl persists it won't take long before she finds a male who is willing give her drugs and show her the ropes. She has taken an important step which deteriorates her self-image still further; she has become a 'junkie'.

A girl who is young, fresh and a newcomer to the scene, usually doesn't have difficulty obtaining drugs. She finds a boyfriend who is dealing and who supplies her with drugs, which she pays for with her body. However, she doesn't have to see it that way; usually her definition of the situation is that she is in love with her partner. After all, having sex with your 'fiancé' is accepted in most industrialized countries nowadays. But problems arise when he can no longer supply both of them with drugs, and she has to help out.

Some of the girls try to avoid prostitution by finding a new boyfriend who can provide them with narcotics. However, this strategy doesn't work for long; after a while the same situation arises and one fiancé succeeds the other. Sooner or later she reaches the end of the line; when she is no longer new and fresh it becomes increasingly difficult to find someone willing to supply 'free' drugs. She then must try to keep the partner she has; which entails contributing to the family economy. Of course she can earn money through crime, and some in fact do so, but there is an 'easier' option. Initially she does it 'for the sake of their love'. It is only a one time thing to make it through an acute crisis. But the same 'crisis' arises repeatedly and it usually doesn't take long before prostitution becomes a daily routine.

Some of the girls choose another survival strategy, but the end result is the same. From the very start they try to stay with the same partner and walk the streets 'for the sake of their love for their fiancé'. But not even this is always sufficient. On the drug scene sexuality is not based on mutual feelings and respect, but on power and exploitation. He not only uses her body as a source of income, he may well demand that she participate in an increasing number of extreme sexual variations; not because diversity and rejuvenation stimulate mutual pleasure, but as an element in a relationship built upon contempt, exploitation and submission. As one problematic consumer told me: he forces his girlfriends to participate in an increasing number of sexual variations which he finds repulsive, just to see how far he can get them to go. The more she acquiesces, the more disgusting he finds her, and the more he despises her; and himself. He added that he wished it were otherwise, but he can't seem to stop himself. He finally becomes so repulsed that he leaves her; only to repeat the same behaviour with another woman: and his former girlfriend starts all over with a new partner.

Regardless of whether a girl chooses to go from one partner to another, or if she tries to stay with the same man, the end result is usually the same: she has many partners and also works the streets. The longer she is on the scene the more her sexuality deviates from what is considered 'normal' in our society. And for every step she takes, she devaluates her self-image, which in turn makes the next step possible. She is dragged downwards in a deviance spiral.

Birgitta Stenberg illustrates this process in her autobiography. When we enter the story, she has not been taking narcotics very long, and is discussing a mutual acquaintance with her boyfriend, Baku:

> 'How does she manage?' I wondered.
> 'Loose living' he replied. Baku stared at the ceiling and a smirk crossed his face, possibly due to the way he expressed himself, or maybe because of my stupid question. Jealousy rose within me.
> 'Have you been a pimp?'
> He's no longer smiling. There is an eerie silence in the room. I tense my muscles so I can get out of the way if his anger should turn to violence.
>
> (Stenberg, p. 18)

A little later Baku asks:

> 'Do you find me repulsive?'
> I shake my head vigorously so he will feel it against his back.
> 'It's almost always like that with junkies', he continued. 'Ask anybody.'
> 'I hardly know anybody but you.'
> 'Think about it.'
> We go through a number of names.
> 'But they can't all be pimps?'
> 'Depends on what you mean. All of them haven't done time on that charge. But a chick's gotta help out sometimes. We need the bread... You've already sold some of your things.'
> 'Well I'm not going to start selling my ass. Not me! Not me.'
>
> (Ibid., p. 18f)

'She stoops to working the streets, and he excuses it for their mutual benefit, and sinks as well. Then they blame each other' (ibid., p. 20).

HOUSING

Because almost everybody who starts using narcotics does so as a teenager, many are still living with their mothers (and sometimes a father or step-father). As previously noted some have been thrown out of their families, placed in boarding schools, sent to other countries, or become wards of the social welfare system. Among those problematic consumers who haven't been forced out, most choose to leave their parents' home earlier in their lives than other adolescents. With luck they may be able to find a place to live; a sublet, a short-term contract in a condemned building, an apartment shared with peers, squatting, etc.

Some problematic consumers even manage to find housing of their own. But the longer they're on drugs the harder it is to keep their living quarters as they often can't afford to pay the rent, or the apartment becomes a shooting gallery and the neighbours' complaints lead to eviction. Some other reasons for winding up on the street are that when a problematic consumer is apprehended he loses his apartment, the person from whom he is subletting returns, those with whom he is living ask him to leave, the police evict squatters, etc. In her study of substantial consumers at Serafens LVM Home in Stockholm, Fugelstad (p. 17) found that approximately one-fifth of her subjects had their own apartments, another fifth sublet or lived with relatives, and 60 per cent were homeless.

When a person is homeless it is nearly impossible to keep himself and his clothes clean, and to sleep and eat adequately. His health deteriorates and his appearance becomes increasingly shabby. Other people shy away from him and the labelling process accelerates. For example early one Sunday morning I sat with a couple of problematic consumers in a subway station. One of the few other people there was a child of about four who approached the substantial consumers and chatted with them until the train came. After we boarded, one problematic consumer correctly noted that 'kids are the only ones who talk to guys like us'. Grown-ups are often afraid or uneasy when they see someone who is down and out, and keep their distance. When others are doing their utmost to avoid you, the message is clear enough. Being reminded numerous times every day that others find you repugnant helps to increase the rate of the deviance spiral.

FAMILY AND CHILDREN

In a survey Olsson (p. 20) found that 76 per cent of the substantial consumers who were parents did not have custody of their children. In her LVM survey, Fugelstad (p. 15) found that: 'In almost all cases, their offspring had been taken into care, or were cared for by the other parent.... Most of the clients lived alone or had temporary partners.'

Being alone is difficult enough, but the burden is even heavier knowing that you are not taking care of your own children. Parents who neglect their offspring do not need negative comments from others to create a labelling process. By breaking one of the most basic norms of society, and by not responding to what presumably are biologically inherited 'parental instincts', the fire of self-reproach is stoked, and the individual propels himself into the deviance spiral.

WORK

In industrialized countries the self-image of adult males (and increasingly females) is closely associated with their position in the workforce. In our own eyes, and in the eyes of others, we *are* our profession. For instance few people say: 'I earn my living as (whatever profession they have)'. Instead people say: 'I *am* a . . . '. This gives rise to the question; what *is* a person who doesn't have a job? 'A pariah', 'a bum' or perhaps worst of all 'nothing' comes to mind.

My basic assumption is that for an adult to maintain a positive self-image he must feel that he has something to offer that others are interested in. One way to accomplish this is to be a parent: children need parents. But as we have already seen, those who have been on narcotics for a long time usually do not fulfil this role.

Another way of gaining personal worth is to have a job. In exchange for one's skills, time and energy, the gainfully employed are given both pay and recognition. Pulling one's own weight is a prerequisite for achieving status as a useful member of industrial societies.

Even my research subjects believe that adults should earn their keep and not be a burden to others. Unemployment therefore contributes to the deviance spiral. When a person hasn't had a job for a long time the chances are that he will not only be reprimanded by others, he may well start asking himself what good he is. Most problematic consumers I met in the field had gone even further; they questioned their right to exist.

Like almost everything else in the life of substantial consumers, their relationship to work is contradictory and ambiguous. On the one hand they want to become like everyone else; yet at the same time they don't believe it's possible. Furthermore, after all the negative acts they have committed they don't think they deserve a decent life. So they vacillate and are unable to maintain a steady course in any direction.

In spite of this, almost all of them occasionally 'decide' to try to get a job and live like everyone else. But we misconstrue the situation if we believe that this 'decision' is definite, and that they are determined to effectuate it. Instead the substantial consumer takes a cautious step towards society, and waits to see what happens. If he is rejected, i.e. does not find a job, he interprets this as further proof of how worthless he is. This fuels the deviance spiral and makes it even more difficult to take steps toward society in the future.

But even if he should succeed in getting work, it does not necessarily mean that the deviance spiral will grind to a halt, or even slow down. Earning one's keep is incongruent with the problematic consumer's extremely negative self-image. Furthermore by taking a job he must face demands he is not used to; such as taking care of his personal hygiene, maintaining 'normal' daily routines, being punctual, associating with people who are not on drugs and looking them in the eye, etc. All this entails an immense and difficult adjustment, giving rise to the feeling that the problems are insurmountable.

Moreover, as it takes so much time and money to acquire narcotics it is all but impossible to combine problematic consumption with a steady job. So even if a substantial consumer manages to find a job, the odds are that he won't keep it for very long.

There are a number of ways not to work even if you have 'decided' to have a job. For instance, you can see to it that nobody employs you. Being stoned, looking unkempt, or behaving aggressively or discourteously during the interview usually does the trick. The job is given to another applicant, and once again the problematic consumer has been given confirmation that nobody is interested in what he has to offer. If he should get a job he doesn't necessarily have to show up. Or he can be tardy or truant, dress inappropriately, behave discourteously, neglect his duties, etc. Getting fired is yet another confirmation of his negative self-image, or even worse, further fuel for the deviance spiral.

If he is not dismissed despite his provocations, the incongruence usually becomes so pronounced that he will either give in his notice, or just depart one day and never return. To do so is a step backwards, but the longer he has held the job, the more his negative self-image has been shaken. He has actually held a job without being fired. Maybe he isn't completely hopeless after all. This revelation can form a basis for better performance the next time he finds employment.

Almost all of the substantial consumers in Fugelstad's LVM study were out of work. 'Normally clients use their social welfare benefits for sustenance and finance their abuse with crime or prostitution' (ibid., p. 18). Put concisely, problematic consumers do not pull their own weight, and they debase themselves to get money. As neither we nor they are likely to forget this, the labelling process and the deviance spiral continue.

SELF-DESTRUCTIVENESS

There is some evidence that the future problematic consumer's self-destructiveness starts in childhood. Chein et al. (p. 118) compare four segments of their population and write: 'It may be a coincidence, but the two user groups have a higher incidence of serious accidents (e.g. a broken leg) than either of the nonuser groups, with the control group reporting the smallest number.' We can't be sure that this should be interpreted as aggression directed toward oneself, but repeated accidents during childhood and adolescence may be a sign of self-destructiveness which in later life manifests itself in the form of problematic consumption of narcotics.

Another indication of self-destructiveness is that prospective problematic consumers are well aware of the negative effects of narcotics before their debut; but this doesn't deter them. 'Their first use clearly did not express ignorance, but rather disregard for what they knew about the long-range probabilities of harm and trouble' (ibid., p. 305). This knowledge has been gained by associating with problematic consumers and observing life on the scene before beginning to take drugs. Furthermore, they do not heed when older substantial consumers warn them not to get involved.

Even withdrawal is well known before the future problematic consumer starts using heroin. Either he has seen someone going through withdrawal, and/or heard about it. I have previously mentioned that today's heroin addicts do not suffer the extreme physical withdrawal symptoms reported in early literature, but they can still put on a tragic show and often exaggerate when they talk about abstinence and withdrawal. This should suffice to scare off anyone interested in self-preservation.

While some may argue that this is proof of intellectual deficiency, my interpretation is that potential substantial consumers are self-destructive and therefore attracted to that which can harm them.

CATHARSIS

Chein et al. (p. 249) discuss withdrawal as means of achieving catharsis. They believe that drug consumption and withdrawal can be seen as:

> enacting a drama of sin and penance; they deserve to suffer for the misdeeds of their addiction, and through suffering they achieve catharsis. Generally speaking, these are the oldest and most experienced addicts, who are among the quickest to relapse after leaving a hospital, since they feel that suffering has undone their misbehaviour and that they are free to sin again.

In this view the propelling force behind penance is *the desire to continue with drugs*. While this may be true in some instances, exactly the opposite can also be the case, providing yet another example of how drugs can be used for diametrically opposite purposes. In the previous chapter I used catharsis to describe how some problematic consumers, whose situation has become desperate, turn to penance in an attempt to leave the scene. In other words they are motivated by *the desire to get off drugs*. By expiating their sins, they hope to be able to stop punishing themselves.

Maybe self-mutilation among substantial consumers should be interpreted as a drastic attempt to achieve catharsis; although I have never heard a problematic consumer make such a claim. Their explanations of self-mutilation are unrelated to this kind of reasoning. For instance, in an autobiographical novel former heroin addict William Burroughs (p. 16) claims that he was 'on a Van Gogh kick' and cut off a finger to impress a woman he was interested in. I find little substance in this type of explanation. Instead it is probably more reasonable to regard narcotics addiction as a drawn-out process of self-mutilation. Perhaps problematic consumers nurture the hope that at some point they will have suffered enough to have paid their debt to society. Having thereby earned the right to exist they will no longer need to destroy themselves with drugs.

ROCK BOTTOM

Many problematic consumers appear to have a line below which they will not stoop; that is, there is a limit to what they will allow themselves to do. When they feel that they are in a situation where they must do things that are *too* incongruent with their self-image, they decide to try to get off narcotics. What it takes to evoke the feeling that one has hit *rock bottom* differs from individual to individual, and is presumably dependent upon how negative the self-image is. As previously noted some people leave the scene after their first negative experience. And for each new stage in the downward process, some abscond.

Even those who have followed the deviance spiral to great depths can get to the point where they no longer are willing and/or able to go on. The following example is taken from my fieldwork.

A dealer, Richard, received a large shipment of narcotics on credit from Bill, a wholesaler living in another country. Richard sold the drugs but as he suspected that the police were on his trail he didn't dare to keep so much cash at home while waiting for Bill to return to Sweden. For a fee, Richard's 'friend' Earl agreed to keep the money in his apartment. Yale, another of Richard's 'friends', was living with Earl at the time and knew there were large amounts of cash in the apartment. Yale told another of Richard's 'friends', Joe, about it and the two of them could not withstand the temptation. They took most of the money and went off on a spree in southern Europe. They left a note to Richard along with the little cash they didn't take, apologizing for what they had done, and telling him that he shouldn't have subjected them to such an irresistible temptation. They added that they weren't burning him as he could just tell his supplier that he had been ripped off.

It appears that Yale and Joe tried to convince themselves that what they did to their friend wasn't so bad. However, they had in fact endangered Richard's life. Bill was left with two choices; he could either accept that Richard had been burned or decide that Richard was ripping him off. If Bill had come to the latter conclusion he would have had Richard killed. This time Bill chose to accept Richard's explanation.

But Richard's problems were far from over. He now had to choose between eliminating Yale and Joe or stop dealing. Otherwise the word would have spread that you can burn Richard with impunity and he would be ripped off time and time again. His suppliers would then either refuse to do business with him, or have him murdered for not paying his debts.

Psychologically Richard could not get himself to order an execution. In our conversations during that period Richard told me time and again that he was many (bad) things but he wasn't a murderer. To be involved in the taking of someone's life would have been a grave step downward in the deviance spiral, and Richard couldn't or wouldn't take it. He had reached rock bottom. After many years of indecision, this became the turning point which eventually led to his leaving the scene entirely. Had he been unable to do so all that would have remained was murder or suicide.

SUICIDE

An all too frequently used means of leaving the scene is suicide. After following the deviance spiral to rock bottom, substantial consumers have come to the point where they can no longer continue. They feel they can't go on suffering and they haven't achieved catharsis. At this point they do something desperate, such as taking 'a witches brew' (see p. 96). Those who survive such a desperate act may interpret it as an omen that they were not destined to die quite yet. This can be the spark which sets them off on the long and difficult battle to persevere (get off drugs). Others do not survive their witches brew and die of an overdose. 'The mortality rate for LVM patients who were narcotics abusers is 60–70 times higher than the normal population in the same age group in Stockholm' (Fugelstad, p. 28).

Whether the excessive death rate among problematic consumers of narcotics is due to accidents and/or unintended side-effects of drugs, or if it is caused by intentional suicide, is an open question. Obviously we can't enquire about a person's intentions when he's dead. But the fact remains that life on the scene is a dance with death. When a person decides to start taking narcotics, and then follows the deviance spiral into the depths, while observing that his acquaintances are dying and his body is deteriorating, it seems to me that he is intent on hastening the process which is the unavoidable fate of everything living.

The deviant career model helps us understand why many of our current attempts to get problematic consumers off narcotics are doomed to fail. Punishment, threats, coercion and scare tactics are extremely ineffective ways to help an individual feel that he deserves to exist.

Part III
Narcotics Policy

11 Can We Cut the Supply?

INTRODUCTION

There are four principal links in the chain between production and consumption of narcotics.

1. *Production*. Raw material must be produced and then refined into narcotics. For instance opium, morphine and heroin are extracted from poppy, cocaine and crack from coca, and marijuana hashish and THC from cannabis. Synthetic narcotics such as amphetamines, LSD and methadone are also refined from raw materials, although these aren't of vegetable origin.
2. *Smuggling*. Narcotics must be transported across national boundaries, from producer to consumer countries.
3. *Dealing*. Once in the country of destination drugs must be distributed to consumers.
4. *Consumption*. There must be a sufficient number of buyers who are willing to pay enough so that all earlier links are making ample profit to find it in their interest to continue.

If one believes that the narcotics themselves are the problem, it is logical to maintain that it would suffice to break any of the links in this chain to solve 'the narcotics problem'. Obviously, if no narcotics are produced they can't be consumed; or, if no drugs enter the country the populace can't take them, etc.

Two concepts from classical economic theory, *supply* and *demand*, have played a central role in the international narcotics debate. Supply refers to the first three links mentioned above, i.e. everything that makes it possible to buy narcotics. Demand designates those factors which contribute to making people want to purchase these substances. However, it is important to note that some people believe that supply is one of the most (if not *the* most) important causes of demand. They argue that the very fact that narcotics are available creates demand. For instance, Bejerot (1975, p. 25) states: 'the availability of the drug is the most important factor in the spread of [epidemic] abuse'. Those who accept this premise believe that reducing supply is the key to drastically reducing demand.

Rather than examining whether or not this postulate is correct, I will devote this chapter to an investigation of the first three links in the chain; i.e. analyse the practical possibilities of reducing the availability of narcotics in the western world. In the final three chapters I will focus on different models for reducing demand.

THE THIRD WORLD

Plants which can be used for the production of narcotics grow and are cultivated in almost all parts of the world. Furthermore, anyone proficient in chemistry can produce amphetamines, LSD, ecstasy and other synthetic drugs. It is now also possible for chemists to custom design drugs; i.e. they can take a drug that is classified as a narcotic and change its chemical properties just enough so that it will be considered a different compound, without significantly changing its psychoactive effects. The newly created drug can then be sold legally in those countries which have not changed their legislation to meet these new conditions. Some of these substances are currently marketed on the Internet. In the not too distant future we can expect that the sale of narcotics on the web will be a prevalent form of cybercrime.

Why are narcotics being produced in so many parts of the world? I shall limit my presentation to some contributing factors, i.e. the political and economic situation in a few countries. That only a small number of nations will be discussed is neither because they are the only ones involved in narcotics traffic nor because they are more 'guilty' than others. In the space available I cannot do more than exemplify the depth to which high government officials, intelligence agencies, the military and the police of some countries have been involved in narcotics trafficking. However, before we begin it is important to emphasize that the problem is not merely that certain highly placed individuals behave abhorrently. Replacing these people with others is not a solution. The narcotics trade has deep historical and economic roots which are independent of any given individual, and therefore cannot be easily remedied.

Laos

It has been well known since the 1960s that much of the heroin being consumed in the industrialized world originates in the 'Golden Triangle', an area encompassing parts of Myanmar (Burma), Thailand and Laos. My discussion of Laos is based on Alfred W. McCoy's pioneering work on the importance of Southeast Asia for the heroin trade.

> This impoverished little kingdom appears to lack all of the economic and political criteria for nationhood. ... Laos has been plagued by fiscal problems ever since independence in 1954. Unable to finance itself through corporate, mineral, or personal taxes, the Royal Laotian government has filled its coffers and lined its pockets by legalizing or tolerating ... the smuggling of gold, guns and opium. (McCoy, p. 249)

> Desperate for a way to finance their clandestine operations, French intelligence agencies expropriated the hill tribe opium trade in the last few years of the First Indochina War and used military aircraft to link the Laotian poppy fields with the opium dens in Saigon. (Ibid., p. 252)

> After France's military withdrawal in 1954, several hundred French war veterans, colonists and gangsters stayed on in Laos. Some of them ... started a number of small charter airlines, which became colorfully and collectively known as 'Air Opium'. Ostensibly founded to supply otherwise unavailable transportation for civilian businessmen and diplomats, these airlines gradually restored Laos's link to the drug markets of South Vietnam that had vanished with the departure of the French air force. (Ibid., p. 253)

> ... the South Vietnamese government had adopted an intolerant attitude toward the opium traffic that seriously hampered their operations. In 1955 South Vietnam's puritanical President Diem closed most of Saigon's opium dens and announced his determination to eradicate the drug traffic. ... However, only three years later President Diem's chief adviser, Ngo Dinh Nhu, reopened the dens to finance his secret police. (Ibid., p. 254)

He also became a silent partner in Air Opium.

Pathet Lao, a left-wing movement, won the election in 1958. The US found this so alarming that it took political measures to 'defend American interests'; all American aid was cut off, and the CIA chose Phoumi Nosavan to organize right-wing forces. When Phoumi was appointed to the government in 1959 American aid was reinstated. But in 1961, in an effort to avoid a military conflict with the Soviet Union, the US changed its policies in the region, and tried to get Phoumi to establish a coalition government. After his refusal American aid was once again withdrawn. 'Phoumi turned to the opium traffic as an alternate source of funds for his army and government. Although he had controlled the traffic for several years and collected a payoff ... he was not actively involved' (ibid., p. 259). 'The obvious solution to General Phoumi's fiscal crisis was for his government to become directly involved in the import and export of Burmese opium. This decision ultimately led to the growth of northwest Laos as one of the largest heroin producing centers in the world' (ibid.).

Phoumi was overthrown by a military coup in 1964 and general Ouane Rattikone seized control of the opium traffic in northwestern Laos. He thought he could run the opium air traffic himself, and put an end to Air Opium. But the war in Vietnam had begun and the CIA was involved in its own 'secret' war in Laos. Airplanes from Laos were needed for bombing raids, leaving Ouane with no aircraft for opium transport.

Meanwhile due to the war the Meo, an ethnic group employed by the CIA to combat Pathet Lao, became increasingly dependent on growing opium for their survival.

> Without air transport for their opium, the Meo faced economic ruin. There was simply no form of air transport available in northern Laos except the CIA's charter airline, Air America. ... Air America began flying opium from mountain villages ... This opium was probably destined for heroin laboratories in Long Tieng or Vientiane, and ultimately, for GI addicts in Vietnam. (Ibid., p. 263)

In other words, the CIA chose to finance their secret war against the left wing in Laos with drug money that was earned, at least in part, by selling heroin to American soldiers who were fighting in Vietnam. 'Although American officials in Laos vigorously deny that either Vang Pao or Air America are in any way involved, overwhelming evidence to the contrary challenges these pious assertions' (ibid., p. 281). I cannot render McCoy's argumentation here, but it is convincing. For our purposes, one of McCoy's more important conclusions is that the Golden Triangle 'is capable of supplying ... unlimited quantities of heroin for generations to come' (ibid., p. 353).

As the political situation in Southeast Asia is often in a state of flux this may instil hope that some day the narcotics trade may no longer be of vital importance to any government, political group or individual who wants power in that part of the world. Unfortunately, there is little in the history of the region which points to such a development. That Thailand took over much of the trade from Laos in the 1980s and Burma from Thailand in the 1990s (Emerson, p. 25) changes little on the world's drug scenes. During the past half century, those in power in this part of the world, and/or their adversaries, have found it necessary to supply themselves with drug money. A reasonable assumption is that poppies will be growing on the slopes of Southeast Asia in the foreseeable future.

Although the US probably bears the highest burden for the narcotics trade, American governments have not given drugs particularly high priority; even if both presidents Reagan and Bush solemnly declared war on narcotics. When the American government feels that other important political goals are at stake, the war on drugs is placed on hold, or (as we have already noted) the US itself gets involved in the narcotics trade. In the face of 'the national interest', addicts are not the first order of business. A number of authors have illuminated this premise. For instance Michael Levine, a longtime agent of the Drug Enforcement Administration (DEA), the American narcotics agency responsible for waging the war against drugs outside the US, writes:

> It is both sobering and painful to realize, after twenty-five years of undercover work, having personally accounted for at least three thousand

> criminals serving fifteen thousand years in jail, and having seized several tons of various illegal substances, that my career was meaningless and had had absolutely no effect whatsoever in the socalled war on drugs. The war itself is a fraud. (Levine, Author's Note)

The rest of Levine's book very clearly illustrates how he reached this conclusion through his own experiences in Bolivia, Panama and Mexico. However, instead of delving into Levine's book I shall illustrate the low priority given to the war on drugs using Honduras as an example.

Honduras

The background to the situation in Honduras was that the US wanted to oust the Sandinistas from power in Nicaragua. To that end they needed bases close to Nicaragua from which the 'contras' could operate. President Oscar Arias refused to permit bases in Costa Rica, and the civil war made the situation in El Salvador too unstable to use that country. That left Honduras. In a well-substantiated article, Mort Rosenblum reported that Frank McNeil, who had been both US ambassador in Costa Rica and assistant secretary of state in charge of intelligence operations, told him that: 'You can hardly peel a banana in Honduras or Costa Rica without US intelligence knowing about it ... CIA people knew which military officers and public officials were corrupt. Jungle airstrips did not escape National Security Agency satellites' (Rosenblum, p. 106). Rosenblum reports that that DEA agents felt that upwards of three tons of cocaine per month were shipped from Honduras to the US (ibid., p. 116). If that figure is anywhere close to the actual amount cocaine is an important source of income for the second poorest country in Latin America. Honduras has economic motives for permitting smuggling, so why did the US close the DEA office in Tegucigalpa instead of intervening? In a nutshell McNeil's answer is: 'Our emphasis is 90 percent Communism and 10 percent drugs' (ibid., p. 106).

McNeil appeared before the Senate subcommittee on terrorism, narcotics and international operations, and reported that Honduran general José Bueso Rosa had tried to smuggle cocaine worth about $20 million into the US. He had planned to use the money to finance the assassination of Roberto Suazo Cordoba, the first democratically elected president in Honduras in a decade. The Justice Department called it 'the most significant case of narco-terrorism yet discovered. This, McNeil pointed out to Congress, was not only drugs and terror but also a murder plot against an ally who was supposed to exemplify Reagan's goals for democracy in Central America' (ibid., p. 114). In spite of this, neither Bueso Rosa nor any other Honduran in a position of power has been convicted for narcotics crimes in the US. Bueso Rosa's assistant was given a 30-year prison sentence, but all of the narcotics charges against Bueso Rosa himself were dropped. He was given a five-year sentence for conspiracy and did his prison term in what McNeil describes as a 'luxury hotel'. According to Rosenblum, Oliver North (who was convicted in the Irancontras scandal) 'warned in a memo that if Bueso Rosa were not kept happy he would "start singing songs nobody wants to hear"' (ibid.). Having to explain why the US chose to overlook the Honduran (and a number of other countries') drug trafficking would have caused political difficulties for a president who claimed he was waging a war on narcotics.

The example above illustrates 'narco-terrorism' engineered by right-wingers. But the political right has no monopoly on such activities. American researcher Rachel Ehrenfeld ardently proposed that communist governments were deeply involved in *narco-terrorism*, which she defines as 'the use of drug trafficking to advance the objectives of certain governments and terrorist organizations' (Ehrenfeld, p. xiii). That she says 'certain governments' in her definition is because she is only interested in left-wing activities. In spite of this serious shortcoming her book contains much of interest.

Lebanon

At least four different ethnic groups were involved in the civil war which raged in Lebanon from the mid-1970s into the 1990s. 'It has been estimated that Lebanon has some 80,000 men under arms, not counting the regular army and the 43,000 occupying Syrians. And this, in a country with a population of 2,800,000 people … One question never asked is this: with a ruined economy, who pays for all those gunmen, who, after all, represent a large percentage of the labor force?' (ibid., p. 52). Ehrenfeld's answer is: 'Lebanon flourishes not only as a producer, but also as a refiner and distributor of hashish, heroin, and cocaine. Much of the fighting that occurs in Lebanon concerns who gets what in the narcotics business' (ibid., p. 53).

> Beginning in the 1960s, the fear, if not the panic, of the Maronite Christian community led its leading families the Chamouns, the Franjiyehs, and the Gemayels to become deeply involved in what had been the traditional drug trade in Lebanon: hashish from the Bekaa Valley and opium and heroin from Asia. Shipped from Christian-run ports, Christian militias protected the product. In this way the Christians earned the huge sums of money needed to buy arms.
>
> Until the late 1970s, the three principal Christian clans divided the trade among themselves much as they had parceled out the real power in Lebanon for a generation; power, drugs and politics become one.
>
> (Ibid., p. 58)

It might have remained this way had not the Muslim population increased at a faster rate than the Christian. As ethnic antagonism increased, income from hashish production became even more important.

The Christians lost their drug-trade monopoly in 1975 when Syria gained control of the Bekaa Valley. All of those involved, Christians, Sunnis, Shiites, Druze and Syrians, needed money for weapons, and all of them recognized narcotics as an important source of income.

> In 1986, more than four million pounds of hashish were harvested in the Bekaa, representing some 75 percent of world consumption. ... Drugs now have become its mainstay, its single most important export, worth several billions of dollars. There are no other known sources of income to generate enough money to support the ongoing war. (Ibid., p. 59)

But not even the enormous income from hashish sufficed. 'In 1982, poppy growers from Turkey were brought into the Bekaa Valley, and their guidance made possible the production of opium, morphine base, and heroin. This was inevitable. Opiates per weight are at least ten times more profitable than hashish' (ibid., p. 60). In 1990, it was estimated that at least five tons of pure heroin were produced from poppy grown in Lebanon, and Syria and the Lebanese factions also took up the very lucrative cocaine trade (ibid., p. 61).

Syria also established partnerships with the Italian Mafia.

> On March 13, 1986, Italian authorities seized the Fidelio, a 400-ton Honduran-registered boat off the southern coast of Sicily ... drugs were found aboard: three tons of hashish and several kilos of heroin and morphine base. Even more interesting was the drug-running team itself, comprised of a dozen Syrian soldiers in uniform and Sicilian Mafiosi. The captain of the boat was a member of the Sicilian Cuntrera crime family. (Ibid., p. 67)

The PLO has also been involved in narcotics trafficking. Ehrenfeld refers to a number of cases where PLO agents have been convicted for narcotics violations in Australia and the US. Victor Ostrovsky, a former officer in the Israeli secret service, Mossad, describes in detail an example of PLO involvement in the narcotics trade. His primary purpose in doing so is not to humiliate the PLO, but to criticize Mossad. In brief the situation was as follows: Israeli intelligence uncovered a PLO plan to sell a large amount of Lebanese hashish in Europe, to finance the purchase of arms. The Mossad devised a plan to prevent Arafat from acquiring weapons, take over the hashish themselves, and lure a Swiss banker into believing that he was lending money to the PLO while the Mossad took the money and the PLO would have to repay the debt. How the Mossad accomplished all this is described in detail in Ostrovsky and Hoy (pp. 255ff). There are two points of interest here: the PLO has been directly involved in narcotics trafficking; and the Mossad was just as willing to deal in narcotics when they deemed it in their interests as the French and American intelligence agencies had been in Southeast Asia.

The picture that emerges is clear. We have a number of governments in different parts of the world, warring factions, intelligence agencies and terrorist/liberation groups, which have shown themselves ready, willing and able to use drug money to achieve their goals. To counteract this, we have UN programmes to help poor farmers replace drug crops with other produce. At best, replacement crops may help some poor farmers survive, but they will not give all of the other groups mentioned above the income they feel they need. This in itself gives sufficient reason why replacement crops have not and cannot have any significant effect on the narcotics trade.

Nordegren and Tunving (p. 193f) give further reasons when they describe the UN project in Lebanon to replace cannabis with sunflowers. The UN's Food and Agriculture Organization (FAO) wrote in their evaluation: 'it seems that the attempts to raise sunflowers instead of cannabis in nonirrigated areas have totally failed'. The problems were not agronomic, as the growing conditions for sunflowers were almost ideal.

> The sunflower project had similar problems to those of many other replacement programs. Following the law of supply and demand, when farmers in an area were reimbursed for not sowing cannabis crops, the market price of hashish and marijuana rose. This made cultivating cannabis even more attractive in nearby areas.
>
> The UN sunflower project was unsuccessful. While it was in effect there was a drastic increase in cannabis exports from Lebanon to Western Europe. Land owners and public officials embezzled the money and sabotaged the project. (Ibid., p. 194)

The Price of Production

The narcotics trade not only produces profits for the producing countries; there is also a price to be paid.

1. *Inflation.* Narcotics generate a lot of money. Pumping huge sums into a weak economy causes a rise in domestic prices for many goods and services. For instance, if the drug lords build luxury homes, the country's limited construction capacity will be focused on these projects, while other undertakings of national importance are set aside. A growing shortage of commercial buildings and ordinary housing increases the price of real estate. Small businesses are forced into bankruptcy and it becomes increasingly difficult for the general public to find affordable accommodation.
2. *Violence.* The violence between competing drug cartels is well known, but this is only a fraction of the drug-related brutality in the producing

countries. Poor farmers and native minority groups may be eradicated to get at their arable land. Anyone the local drug lords consider a potential enemy, i.e. policemen, journalists, politicians, judges, and local citizens who refuse to cooperate with the cartels, risk being killed.

3. *Isolation.* If the violence is widespread, such as in Colombia during the early 1990s, it affects foreign investments, and tourists spend their money elsewhere. The nation may also be subjected to political sanctions, i.e. curtailing economic aid, limiting political contacts, minimizing cultural exchanges, etc.
4. *Increased domestic drug consumption.* To increase profits, producing countries eventually start refining narcotics rather than merely exporting raw materials; thereby making drugs readily available to their own population. Because many of these countries are poor and the prospects of a decent future limited, the stage is set for a drastic increase in problematic consumption, leading to still greater destitution.
5. *A state within the state.* In those countries where the state is not the primary beneficiary of the profits from narcotics production, the drug cartels may eventually become a state within the state. For instance, the drug lords may use their resources to gain control over vital economic institutions such as banking and industry, and also control politicians and officials at various levels. In some countries drugs cartels have even gained control over whole regions by establishing armies which are capable of defending the area against the armed forces of the central government. Drugs can then be produced and sold openly.
6. *One-sided economy.* When narcotics profits are higher than those of other business activities, the country's economy becomes increasingly dependent on that one source of income. Alternative industries are neglected and the country becomes extremely vulnerable to fluctuations in the narcotics market.

It is not without cost that a nation enters the narcotics trade. But clearly there are many willing to pay the price, and the number of producing countries is rising.

The only logical conclusion is that in the foreseeable future our chances of preventing narcotics from being produced and refined are nonexistent. Whatever the industrialized world does, the supply of narcotics will be immense. But maybe we can prevent smuggling?

SMUGGLING

Governmental involvement in the narcotics trade does not end with producing raw materials and refining drugs. The leaders of a number of countries are also involved in smuggling and money laundering. In some instances the governments participate directly, while in others private businesses, such as banks, do the job with clandestine support from the government. The quantities of narcotics passing through certain countries is so extensive that it seems highly unlikely that it would be possible without governmental and/or military participation. As there are so many countries involved the subject is well worth a book of its own. I shall present Bulgaria as an example.

Bulgaria[1]

Bulgaria is situated between Asia Minor and Western Europe and is one of the transport routes for opiates from Turkey and narcotics from the Middle East. That Bulgaria is also a major dealer in light handguns is related to narcotics. For many years the primary player in the Bulgarian narcotics trade was a state-owned export company called KINTEX. A report by the American Department of Justice describes a 'typical' scenario:

> A European arms dealer, a sanctioned customer of KINTEX, purchases weapons from Western or Eastern European countries through licit or illicit channels. The arms dealer sells these weapons to KINTEX through a representative in Sofia. These weapons, in turn, are resold to a Middle Eastern trafficking group, which then supplies an insurgency group. Payment to KINTEX from the Middle Eastern group may take the form of heroin in selected cases. The heroin is then sold through KINTEX to selected Western European trafficking groups.
>
> (Ehrenfeld, p. 8)

In the 1970s, Bulgaria's income from narcotics was estimated to be billions of dollars. The money earned through the narcotics and weapons trade was laundered in Swiss banks by using accounts issued to nonexistent companies. It is difficult to see how it would be possible to launder money in a country's banks unless the banking laws permitted it. As legislation is the responsibility of the government, the political leadership of any nation which permits money laundering is at least indirectly involved in international drug trafficking.

In the early 1980s, the US focused some attention on KINTEX and as a warning to Bulgaria, cut off all normal contacts between American and Bulgarian police authorities. In 1983 the American government underscored the message by entering into the Congressional record an official statement to the effect that it suspected the Bulgarian government of being involved in narcotics trafficking.

According to the DEA, one of the favourite methods for the Bulgarians to smuggle narcotics is to use TIR trucks equipped with hidden compartments.

[1] The discussion in this section is based on Ehrenfeld, Chapter 1.

TIR (Transport International Routier) is an international agreement created to make it easier to ship goods between countries by reducing bureaucracy. If the customs authorities in a transit country do not have a specific reason (such as a tip-off) to suspect a given TIR vehicle, it is usually permitted to pass through the country without inspection. Customs clearance does not take place until arrival in the country of the consignee. Obviously this facilitates smuggling. During the mid-1980s, approximately 25 000 TIR trucks left Bulgarian territory annually.

Customs

Within the EU, customs control is extremely difficult. The Treaty of Rome, Article 7a, establishes the principle of free movement for goods and people between the signatory countries. This implies that border controls are to be abolished. In principle, random checks (which have long been used by customs authorities) are no longer permitted within the 'inner market'. In practice the customs authorities in some countries have interpreted this to mean that they can't stop every nth person or vehicle, but they can check anyone or anything that arouses reasonable suspicion. Thus far the legality of this activity has not been determined by the EU courts. But even if intuitive customs checks should be deemed legal, once goods have entered any EU country it will not be difficult to smuggle them to other member states. Thus far there are no signs that the increased cooperation between police and customs authorities within the EU has significantly impaired smuggling.

Customs controls are also limited by political and economic factors. For instance, in an elaborate and determined effort to reduce the flow of marijuana from Mexico, the US started 'Operation Intercept'.

> Along the 2,500 mile border, on land as well as in the sea and air, the surveillance network was intense, particularly so at the border crossings where vehicles and passengers could be individually searched. Within an hour after it all started, automobile traffic began to pile up as each vehicle waited to go through inspection. In no time, the backups were three miles [5 km] long, and in some places they extended to six miles. Members of Congress and other officials immediately began to receive complaints from Mexico because the effort was hurting tourism, from merchants on both sides of the border because it was affecting business, and from the American travelers who had spent many extra hours waiting to return home.
>
> Twenty days later Operation Intercept was abandoned.
>
> (Inciardi, p. 42)

A further limiting factor is cost in relation to efficiency. There are differences of opinion as to the resources needed to maintain 'reasonable' border security. But whatever the amount deployed, it is impossible to safeguard a nation's borders against narcotics trafficking. In the US, for instance, 'federal disbursements for supply and demand reduction from 1981 through 1988 totaled some $16.5 billion. ... Customs, Coast Guard, and Drug Enforcement Administration (DEA) officials had readily admitted that ... seizures likely reflected only 10% of the marijuana and cocaine entering the country' (ibid., p. 238).

To better understand why the authorities have had so little success, we shall take a look at some of the ways smugglers operate.

Some Methods Used by Smugglers

I have already mentioned TIR vehicles equipped with secret compartments. Obviously, hidden recesses can also be built into cars, suitcases, imported goods, etc. Furthermore drugs are concealed in the human body in every imaginable way; i.e. in condoms inserted in the rectum or vagina, condoms filled with drugs are swallowed before the smuggler passes the border, and retrieved when they leave the body in the faeces, etc. As this is well known I will not delve further into these and other more obvious smuggling methods such as hiring a courier, hiding drugs in the hold of a ship or plane, etc. Instead we shall take a closer look at a few lesser-known but extremely effective methods.

Coastal Countries

My first examples of the difficulties coastal countries have in protecting their borders are taken from Sweden. An almost 3000 km (2000 mile) long coastline with archipelagos, islets, bays, shallows, etc., provide a multitude of possibilities for smuggling. The very length of the coast makes surveillance all but impossible. There are also an enormous number of pleasure craft in the country, making it relatively easy to sail out to international waters and return without being noticed.

In 1983, 1500 kg (!) of Lebanese hashish packaged in plastic bags floated ashore on the Swedish Atlantic coast. The cannabis had either been anchored on the ocean floor and broken loose, or stashed on an island off the coast of Sweden or Denmark. Most likely the plan had been to smuggle these drugs into Sweden in small boats.

In 1990, a similar incident occurred. This time a plastic sack with 25 kg of hashish washed ashore. The authorities do not know if this was the entire shipment, or only a part of a larger shipment that had been stashed somewhere. In 1991, there was yet another occurrence; 3000 litres (quarts) of 96 per cent alcohol floated ashore in ten-litre containers. And in 1998 smuggled cigarettes were dumped off the ferry from Estonia in the Stockholm archipelago.

Undoubtedly considerably larger quantities of drugs and alcohol than was discovered on these occasions have been anchored on the ocean floor, or stashed on desolate islands; waiting to be picked up and brought ashore in small craft. This method of smuggling is so common that in American street argot those who retrieve drugs from the ocean floor are called 'swimmers' (Williams, p. 9).

Inciardi (p. 88ff) lets one of his informants explain how it's done:

> With the combination of good coordination, good connections, good navigation equipment, good navigation skills, plus a few payoffs here and there, coke can be safely brought in at any time. ... In one operation, we had a guy fly out of Cartagena with refueling stops in Jamaica and Nassau. After a little money changed hands there with the right officials ... he headed towards Miami and dropped the 10 kilo watertight package out the window into the water, to a prearranged spot just a few miles offshore ... Then he landed at Miami International and went through customs like everyone else and came out perfectly clean. That was on a Saturday night. The next afternoon, when the water was full of Sunday boaters, another guy went out with a good set of Loran numbers. He located the exact spot, went over the side with fins, mask, and snorkel and found the thing ... Then he did some fishing and came back late in the afternoon with all the other boaters. He had his girlfriend and her kid with him, so everything looked ordinary and nobody looked suspicious.

Preventing such aircraft drops is no easy task, and intercepting at sea is apparently equally difficult: 'after sailing for a combined 2,347 ship days costing $33,200,000, the US Navy and US Coast Guard seized only 7 ships and arrested only 40 smugglers' (ibid., p. 267).

Diplomats as Couriers

I have already established that some governments deal in narcotics. It is also known that diplomats are used as drug couriers. It is particularly difficult to apprehend them as anyone travelling with a diplomatic passport is allowed to cross national borders without going through customs; unless something exceptional has happened. It would be an insult to a foreign government to even hint at the possibility that their representatives might be doing something illegal by submitting them to a customs check. Yet a number of diplomats have been caught smuggling drugs.

In 1971 a suitcase was confiscated at Orly Airport in Paris. It contained 60 kg of pure heroin and belonged to the Laotian diplomat, Prince Sopsaisana. As he had diplomatic immunity, the French government could do nothing more than declare him 'persona non grata' and demand that he leave the country. No charges were brought against him in Laos.

The heroin in Sopsaisana's luggage had been refined in Long Tieng, headquarters for the CIA's secret operations in northern Laos, financed by the Meo general, Vang Pao, who was the commander of the CIA's secret army. 'Perhaps these embarrassing facts may explain the US Embassy's [in Laos] lack of action' (McCoy, p. 244). During the same year, a Philippine diplomat was arrested in New York in possession of 15.5 kg heroin (ibid., p. 346).

'Customs officers at the Miami airport poked into an arriving passenger's unusually large stock of coffee. Most of it was highgrade coke. The passenger was the Honduran ambassador to Panama and the halfbrother of armed forces commander General Regalado Hernández' (Rosenblum, p. 116).

Even small countries are subjected to the narcotics smuggling of foreign governments. For example, 33 kg of hashish were found on board a Pakistani military aircraft which had brought government representatives on an official visit to Sweden. In 1991, a North Korean diplomat was apprehended in Malmö trying to sell one kg of heroin he had smuggled into the country. As he was accredited in Czechoslovakia, he did not enjoy diplomatic immunity for crimes committed in Sweden, and served several years in prison.

No one knows how much is smuggled by diplomats. If a diplomat has acted on government orders he is taking no real risk other than being deported, as it is unlikely that he will be charged at home. If he has acted on his own he might be indicted in his own country. However, I don't know of any cases where this has actually happened.

Bribes

That which follows it is not meant as a general accusation against customs officers. On the contrary, I assume that most are honourable. But to believe that there are no 'rotten apples' in the corps, or that no customs official will ever find himself in an acute economic and/or psychological crisis and therefore be tempted to accept a bribe, is simply not realistic.

There is very little that a customs officer has to do to make a smuggling attempt successful; and he runs almost no risk in doing so. A possible scenario might be: the bribed officer is working the night shift in a harbour where customs is understaffed. All he needs to know is that the vehicle being used for smuggling is neither white nor red. These colours are so common that there will undoubtedly be several cars of these colours on the ferry. The bribed officer selects a white or red vehicle and spends his time inspecting it. Even if the attempted smuggling should be uncovered, he probably won't be suspected of taking a bribe. He has simply chosen another car. As there aren't enough resources to check every vehicle, he must make an intuitive choice; and nobody's intuition is infallible.

It has been said that Al Capone believed that everyone has his price; anyone can be bribed. From his own experience, Capone gave some cause for this opinion; he was known to have corrupted a significant number of police, judges and politicians. That he was eventually apprehended proves that he somewhat overstated the case. But to smuggle narcotics it is not necessary to bribe everyone; paying off a few is sufficient.

In conclusion, there are too many ways to smuggle narcotics for any country to even come close to being narcotics free in the foreseeable future. Customs can and should try to stop drugs at the border, but it is unrealistic to believe that any nation will be able to thwart more than a fraction of all smuggling attempts. Most current estimates indicate that customs has a success rate of 5–10 percent.

DEALING

Many argue that we can successfully tackle 'the drug problem' through law enforcement, although there are different opinions as to how this should be done. Roughly, there are three different standpoints:

1. concentrate on organized crime;
2. focus on street-level dealing;
3. divide resources between both of the above.

The assumption behind all of these strategies is that supply is a major cause of abuse. Therefore eliminating sellers is seen as way to drastically reduce narcotics consumption.

The Police against Organized Crime

Calls for concentrating resources on organized crime are usually based on economic and/or moral arguments. It is claimed that without big money the drug market would collapse and/or that the kingpins behind narcotics are cold-blooded monsters whose only interest is making huge profits, without concern for how many lives are laid to waste in the process. Therefore they must be stopped, whatever the costs. What are the practical implications of this strategy?

Organized crime is organized; that is, we are not primarily dealing with petty criminals (although those who do the dirty work might well be classified as such). To be successful in big-time criminality one needs many of the same resources necessary for any major business operation, i.e. long-term planning, leadership, organization and coordination, economic and material resources, political connections, strong will, etc.

To combat organized crime one must be powerful. From the point of view of police strategy, this implies that to have any hope of success law enforcement agencies must be granted exceptional powers. In many countries, the necessity of fighting organized crime (primarily narcotics syndicates) is used as an argument to justify demands for granting powers to the police which they previously haven't had, because such powers can lead to infringements of the civil liberties of the general population. In other words the need to free ourselves from narcotics is an important argument in the arsenal of those who would tip the balance between civil liberties and police power towards the latter.

For instance, Sweden has heretofore taken a middle of the road stance and maintained most civil liberties; at the cost of making the work of the police more difficult, and possibly less effective. 'In drug cases the police can employ such methods as wiretapping, evidence provocation, controlled deliveries and disinformation. On the other hand the Swedish police do not, for example, make use of criminal provocation or secret bugging' (SNIPH, p. 20). The police, however, want otherwise, and there has been a debate on the subject at least since the 1970s. The National Swedish Police Board (RPS) is of the opinion that 'wiretapping with long-range or hidden microphones (bugging) and concealed TV surveillance equipment are effective methods in combating serious drug offences, and should therefore be permitted after court approval' (Rikspolisstyrelsen, p. 25). Furthermore, RPS wants to expand 'the legal use of so-called controlled deliveries, infiltration, undercover work, crime and evidence provocation, and the use of movement detectors and videolink transmissions in connection with surveillance' (ibid.). Opposition to these kinds of measures has come from two sources: those who advocate a different police strategy, and those who feel that the protection of civil liberties is more important than arresting drug offenders. We shall discuss the first category here and return to the question of civil libertarians in the next chapter.

Bejerot and Hartelius (p. 2) write:

> The proposed measures imply an escalation of the tactics compared with the current methods, such as wiretapping, mail checks, etc. Thus far these tactics have been unable to prevent the development of well-organized crime syndicates, which operate with the help of increasingly sophisticated methods. ... The objective of police strategy is to cut off the supply of narcotics by closing in on international narcotics criminality. Efforts are especially focused on 'major' narcotics traffickers and the kingpins of international organizations. ... At times and for short periods, this strategy has resulted in dramatic changes in the level of abuse, but the results are of short duration. ... Narcotics production and cartels cannot be eliminated, even if the customs and the police, by spending enormous sums and continually escalating the use of technical and legal measures, can slow them down. However, the producers will quickly adjust to changing conditions. ... *We maintain that the war on drugs cannot be won with*

> *the proposed escalation of police powers; we will wind up with the National Swedish Police Board waging its own never-ending Vietnam War.* (emphasis in original)

Bejerot and Hartelius are probably correct in saying that it is impossible for the police to put a halt to organized crime once and for all. But what would happen if the police were to become more effective in arresting the kingpins? Not even the police themselves think that this would rid us of wholesalers. The National Swedish Police Board writes that there 'will always be organizations and individuals who for economic or other reasons are prepared to deliver narcotics' (Rikspolisstyrelsen, p. 27). If the police obtain more effective weapons, the kingpins are forced to become even more sophisticated, and only the most proficient will remain in business, the result being that those who are still in operation are more cunning, have fewer competitors and higher profit margins. Vast resources will be concentrated in the hands of a relatively few major criminals. We can't be sure how these individuals will use their cunning and economic resources, but during Prohibition in the US organized crime minimized risks by using some of its enormous profits to bribe the police, customs officers, judges and politicians, thereby contributing to the corruption of central parts of society. A similar development can be observed in many parts of the world today.

The Police against Street Dealing

Because almost all problematic consumers of narcotics at least occasionally sell drugs to support their own consumption, the goal of eliminating street dealing implies that the police must arrest every substantial consumer. Eleven Conservative Party MPs have made two official proposals to the Swedish Parliament stating that street-level measures are effective in combating narcotics. In one proposal they call for giving the police increased resources (Dahlberg et al., Ju827, p. 18) while the other demands that the government and Parliament send an unequivocal message to both current and prospective abusers that drugs are not tolerated (Dahlberg et al., Ju826, p. 3). Among the suggested means for achieving this are:

1. Absolutely all narcotics offences must be brought to trial (ibid., p. 8).
2. Only under exceptional circumstances should drug crimes be classified as petty (ibid., p. 5).
3. Penalties for drug offences should be increased; in serious cases up to life imprisonment (ibid., p. 7).

Calling for stiffer penalties is nothing new in Sweden. 'Prison sentences for narcotics crimes have tripled since the late 1970s. The long sentences and the increased control of narcotics has clearly helped to worsen conditions in prisons' (Tham, 1998, p. 17). And in countries such as Sweden and Norway narcotics crimes can already attract longer sentences than taking someone's life. Two Norwegian researchers, Kåre Bødal and Inger Marie Fridhov (p. 43), write: 'There are legal precedents in Norway indicating that the *presumed damages* of narcotics smuggling are deemed more serious than the *actual damage* of violent acts' (my italics). They present several examples, for instance, three men were given 12-year prison sentences for assaulting an elderly pair of siblings so seriously that the sister died and the brother was disabled. This can be compared with a case where a smuggler of two kilograms of heroin was sentenced to 14 years (ibid.).

In another parliamentary proposal the Conservatives make further suggestions. 'The police should be given the right to perform blood and urine tests on people under the age of 15 if they are suspected of having used narcotics' (Hellsvik et al., p. 9). The same political party also wants to change a law which prohibits social workers from giving information on adolescents and their relatives to the police (ibid., p. 11). Furthermore they want the police to register youths under 15 who are suspected of crime (ibid., p. 13) and would re-establish prisons for 15–17 year olds (ibid., p. 15f). The Conservatives also believe that 'it is unavoidable that youths sometimes must be placed in isolation' (ibid., p. 18). Behind these proposals is the belief that we can deal with narcotics by getting tougher with adolescent consumers.

Fighting narcotics in the streets is common practice in many countries.

> The purpose of drug control at street level is to reduce the supply of drugs by disrupting the trade. Pushers on the street are arrested and drugs traded on the streets are confiscated, the idea being to knock out drug trading in public places, so that no single place will become known as a sale [*sic*] outlet for drugs. In this way the drug market will become less 'visible' and pushers and customers will have less chance of finding each other.
>
> (SNIPH, p. 21)

In Sweden this strategy was proposed by Bejerot in the 1970s and law enforcement agencies have attempted to implement it many times since then. For instance, in the early 1980s the police carried out a nationwide drive against street dealing. Among the objectives were to 'reduce the damaging effects of drugs, especially property crimes, by taking action against abusers and street dealers thereby interfering with and disturbing the narcotics market' (Eriksson and Eriksson, p. 11).

Concurrently, a memorandum from the Office of the Prosecutor General indicated a change in policy. The then common practice of not prosecuting suspects caught with small amounts of certain drugs was now to be greatly restricted.

Evaluating the results of these measures cannot be done in an unequivocal way, but a serious attempt was made by two researchers at the Swedish

National Council of Crime Prevention (BRÅ), Inger Eriksson and Ulla Britt Eriksson. After investigating whether police activity actually disturbed the narcotics market, they conclude: 'Statistics on the number of reported narcotics offences in conjunction with the police campaign do not reveal any general tendencies' (ibid., p. 5).

The same researchers also examined whether these measures reduced the level of property crime and conclude: 'Our impression is that neither the memorandum from the Office of the Prosecutor General nor the street-level activities of the police have had any tangible effect' (ibid., p. 47).

International Police Cooperation

The International Criminal Police Organization (Interpol) dates back to 1914. 'Interpol aims to encourage cooperation between police services combating international crime but is not an operational organization as it cannot deploy police investigators exercising supranational authority' (EMCDDA, 1996, p. 7:11). In the 1970s a Drugs Subdivision was created to analyse drug trafficking and associated crimes. More than half of the 40 000 international criminals in Interpol's archive are connected to drug trafficking (ibid.).

EU member states are in the process of building Europol. The first phase was the Europol Drug Unit (EDU) which became operative in 1994. As is the case with Interpol the EDU is a non-operational body whose main function is the exchange of information between member states. 'Though in the first instance a receiver and user of information, the Europol Drug Unit will become an information producer by disseminating a database progressively fed by the Member States and its partner international organizations' (ibid., p. 7:10).

I am unable to present an evaluation of international police cooperation but as J. W. Brinkman (p. 6) Chief Constable of the Rotterdam-Rijnmond regional police in the Netherlands laments: 'international cooperation in the fight against drug crime is still at the developmental stage, whereas organized crime is operating on a truly international basis'. Thus far nothing indicates that international police cooperation will be able to strike a decisive blow against the international drug trade.

Secondary Harm

Usually attempts at controlling certain behavioural patterns in the population do not only have positive effects but also negative consequences. These undesirable side-effects are often called *secondary harm*. I shall now explain some of the secondary harm arising from police actions against street dealers. Secondary harm in conjunction with other aspects of narcotics policy will be discussed in the next two chapters.

Substantial consumers commonly have an extremely negative attitude toward the police: not as individuals, but in their role as tangible representatives of societal labelling, and as the identified source of much of the fear and 'paranoia' which is an integral part of problematic consumption. In my fieldwork I observed that during periods when the police paid less attention to the scene, the atmosphere became more relaxed and a little more of the substantial consumers' energy was used to ponder upon their emotional and personal difficulties. But when the heat was on, the situation deteriorated. Feelings of rejection and exclusion were magnified, increasing the risk of accelerating the pace of the deviance spiral. Instead of reducing problems, extensive street-level intervention was experienced as labelling.

Another problem is that thus far all attempts from the police to get dealers off the streets, even in a single area, have been unsuccessful. For instance, in 1991 the police decided (once again) to rid downtown Stockholm of street dealers. According to an article in the country's largest morning newspaper, 30 police officers were assigned to the job; and the County Police Commissioner (once again) proclaimed success. But the heads of the narcotics units in several of Stockholm's suburbs expressed another opinion. They couldn't see that anything had been accomplished (see Flores, p. D1).

It is possible that both parties were correct. On a short-term basis, it is possible to rid a certain area of street dealers. But in the long run, there are no positive effects. As soon as the police ease the pressure the dealers return and it's business as usual. If the police continue surveillance on a given place for a longer period, the scene moves elsewhere. If the police follow after, the previous area is re-established. Writer David Simon and former police officer Edward Burns (p. 476) write:

> there will be no victory. Not if you come up Fayette St with bulldozers and knock over every rowhouse ... slingers and fiends would be out here in the rubble, slinging pink-top vials. Not if you call out the National Guard or put police officers on every corner; do that and they'll move five blocks, or ten blocks, or twenty, until there's an open-air market savaging some new neighborhood and you've run out of cops and guardsmen.

It is unrealistic to believe that all areas can be kept under surveillance simultaneously. If the police choose to use more of their assets for narcotics surveillance, sooner or later these resources will be needed for other duties. Part of the secondary harm in conjunction with combating narcotics on the street level is that personnel must be diverted from other tasks. For instance, in conjunction with the above mentioned nationwide campaign, researchers estimated that 'between 150 and 200 policemen per month were assigned to narcotics duties'. These officers were primarily taken from anti-crime divisions, surveillance units and county highway patrols (Eriksson and Eriksson,

p. 15). Certainly this drainage of resources had negative effects on the operations of these departments.

Yet another aspect of secondary harm is described by Chein et al. (1964, p. 369f):

> The very effectiveness of efforts to suppress the traffic creates a situation in which prices rise if there is no corresponding decrease in demand. From a business viewpoint, all that this means is that an increase in risk is balanced by an increase in potential profit. ... Thus, it is not enough that the police activity be moderately successful in catching and convicting violators of the narcotics laws; it must offer the promise of being almost perfectly successful for a long period before we can take it seriously as a measure of control.

In other words, the only way that the police activity might be able to stop the dealing is to remove all problematic consumers from the streets within a very short period of time. But what would this entail? How many police would be needed to apprehend all substantial consumers almost simultaneously? What would it cost to train and equip all the necessary new policemen?

After the police have detained all of these substantial consumers, what should we do with them? How many extra courts, judges, district attorneys and lawyers will be necessary to ensure that all are given a fair trial? How long will it take and how much will it cost to educate these people? How shall we finance the trials?

How many new treatment centres and penitentiaries will have to be built and how many new therapists and prison guards will have to be trained and paid to keep these people in secure custody for years to come? Whence shall all these moneys come? As Simon and Burns (p. 161) put it: 'Soon enough, you're spending more money to lock a man down than it would cost to send him to Harvard.'

Aside from being economically unfeasible, the entire scheme is morally unjustifiable. If a country were to implement a plan of this nature, there would be so many people in prison that it would be in order to speak of a new Gulag. Moreover, it would take so long to try all of these individuals that we would be risking moral disintegration: the general public would probably start having misgivings about the country's laws and judicial system.

This discussion of secondary harm does not imply that the police do not have a role to play. Police activity can help reduce recreational consumption by seeing to it that drugs are not readily available. Those who are unwilling to expend a great deal of effort to acquire drugs, will most probably reduce their consumption.

Police actions, if they are in moderation, can even have positive effects on problematic consumption by making it difficult to make easy money by dealing or through other kinds of crime. At least to some extent the more money problematic consumers have the greater their drug consumption. By for instance confiscating drugs the police can help to reduce the amount of money substantial consumers have to spend. But if the police apply too much pressure, they accelerate the pace of the deviant spiral. In other words, up to a point police activities can have certain positive effects on the drug scene. However, if they exceed this point secondary harm escalates. For this reason police operations cannot deal a lethal blow to the drug scene.

CONCLUSION

Based on the arguments presented in this chapter I find it difficult to draw any conclusion other than that as long as there is a demand for narcotics they will be available to those who are willing to make an effort to obtain them. There is going to be a supply, but can we eliminate the demand?

12 Prohibition – Swedish Narcotics Policy

Prohibition has long been the dominant paradigm upon which international treaties and the narcotics policies of many countries have been based. But due to various forms of secondary harm originating in prohibitionary measures there has been increasing opposition all over the world. An alternative paradigm, most commonly known as harm reduction, has been evolving since the 1960s. Prohibition and harm reduction represent opposite poles in the increasingly polarized international narcotics debate. Each constitutes a primary theoretical foundation for a major European drug policy organization.

Disenchantment with prohibition led representatives from some of the major cities in Europe to meet in Frankfurt in 1990. The 'Frankfurt Resolution', dedicated to developing harm reduction policies as an alternative to prohibition, was signed by 18 cities.[1] At the same time a network was founded: European Cities on Drug Policy (ECDP), seated in Frankfurt.

Concerned by the growing threat to prohibition constituted by the ECDP, another network was founded in 1994 through the signing of the 'Stockholm Resolution'.[2] European Cities Against Drugs (ECAD), with its seat in Stockholm, is an organization dedicated to the preservation and further development of prohibitionist narcotics policies.

In this chapter we shall take a closer look at prohibition. Although the major force behind this model is the US, I shall not present the American war on drugs here, as it is well documented elsewhere (i.e. Inciardi; McCoy and Block). Instead I will look more closely at Swedish narcotics policy ('the Swedish model'), which can be seen both as a small country's attempt to implement prohibition and as a source of inspiration for ECAD. In the next chapter I will examine narcotics policy in the Netherlands, which has been important for ECDP and the development of harm reduction.

[1] Initial signatories of the Frankfurt Resolution were Amsterdam, Arnhem, Basel, Charleroi, Dortmund, Empoli, Prov. di Forli, Frankfurt-am-Main, Hamburg, Hannover, Kalithea, Ljubliana, Luzern, Rome, Rotterdam, St Gallen, Provincia di Teramo, Zagreb and Zurich. ECDP cooperates with the Drug Policy Foundation and the Lindesmith Center in the US.

[2] Initial signatories of the Stockholm Resolution were Berlin, Budapest, Dublin, Gdansk, Gothenburg, Helsinki, London, Lugano, Madrid, Malmö, Moscow, Oslo, Paris, Prague, Reykjavik, Riga, St Petersburg, Stockholm, Tallinn, Valetta and Warsaw. ECAD cooperates with American Cities Against Drugs.

THE EVOLUTION OF SWEDISH NARCOTICS POLICY

The Liberal Prescription Experiment

As was the case throughout the western world, narcotics consumption in Sweden began to increase in the 1960s, and there was great uncertainty as to what should be done. In 1965, as an experiment, permission was granted to a few physicians to prescribe narcotics. It was thought that by giving substantial consumers unadulterated drugs in known quantities, their medical status would improve. Other supposed benefits were that problematic consumers wouldn't have to commit crimes to purchase narcotics, and they would establish a relationship with medical personnel who could help them with treatment should they decide to stop taking drugs. The project was based on 'liberal prescription', which was defined by Sven Erik Åhström, the most active physician in the programme, as 'the patients themselves choose the doses, and the doctor is more an adviser, even if he, of course, has a veto' (Narkomanvårdskommittén, 1967, p. 125).

In 1966 a government commission, the Drug Treatment Committee, was appointed, and as a part of its work Jacob Lindberg was given the task of evaluating the liberal prescription project. Lindberg later became the Deputy Director-General of the Swedish National Institute of Public Health (hereafter abbreviated SNIPH) and was responsible for a summary of Swedish drug policy, which he wrote together with representatives from three government ministries: Health and Social Affairs, Justice, and Finance (SNIPH, 1995). I shall refer to this document as 'the official narcotics policy report'.

Based on Lindberg's study, the official narcotics policy report claims that the liberal prescription project did not lead to less criminality:

> the number of individuals committing criminal offences during the years when they were issued with drugs was roughly the same as for the years immediately preceding. The number of crimes per individual actually showed a slight increase. Drug offences discovered by the police within the group of patients virtually disappeared during the legal period, whereas *all other types of crime increased.* Both 'crimes against the public' and, for example traffic offences increased in both relative and absolute figures.
>
> (SNIPH, p. 8) (their italics) (see also Lindberg, p. 380)

However, while the official narcotics policy report stops here, Lindberg's original text continues: 'a greater number of the most criminally active were out of prison during the legal period than in any of the years used as comparisons. This is the most reasonable explanation for the increasing crime rate' (Lindberg, pp. 380, 385).

In other words the official narcotics policy report, in stating that crime increased, gives a more negative impression than can be supported by available data. On the other hand there is little evidence that the liberal prescription programme achieved its aim to reduce criminality. We cannot with any degree of certainty say what effects this project had on criminality. Most of the 156 participants were criminally active before receiving legal drugs and it appears that at least in the short term they did not become law abiding citizens.

Some of the other criticisms directed at the programme were that excessive doses were prescribed (Bejerot, 1970, p. 177), considerable 'leakage' on to the black market occurred (ibid., p. 180), drugs were passed on from patients to other people (ibid., p. 182) and there was a lack of written records (ibid.). The impression given by Bejerot is that the programme was mismanaged, failed to achieve its goals and had undesirable side-effects.

Professor of Social Work, Sune Sunesson (p. 23) notes that Bejerot's study 'is methodologically unacceptable, as it is based on uncontrolled anecdotes and statistics on deviance which lack comparative figures'. In spite of this, Bejerot's conclusions are generally accepted in Sweden today. The liberal prescription experiment was terminated in 1967.

Methadone Maintenance

Another experimental project initiated in the mid-1960s was the methadone maintenance programme in Uppsala. It has always been well managed, and very little legally prescribed methadone has ever been available on the black market in Sweden. Today three methadone maintenance programmes are operative in the country.

To some extent the liberal prescription project has been used as a scapegoat to explain why an increasing number of people in Sweden started using narcotics in the mid-1960s. Some believe that leakage from the project helped to spread illegal drugs to people who otherwise never would have become involved with psychoactive substances. To this day this programme is presented as 'proof' that prohibition is the only realistic and humane approach. That existing methadone maintenance programmes provide an obvious counter-argument is simply ignored. In the 1970s and 1980s prohibitionists did what they could to abolish methadone, and almost succeeded. However, at present the existing methadone maintenance programmes appear to be relatively unthreatened.

The Narcotics Drugs Act of 1968

The Drug Treatment Committee presented a programme consisting of ten measures to combat narcotics; the most important of which were developing drug-free treatment, providing information on narcotics, enlarging the police and customs, and drastically increasing penalties for serious drug offences. These principles were enacted into law in the Narcotics Drugs Act of 1968 and still form the basis of the Swedish model.

During the 1970s various combinations of these tenets were applied. A number of drug-free treatment centres, based on different theories such as milieu therapy, psychotherapy, transactional analysis, confrontational methods, the so-called Hassela pedagogy, etc. were established. That treatment could get people off drugs was taken for granted; the major point of contention at the time was what the treatment should consist of. To some extent this optimistic view of treatment still exists today. For instance, the official narcotics policy report categorically states that: 'drug abusers *can* be rehabilitated' (SNIPH, p. 11) (emphasis in original).

Parallel with attempts to develop effective forms of treatment, allocations to the police and customs were repeatedly increased. An increasing number of activities were made illegal, and penalties were successively made more severe.

The Narcotics Debate

In the 1970s two client groups with different ideologies participated in an ongoing narcotics debate. The Swedish Association for Help and Assistance to Drug Abusers (RFHL) emphasized that drug abuse should be seen as a result of adverse social experiences and that solutions should be sought by improving societal conditions and through voluntary therapy. One of their slogans was: 'Abused people become abusers'. The other group, the National Association for a Drug-free Society (RNS), demanded further use of the criminal justice system, and rejected the idea of therapy. In their view problematic consumers are just ordinary people who haven't been properly brought up, and therefore treatment was a matter of pedagogy; i.e. teaching these people to behave correctly. Furthermore as substantial consumers are seen as having lost control over themselves, treatment should not be voluntary. Society has the right to demand that they change. RNS insisted that problematic consumers should be placed in treatment and held there through the use of coercive legal statutes. This was to ensure that if they should leave the treatment centre the police would have the right to apprehend them and bring them back.

Parallel with this discussion was a debate concerning the role of law enforcement. In the early 1970s the main thrust of police activity was on the kingpins of the drug trade. On occasion there were raids against street dealers and consumers, but these people were not considered the primary target. In fact for most of the 1970s possession of cannabis equivalent to one week's consumption was usually not prosecuted. In the early 1980s law enforcement strategy was changed and to this day the emphasis is on street-level intervention. Arresting problematic consumers (and sometimes recreational consumers) makes for imposing statistics, gives the impression of determination, energy and drive, and is thought to scare off experimenters. It is also one of many examples of one of the most basic and recurrent themes of Swedish narcotics policy: the importance of driving home *the message*: i.e. drug consumption will not be tolerated. There are no exceptions, excuses or extenuating circumstances. There is no other way to relate to drugs than to 'just say no'!

Since the early 1980s there hasn't been much of a narcotics debate in Sweden. *Either/or thinking* appears to be the rule. The alternatives have been reduced to two: either you support the current drug policies or you are a 'drug liberal'. Classifying opponents as drug liberals is one of the means used in Sweden to avoid debate. Originally the term designated those who supported the liberal prescription project. As this project is generally considered a failure the denotation has now become that there is no need to take the arguments of drug liberals seriously. People have thereby been led to believe that there are no reasonable alternatives to prohibition. As Nils Bejerot, one of the dominating voices in the Swedish drug debate during the 1970s and 1980s, put it:

> After 12 years of debate there are still some points to be settled. How prevention and narcotics policy in general shall be drawn up (strict, restrictive and consistent or lax, liberal and inconsistent).
>
> (Bejerot, 1979, p. 8)

That drug policy could be formulated from a wider range of choices appears to be out of the question. From this premise those who challenge the Swedish model disqualify themselves. If they persist in their criticism they may well find their intellectual faculties and/or morality put to question, and may even have to leave their jobs. To be effective *the message* must be unequivocal. There is no room for doubt about our goals, or of our will and ability to achieve them. To a great extent the model propagated by RNS has emerged victorious. 'There is in Sweden today an extensive community of values concerning the focus of drug policy' (SNIPH, p. 12). However, since this statement was made in the official narcotics policy report, awareness has grown that the new millennium will require new solutions.

THEORETICAL FOUNDATIONS

The basic idea behind prohibition is that narcotics constitute a grave peril to society and therefore must not be permitted. With the help of the criminal justice system prohibitionists believe that it is possible to create, or at least approximate, *a narcotics-free society*. They are of the opinion that by formulating political and legal measures directed at drugs, it is possible to significantly reduce the levels of consumption. Narcotics policy is therefore seen as an effective means to reduce demand.

All drug policies are based on a theoretical understanding of the roots of the problem. Fundamental to prohibitionist thinking is the idea that narcotics consumption has a vast growth potential. For instance, the official narcotics policy report concludes:

> Drug abuse is dependent upon supply and demand. If drugs are readily available and society takes a permissive attitude, the number of persons trying drugs will increase. In other words, even people in a favorable social and psychological situation will come to use drugs. (Ibid., p. 32)

Careful readers of the above quote will note that it starts by discussing drug *abuse* and ends by discussing drug *use*. Swedish prohibitionists believe that 'all non-medical use of narcotics is abuse', and therefore tend to slide back and forth between the two terms, using whichever best suits their purposes for the moment. That which is true for users (recreational consumers) is taken as being true for abusers (problematic consumers). Equating use and abuse is based on the assumption that few (if any) are immune to the biochemical properties of narcotics which cause dependency. In the long run it is not possible for the individual to control drugs; if he starts using them sooner or later they will control him.[3] It is therefore of utmost importance to reduce the supply of drugs to a minimum. This in turn will reduce the demand as fewer people will become dependent. Supply is seen as a major (if not the major) cause of drug abuse.

In other words consumers are seen as objects in relation to narcotics. People cannot be given the freedom to choose to take drugs or not, as if they should start experimenting sooner or later they will lose their ability to abstain due to the chemical effects of the drugs.

As everyone is threatened by them, drugs are seen as an urgent problem in need of immediate and drastic measures. For instance, the official narcotics policy report states that narcotics abuse is 'one of society's greatest social and medical problems' (ibid., p. 7). When a problem is given such monumental proportions there is a risk that the ends will justify the means. I don't believe that most Swedes find expansion of the criminal justice system, fear arousing campaigns and emotionally charged appeals particularly appetizing; indeed these are rather foreign to Swedish culture. However, narcotics have been presented as an urgent threat in need of drastic countermeasures. The fact that emotionally charged appeals are so rarely used in Sweden may be an important part of the explanation as to why these measures have met so little

[3] This is a direct analogy to a commonly held idea about alcohol in Sweden, as witnessed by the proverb: 'First you take a drink, then drink takes you.'

resistance. Perhaps many people reason that the government would not use such terminology if the situation wasn't extremely precarious.

CENTRAL CONCEPTS IN SWEDISH NARCOTICS POLICY

One way to quickly get an overall view of how a problem is understood is to list the central concepts being used.

A Narcotics-Free Society

The primary goal of Swedish narcotics policy, as stated by the Swedish parliament is a narcotics-free society (SNIPH, p. 10).

> A drug-free society is a high objective expressing society's *attitude* to narcotic drugs: we do not accept the integration of narcotic drugs in society, and our aim is a society in which drug abuse remains a socially unaccepted form of behaviour ... A drug-free society is a vision expressing optimism and a positive view of humanity: the onslaught of drugs *can* be restrained. (Ibid., p. 11) (emphasis in original)

Prevention

Swedish researchers and some government documents discuss three different types of prevention: *primary prevention* (stopping the problem before it arises), *secondary prevention* (early intervention after a problem has arisen) and *tertiary prevention* (maintaining the problem on a certain level, or inhibiting further deterioration, a chronic condition or recidivism) (see Socialtjänstkommittén, p. 112f). However, in the official narcotics policy report, the entire section on prevention is devoted to different means of dispersing information about (the dangers of) narcotics (SNIPH, pp. 16ff). The societal factors briefly mentioned elsewhere in the publication, i.e. unemployment, segregation and social deprivation, are evidently not seen as guidelines for prevention. Combating the negative effects of societal problems is thereby reduced to a matter of disseminating information. This is another example of the importance placed on driving home the message. Sociological and economic factors have been relegated to the back bench.

Mobilization of Public Opinion

Yet another major means of getting across the message is the mobilization of public opinion. For more than a century voluntary organizations in Sweden have been active in social issues, especially alcohol. This tradition has been carried over to narcotics, and the government has allocated considerable sums for the purpose. Just about any voluntary organization willing to carry out a campaign against drugs has been granted government funding. For instance, a former problematic consumer told me that he applied for money for a campaign to be run by Täby Hockey Club. The first year funds were awarded but the second time he sent in an application somebody responsible for the grants noticed the initials of the club and got suspicious.[1] It was then discovered that the organization did not exist.

As prevention is defined in terms of giving information, and finances are provided so that the public at large can participate in the process, many people have come to feel that they are part of a national movement, and that they are an important link in the defence of the children of the country – maybe even the country itself. In this way groups of non-critical 'part-owners' of the Swedish model have been created.

Restrictive Control Policy

The assumption behind restrictive control policy is that by using the criminal justice system it is possible to drastically reduce narcotics consumption. This has led to a repeated escalation of both the kinds of acts which have been brought under the penal code, and the penalties for those convicted of transgressions.

Care and Treatment

Professor of Social Work, Bengt Börjeson (1991, p. 4) writes: 'Repression is when a person is expelled, treated ignominiously or placed in a situation where he cannot defend himself.' In practice, repression is exerted by a relatively small number of people 'but it is supported by the silence and non-activity of large groups of people and important organizations' (ibid., p. 13).

As Sweden prides itself on being libertarian, it is difficult to have a policy which is heavily dependent on inherently repressive restrictive control measures. Opposition would almost certainly have been greater if prohibitionists hadn't been able to convince the populace that the repression is being counterbalanced by humanitarian measures; most notably drug-free treatment. 'The Social Services Act is based principally on voluntary participation. Therapeutic work derives its motive power from the individual drug abuser's personal motivation for change, and the social worker and drug abuser decide between them what support and care are needed' (SNIPH, p. 26).

However, the Act on Treatment of Alcoholics and Drug Misusers (LVM) and the Care of Young Persons (Special Provisions) Act (LVU) came into

[1] THC is an abbreviation for tetrahydrocannabinol, the psychoactive ingredient in cannabis.

effect in 1982 together with the first Social Services Act. LVM and LVU are repressive measures with provisions for *compulsory care*.

> In acute phases of abuse... the social worker can take over responsibility for assessing the individual's caring needs. ... it [is] possible for drug abusers to be admitted to care against their wishes... [if he] is a direct danger to himself or to others. The purpose of the intervention is not to coerce the individual through a complete program of rehabilitation, but instead, through short-term intervention, to overcome a life-threatening situation and motivate the individual for continuing care on a voluntary basis. (Ibid.)

The lobby in favour of LVM and LVU argued that this legislation was a way of expressing that society cares about drug consumers. Those who were opposed to these laws saw them not as care but as repression and as a repudiation of the humanitarian Social Services Act, which begins by declaring that social services 'shall be built upon respect for the individual's self-determination and integrity'.

The balance between humane and repressive measures is delicate and subject to revision. LVM was modified in 1989, becoming even more repressive. In the original law a person could be held in coercive care only if his own life was in danger, while the new law could be applied to protect others. Furthermore, people can now be held in compulsory care for six months instead of four.

A modified Social Services Act was passed in 1997, and for the most part it retains its humanitarian profile. However, before it as much as came into effect in 1998, a new commission to suggest further modifications was appointed.

The Caring Chain

When care was at its zenith in Sweden it was organized in a chain of specialized units, each adapted to the drug user's needs in a particular phase in his career; i.e. detoxification, outpatient facilities, voluntary residential care, coercive residential care, supervision after discharge, etc. Many municipalities also started a *caring base* which most often consisted of social workers who actively sought out problematic consumers and tried to get them into the most suitable unit for their needs at the time. However, almost all of the caring bases have now been dismantled.

Street-Level Intervention

> The purpose of drug control at street level is to reduce the supply of drugs by disrupting the trade. Pushers on the street are arrested and drugs

> traded on the streets are confiscated, the idea being to knock out drug trading in public places, so that no single place will become known as a sale [*sic*] outlet for drugs. In this way the drug market will become less 'visible' and pushers and customers will have less chance of finding each other. In this way too, the work of the street trading groups has an effect on the demand for drugs. (SNIPH, p. 21)

Street-level intervention is also seen as yet another way of driving home the message. 'Police measures at street level also have an important effect on public opinion, because they are a clear manifestation of the community's rejection of drug abuse and drug trafficking' (ibid., p. 22).

SWEDISH NARCOTICS POLICY IN PRACTICE

Prevention

As previously noted, prevention is primarily understood as disseminating information. Considerable resources have been allocated in an attempt to both control attitudes towards the narcotics themselves and consumers, as well as to influence the way the public discerns the roots of illegal drug consumption. The official goal is to reduce the demand for narcotics; creating the 'correct' attitudes is thought to be an efficient means to that end.

On the Effects of Norms against Drugs

If we were to develop a more tolerant attitude towards narcotics, it would be easier for people to use them, as drug consumption would only be a minor infraction of societal norms and no longer incongruent with the self-image of a great number of people. It therefore seems reasonable to assume that demand would increase.

If one believes that all non-medical use of narcotics is abuse, then it makes sense to conclude that abuse can be reduced by maintaining distinct and unequivocal norms against all consumption of narcotics. However, it is primarily recreational consumption which is diminished in this manner; while problematic consumption, which entails premature death, crime, prostitution, HIV/AIDS and all the other forms of human degradation that we associate with narcotics, is hardly affected. By emphasizing that narcotics are abhorrent we attract those who already have the most negative self-images. The more negative social norms are toward drugs, the more problematic consumers must 'devaluate' their self-image for behaving in such a loathsome way. Consequently, an extremely negative attitude toward narcotics tends to increase the pace of the deviance spiral. Thus, while society's strict stance on narcotics may possibly decrease recreational consumption, it most likely leads to more deviance and greater demand among problematic consumers.

Some people believe that limiting recreational consumption will also reduce problematic consumption. The reasoning is that recreational consumers, by buying drugs from problematic consumers, are a primary source of revenue for the drug trade. While it is true that money from recreational users makes it easier for the substantial consumers to finance their purchases, it is highly unlikely that problematic consumers would abstain from drugs if they were to lose this source of income. After all, nothing has been done to change the factors behind the substantial consumers' drug-taking behaviour. Two opposing forces would be operative simultaneously:

1. A decrease in income would make it more difficult for problematic consumers to maintain their intake at the same level; at least until other sources of revenue were established or prices were reduced.
2. To replace the loss of income from dealing, substantial consumers will resort to more crime and/or prostitution. This will further diminish their self-image resulting in an even greater need for narcotics.

We can't say with any degree of certainty what the result of these opposing forces would be. Lack of money might lead to more deviance to refill depleted supplies. However, substantial consumers may be unable to fully compensate for their loss of income and thereby be forced to decrease consumption. But the decreased demand would probably reduce prices, increasing the demand again until prices become fixed at a lower level. As a hypothesis I would propose that if a society manages to significantly curtail the number of recreational consumers, the total demand will diminish and so will prices. Problematic consumers will lose an important source of income so in spite of the lower prices they will react with more property crime and more prostitution. This will increase the rate of their deviance spiral resulting in an increase in their narcotics consumption.

Another argument concerning the relationship between recreational and problematic consumption is that the latter are recruited from the ranks of the former. Starting on the assumption that the drugs themselves create problematic consumption, some people conclude that the fewer recreational consumers we have, the fewer will get hooked. However, the theory presented in this book repudiates this idea. Here I will simply remind my readers that it is a giant step from trying drugs to becoming a problematic consumer and only a minute per cent take it. Those who do become substantial consumers have prior life experiences which drastically deviate from the rest of the population. In other words, *problematic consumers are not only purchasing drugs, they are buying a self-destructive lifestyle which is so extreme that there is a very limited base from which they can be recruited.*

The self-destructiveness of problematic consumers is neither created by the occasional use of drugs nor tolerant attitudes towards narcotics; but by an extremely negative psychosocial milieu. Reasonably this has to be the basis upon which prevention is built.

Pounding the Fear of Narcotics into the Population

The guiding principle behind most narcotics campaigns in countries subscribing to prohibition has been fear arousal. Instead of giving factual information which adolescents can use to come to their own conclusions, educational efforts attempt to scare young people into saying no to drugs. Misrepresentations, exaggerations, distortions and fear inducement are all too often the ingredients misleadingly presented as 'drug information'.

Since the latter part of the 1960s the media in many western countries have periodically campaigned against the use of drugs. As the articles are often sensational and titillating, one can wonder if their primary purpose isn't increasing single-copy sales and advertising revenues rather than giving factual information.

However, the mass media are not alone in conducting campaigns. Many organizations and public authorities lend both their names and financial support to what is called 'drug information' (anti-drug propaganda). In the US for example:

> Many teenagers and young adults across the nation had become recreational users of marijuana. For most, the psychological reactions they experienced included euphoria, fragmentation of thought, laughter, spatial and temporal distortions, heightened sensuality, and increased sociability. A few experienced fear, anxiety, and panic. Yet what most of the brokers of drug education were saying to users and their peers was something totally different – something reminiscent of Anslinger's pontifications during the 1930s' era of reefer madness. In fact, in the early 1960s Anslinger was still saying essentially the same things about marijuana:
>
>> Those who are accustomed to habitual use of the drug are said eventually to develop a delirious rage after its administration during which they are temporarily, at least, irresponsible and prone to commit violent crimes. The prolonged use of this narcotic is said to produce mental deterioration. ... Much of the most irrational juvenile violence and killing that has written a new chapter of shame and tragedy is traceable directly to this hemp intoxication. (Anslinger and Tompkins, 1953, p. 37f)
>
> With statements such as these coming from the Commissioner of Narcotics, drug educators and parents – statements that for the most part were

contrary to experience and untrue – it is no wonder that the youth of the day turned deaf ears to the anti-drug messages.

(Inciardi, p. 33f)

In Britain, Julian Cohen (1996, p. 153f) found that:

Most past drug education programmes have tried to dissuade young people from using drugs. This is called primary prevention and has been attempted using a number of different approaches. In rough chronological order these have been:

1. the shock/scare approach as exemplified in hard hitting anti-drug videos, talks by ex-junkies or some government TV and billboard campaigns that focus on the horrors of drug use;
2. the information approach where young people are given the facts about drugs (and especially the dangers) on the assumption that if they knew the facts they would not use drugs;
3. the attitudes/values approach whereby the attempt is made to promote a drug free lifestyle, personal responsibility and strong moral beliefs to avoid drugs;
4. the refusal skills approach where young people are seen as easy prey to peer pressure and in need of developing the skills to Say No To Drugs;
5. the decision making skills approach that assumes young people lack the generic skills to make rational choices and that if they had these skills they would not use drugs;
6. the alternative highs approach whereby the attempt is made to replace the excitement of drug use with other forms of risk taking such as pot holing, climbing and abseiling on the assumption that young people will then not need to take drugs;
7. the self-esteem approach where the focus is on the individual rather than drugs *per se* and it is assumed that young people of high self-esteem will not use drugs.

Cohen (ibid., p. 154) concludes that 'evaluations of all kinds of drug education programmes, in this country and all over the developed world show that drug education does not prevent young people from using drugs' (see also Pauloff; Ennett et al.; Dorn and Murji; Tobler).

In Sweden, Nordegren and Tunving (p. 220) discuss some of the secondary harm created by fear arousing anti-drug propaganda.

Some of the adolescents who had smoked hashish believed that they had become incurable drug addicts. Others, based on their own experience and those of their friends, dismissed public information as untruthful or grossly exaggerated, undermining faith in what was being taught in school.

Based on the theory presented in this book, fear arousal has little or no effect on problematic consumption. If there are any results at all they are exactly the opposite of the professed aims. While scare tactics may well dissuade those who don't want to harm themselves from as much as trying drugs, these are not the people who become substantial consumers. On the other hand, those who have strong self-destructive tendencies, i.e. those who are at risk of becoming problematic consumers, become attracted to drugs. They are given clear instructions as to how to satisfy their self-destructive needs and learn that 'people like me take drugs'. However, in time they almost surely would have learned this anyway.

But anti-drug programmes do have other effects, and these must be included on the list of secondary harm caused by current narcotics policy. Fear arousing campaigns have most certainly raised the level of anxiety among parents and caused unnecessary worry. This in itself is bad enough, but it has also helped to pave the way for repressive narcotics policy. Frightened citizens, worrying about how to protect their children and grandchildren, have passively accepted measures which threaten constitutional safeguards. I shall return to this shortly.

Fear arousing propaganda also reveals an attitude towards adolescents which in itself is frightening. This may well contribute to a rift between generations which affects other areas of life as well. Grown-ups do not approach the complexities of narcotics with openness, truthfulness or the will to convey wisdom. Instead of initiating a dialogue with their children, thereby showing respect for the thoughts, experiences and feelings of the next generation, adults choose to lecture. The message is clear; we make the rules and teenagers must submit. The situation is an open invitation to defiance. However, we need not exaggerate the dangers; no one becomes a problematic consumer, i.e. destroys himself, simply because adults aren't sufficiently sensitive when talking about drugs. But if the lack of dialogue and distortion of facts reflects a pattern in the way grown-ups interact with adolescents, this might well constitute a part of a labelling process which can lead to problematic consumption of narcotics. To my way of thinking, our apparent readiness to approach our youth with exaggeration and decrees is one of the most frightening aspects of fear arousing propaganda.

Nordegren and Tunving (ibid.) state that the situation in Sweden has improved since the country started using more modern approaches. 'Information based on scare tactics was replaced after a few years by information on the "underlying causes".' Nordegren and Tunving declare that today's narcotics information is based on 'responsible decision making'.

> The idea being that since sooner or later almost all adolescents will be offered drugs, it is important to discuss the subject with them and teach them how they should behave when the situation arises. Drug information

> should be presented primarily through discussion (two-way communication), role-playing, and drama pedagogy. (Ibid., p. 221)

At first glance, this seems much better than fear arousing anti-drug propaganda, but upon second reading, I have my doubts. The quotation in the last paragraph does not say that there is a discussion with adolescents on how they feel they should deal with the situation if they are offered drugs; it says that they are taught *how they should behave*. In other words, there is only one 'correct' answer, which means that there is no place for two-way communication and drawing one's own conclusions.

Suspicions that such is the case are reinforced upon further reading in Nordegren and Tunving's book. A variant of 'responsible decision making' used in Swedish schools endeavours to 'teach students to make their own independent decisions so that they are able to *withstand peer pressure*' (ibid., p. 231) (my italics). Once again it seems that there is only one reasonable course of action; adolescents must withstand peer pressure and stay off drugs. But suppose a teenager, after careful consideration, makes an independent decision and chooses to try a drug? Is that OK? If it is not permissible to make any decision other than saying no to drugs, then there is no 'responsible decision making'. It seems that the adults are saying: 'You can make any decision you want – as long as it is the one we're telling you to make.'

However, whether we like it or not, it is the adolescents not the adults who have the last say. Just as earlier generations of parents were unable to prevent their children from using tobacco or alcohol, adults of today cannot stop adolescents from trying drugs. If we accept this fact and present young people with unbiased information, we will help them by giving them solid ground on which to base their decisions. Moreover, we will avoid placing them in a situation where they feel that they must choose between submission or defiance. In the words of Jan Ramström (1987, p. 112): 'By negotiating with teenagers instead of simply telling them what to do, we show respect for the adult in the adolescent.' In the final analysis, we should ask ourselves: if adults make the decisions, how then can we expect young people to feel responsible for their actions?

I conclude this section with two quotes from the official narcotics policy report (SNIPH, p. 16):

> The purpose of information . . . is to preserve and reinforce the negative attitudes already existing in Sweden.

> Information today is concerned with supplying basic facts.

It appears that the authors of this document cannot imagine that there might possibly be some contradiction between these two objectives.

But whatever we do, we can neither inform away nor scare away problematic drug consumption; the roots of the problem lie much too deep.

Ideology

The concept of ideology in the particular sense it is used here was developed by sociologist Karl Mannheim, even if its basic implications had been put forth by earlier writers. An ideology is a set of ideas which function as a defence for, and legitimization of, prevailing social conditions. This can be accomplished by:

1. teaching people to concentrate their thoughts and energy on those elements in their life experiences which do not constitute a potential threat to the current social order; and by
2. providing interpretations which make it difficult for people to see the relationships between their life experiences and society's macrostructure.

Put succinctly the function of ideology is to maintain the status quo. To the extent that ideology fulfils this function, the need for society to use other forms of coercion decreases.

Professor of Sociology Göran Therborn (p. 27) writes that ideology influences our consciousness by identifying:

1. what exists and what doesn't, what is what, who we are, what the world consists of, the nature of society, of men, of women, etc. In this way we establish an identity; and define what is right and what is real;
2. what is good, correct, just, beautiful, attractive, enjoyable, etc., and all of their opposites. In this way our desires are structured and normalized;
3. what is possible and what is not. This gives us the feeling that certain aspects of our existence are unalterable.

In Mannheim's sense of the word, some of the dominating thoughts on how to reduce the demand for narcotics are 'ideological'. For instance, by choosing to call drug consumption an 'epidemic', the use of a medical analogy channels our thoughts towards medicine, biology and chemistry and away from society and its institutions.

Another example is reducing drug consumption to the individual user and his 'personal' deficiencies, i.e. his (lacking) personality, his inability to learn, his asocial behaviour, and that he is 'chemically controlled' (dependent on drugs). All of these lead our thoughts away from the fact that problematic consumers are a part of society and that to a great extent their activities are a product of the relationships they have had to other people in society. Ideological explanations reduce the significance or totally ignore the connections between the deficiencies we can observe in the substantial consumer and his social experiences. The individual himself is considered the source of the problem, and we therefore do not have to see drug consumption as a signal that there are deficiencies in our social institutions.

The way in which playing down the importance of society in creating the individual leads to ideological thinking can be exemplified by a news report depicting how a black teenager attempted to hold up a convenience store in New York City. When the proprietor did not hand over the money quickly enough, he was gunned down in cold blood. After the youth was arrested he was asked if he regretted what he had done. He looked surprised at the question and answered: 'He didn't give me the money, did he?'

Should this be considered an example of the 'mindless violence' that some people feel characterizes our modern society? Is this teenager asocial, i.e. should we assume that the reasons for what he did are solely his own, unrelated to the rest of society? To my way of thinking the answer to both questions is no. Instead, we should look at the experiences this youth has had that make it possible for him to murder a stranger in cold blood, without remorse.

It is not difficult to find reasonable explanations for what this teenager has done if we examine the living conditions in Harlem where he grew up. It is obvious to anyone who bothers to look that people in this neighbourhood live in extremely difficult circumstances. Children learn that human life is of little value. Who cares about the addicts on the roof, the alcoholics in the gutter, the kids on the streets late at night without adult supervision, the violence and murder? Who has shown this teenager that it is important to safeguard life; both his own, and others? Most likely the answer is nobody – and in this lies an important part of the social background of his 'asocial' acts.

By discarding the assumption that the individual is asocial (i.e. separate from society) and instead considering human acts as social in nature, we avoid the ideological pitfall. We then understand that we must try to find measures which take into consideration social conditions. If we continue to direct our attention to individuals who conduct themselves in undesirable ways, the environments which shaped these people will remain intact and produce a never ending stream of new perpetrators.

The problems in Harlem are so apparent that it is relatively easy for us to see them. However, other unsuitable social environments are not as easy to identify. This is partially because they are not always obvious, but also because we are (ideologically) taught not to see them. And when the results of these adverse social conditions appear before our eyes, for instance in the form of problematic consumption of narcotics, they are explained away with a multitude of ideological theories.

In Swedish narcotics prevention there is no discussion of how we can change the environments which play an important role in creating problematic consumers. This is because these measures demand enormous resources, and therefore imply that the rest of us must relinquish something. To avoid this insight we are (ideologically) brought to believe that problematic consumption of narcotics is a personal problem which can be solved with little sacrifice from the rest of us. All we can and should do is not take drugs ourselves, and rally behind our current narcotics policies.

Censorship

Some people seem to believe that narcotics consumption would decrease if we could prevent those who question current 'truths' about drugs from spreading their opinions. This view is expressed in the form of demands that certain kinds of music should not be played on the radio, that certain magazines not be printed or imported, that certain pop stars and other so-called drug liberals should be kept out of the country, etc. For instance, criticism was raised against the organizers of a scientific conference on cocaine because they invited, as one of many speakers, Lester Grinspoon, Professor at Harvard University. His critics felt that he was too liberal on drugs to be permitted to speak. The fact that he has written numerous books on the subject, that he is a reputed scientist, and that he has been called as an expert on narcotics to testify in congressional hearings, bore no weight against the risk which his ideas might constitute for our youth (who most certainly do not become party to papers presented at scientific conferences).

Sociologist Mats Hilte (1998, p. 8) writes:

> There are many risks in conjunction with asserting politically incorrect viewpoints. Politicians would lose credibility and public support. Civil servants can lose their jobs or ruin their careers. Correspondingly, drug researchers' careers and grant money are threatened if they publish reports or articles which question politically correct conceptions.

It has gone so far that two of the most well-known figures in the Swedish narcotics debate, Widar Andersson and K. A. Westerberg, published an article on Hassela's home page on the Internet stating that 'freedom of speech . . . should be restricted for people who openly or clandestinely propagate for narcotics' (Andersson and Westerberg, 1996).

These appeals for censorship are based on the supposition that ideas are the most important determinant of how an individual will act. An assumption of this kind turns our attention away from political decisions and social and economic processes which have influenced the individual's experiences throughout his life. Instead of attempting to find macrosolutions, we learn that it is necessary to silence those who say (or sing) 'inappropriate' things. But censorship will not stop problematic consumption; it will only lead to very serious secondary harm. Censorship is a major threat to freedom of speech; one of the cornerstones of democracy. Accepting censorship is a significant step on the road to a totalitarian society. For a century Sweden has been an extremely open society. The need to fight narcotics is now being used to motivate measures which threaten the most basic civil liberties of citizens.

Restrictive Control Policy – Introduction

A Brief History[4]

Some 'modern' attempts to control drug consumption have deep historical roots. More than 200 years ago Frederick II of Prussia tried to ban coffee as he believed it threatened the balance of trade, commercial breweries and the fitness of his soldiers. He created a *coffee monopoly* and a *special police force* whose mission was to sniff out illegal coffee-roasting establishments (a human predecessor to the narcotics dog). These measures were unpopular and corruption flourished within the special police force. Because of this, the monopoly was abolished and replaced by *high import duties*. Yet people continued drinking coffee.

There have also been attempts to stop the use of tobacco with methods we recognize from today's proposals for the control of alcohol and narcotics. In 1634 the Russian policy towards tobacco was *prohibition*. The priesthood saw tobacco as a western (foreign) element and a threat to Russian culture (the prevailing power structure). Among the methods of punishment were flogging, cutting off the noses of those caught using snuff, and *deportation* to Siberia. *Special courts* were established, but in spite of these measures, smuggling and the (ab)use of tobacco continued. New laws were passed with *increasingly harsh punishments* which also included the *death penalty*. Yet the smoking continued!

The italicized concepts are certainly familiar to anyone with a minimum knowledge of modern prohibitionist control policies. At first glance it seems that we have learned little from history.

Official Goals – Operative Goals

There are, however, alternative explanations as to why our legislators continue to use the same old recipes in spite of secondary harm and in spite of the fact that evidence is lacking that such policies are effective. One such explanation is that some people have motives which are not openly declared, and that restrictive control policy is in fact effective with regard to these undeclared objectives.

In writing this I am borrowing an idea from Charles Perrow (p. 369f), an American researcher who has studied how organizations function. Perrow differentiates between *official goals* ('the general purposes of the organization as put forth in the charter, annual reports, public statements by key executives and other authoritative pronouncements') and *operative goals* ('the ends sought through actual operating policy of the organization; they tell us what the organization actually is trying to do, regardless of what the official goals say are the aims'). Put differently, when words and deeds do

[4] This brief history is based on Christie and Bruun, pp. 47–51.

not correlate particularly well, one's understanding of the situation is dependent upon one's assumptions:

Assumption 1 – The official goals are the actual goals.
Conclusion 1 – The organization is inefficient and must develop better methods.
Assumption 2 – The organization is efficient.
Conclusion 2 – The official goals are not meant to be achieved. That which is actually accomplished reflects the operative (real) goals of the organization.

The official goal behind the increasingly restrictive Swedish control policy is to 'solve the drug problem'. Based on the first assumption above, we can explain our limited success by saying that the problem is extremely complex. We interpret that which is being done as an untiring effort to refine our methods.

Based on the second assumption, we ask: what are the real goals? I will now present two plausible answers. Other explanations will be discussed further on.

Relieving Bad Conscience

Based on the assumption that some of the people who propose prohibition understand that we cannot force problematic consumers to stop using narcotics with restrictive control policies, we must ask what alternative purposes are served by continuing along this path? Chein et al. (p. 326) feel that superficial measures help to create an illusion that society is trying to fulfil its obligations and thereby help ease conscience pangs. 'The fortunate can live at peace with themselves, secure in the fiction that that which needs to be done is being done.' Many people happily embrace theories which propose that problematic consumption is the personal predicament of the substantial consumer, and that solutions do not require sacrifices from others.

It is not difficult to understand such reactions. Most of us have enough on our minds as it is and it is a relief not to feel obliged to become involved with all the implications of problematic consumption of narcotics. 'The major goal is to suppress the problem, rather than to deal with its causes' (ibid., p. 327).

Avoiding More Difficult Problems

Christie and Bruun explain why the war on drugs in its present form is an effective way to attain the goal of not having to deal with the more profound problems of society – or, in their own words, why narcotics are *the good enemy*.

Christie and Bruun (pp. 56–61) ask, why aren't tobacco, alcohol and psychoactive medicines combated with the same zeal as narcotics?[5] Their

[5] In the late 1990s the tobacco industry in the US lost several court cases and agreed to pay what in nominal figures appears to be a substantial amount of money to compensate for the damages caused by smoking. In reality this sum is equivalent to a tax of a few cents on each pack of cigarettes sold and does not constitute a serious threat to potent economic interests.

answer is that all of these drugs are defended by powerful industries, making them unsuitable adversaries. 'It is a question of choosing your foe. The perfect enemy meets certain criteria' (ibid., p. 63).

1. Social problems are those problems which outspoken and dominant groups manage to mobilize public opinion against. Obviously a social problem cannot be defined in such a way so as to threaten central positions of power in society. The definition of a social problem cannot be such that it damages or embarrasses industries, powerful unions, important professions, or geographic regions. Nor should they threaten the intellectual elite. The enemy should not be defined in such a way that any potent group in society would find it in their interest to support him... (Ibid., p. 63f)
2. It must be possible to depict the enemy as dangerous, often fiendish, inhuman. ... Exaggerations and fear-arousing analogies characterize the early stages of a war and their use is increased as the war escalates. The ideal situation is to find a group which personifies the evil of the enemy. This group can then be used as the arch-representative for everything that is malevolent. (Ibid., p. 64)
3. Those who are responsible for fighting the enemy have to feel that the country stands behind them. Criticism must therefore wait until the battle is won. In order to gain popular support the warriors must appear credible and not be challenged, even if they should resort to exaggerations when they describe either the adversary or the nature of the problem. The enemy must be portrayed as powerful so that the use of extraordinary measures can be justified.

   A means of achieving necessary support is, at least to some extent, to disengage the societal control mechanisms which normally prevent the abuse of power. Another method is to leave it to those in power to define how the war is progressing. In times of war, censorship makes it difficult for people to assess what is happening. ... The more difficult the war is, the less discussion there is as to how the war should be fought. (Ibid.)
4. Good enemies never die. ... [the strategy] is to continually report successes and partial victories, while at the same time indicating that the enemy is still powerful and cunning and still poses a serious threat. The triumphs of the already successful campaign can be further enhanced if the generals are granted still more material resources and extraordinary powers. (Ibid., p. 65)
5. The perfect enemy is sufficiently tangible that he can be fought when we see him, yet obscure enough that we can never be really sure that there aren't more of them lurking somewhere in the shadows. (Ibid.)

6. But there are limits to obscurity. The enemy must symbolize the opposite of all we consider righteous and correct. (Ibid.)
7. The war on drugs could hardly have reached the proportions and intensity it has...without there being good reason for anxiety about narcotics. ... The enemy exists and is present every day, even if he doesn't take on the proportions and have the power claimed by the generals. (Ibid.)

'No enemy fully matches all of these criteria. ... Some enemies are better than others' (ibid.). Problematic consumers of narcotics have enough of the necessary attributes to serve as the good enemy. Consequently, various countries around the world have declared war on narcotics.

> Wars are not necessarily bad – for those who do not have to pay the immediate price for participation. Enemies are not only a threat; they can also be very useful. They unite the other side, they make it possible to change priorities, and they also help to *direct our attention to a minute part of reality and ignore everything else.* (Ibid., p. 62) (my italics)

By concentrating most of our energy on problematic consumers instead of examining the society we live in, we can avoid open conflict with powerful groups; to the relief not only of politicians but also of large parts of the citizenry.

Restrictive Control Policy in Practice

Introduction

Although the official narcotics policy report states that current Swedish policy is still based on the proposals of the Drug Treatment Committee of 1968, many changes have occurred since then. The use of the criminal justice system has been repeatedly expanded and extended. The Narcotics Drugs Act has been modified time and again, partially as a result of international conventions but also by Swedish initiative.

> As the Act now stands, the supply, production, acquisition (with a view to supply), procurement, ... transport, storage, possession and consumption of narcotics are punishable actions. It is also a criminal offence to promote drug trading, which for example means that anybody putting a seller and purchaser in touch with each other thereby commits a criminal offence.
> (SNIPH, p. 19)

Furthermore, penalties have been drastically increased; from a maximum of one year in the penitentiary, in 1966, to up to 16 years today. In each year in the early 1980s Swedish courts gave prison sentences totalling about 1000 years for narcotics crimes. By the mid-1990s the figure had doubled

(Carlberg et al., p. A4). Parole is no longer granted after half the sentence has been served; a minimum of two-thirds is currently required. Furthermore problematic consumers can be forced into treatment against their will.

Within the space available I cannot present a detailed picture of how Swedish restrictive control policy functions on a day to day basis, but I will present a few examples.

Disturbing Consumers

We have already discussed why street-level intervention by the police cannot eliminate the supply of narcotics. But some people in Sweden believe that if different authorities cooperated with each other we can drastically reduce demand by disturbing consumers. In several municipalities the authorities have made serious attempts to put this strategy into effect; sometimes using exceptional methods. When legal or ethical principles have got in the way of their efforts, some of the most zealous have taken the law into their own hands. I will present a few examples of how the ends have justified the means when it comes to keeping adolescents off drugs.

The Secrecy Act (Sekretesslagen) emphasizes that clients must feel certain that the information they give to the authorities when they seek help is not spread to others (see JO, 1987/88, p. 149). The 'narcotics group' in the city of Örebro, however, felt that fighting drugs was more important than principles. The following discussion is based on Sjöstedt.

The official goal of the narcotics group was to detect drug consumption early on. It was sufficient for an adolescent to look tired in school, or to go to Rockmagasinet (a music club), or to have 'unsuitable' friends, for his name to be put on a list of suspected drug abusers. Information from these lists was then spread to different agencies such as the police, the schools, the social bureau, etc. Once a person's name was on the list he could be clandestinely photographed so others could easily identify him.

The authorities would follow adolescents on the lists when they walked around town, and even sit near them in cafés and try to overhear what they were saying. Social workers could also show up uninvited and unannounced at private parties. Sometimes they brought the police with them and checked everybody's ID. As one teenager put it: 'It got so bad you didn't feel alone when you went to the toilet' (Sjöstedt, p. 12).

The youths were also called to the social bureau to discuss drug consumption. A teenager who needed social welfare claims: 'They lowered or raised my benefits depending upon how they felt I was doing' (ibid.). I have been unable to check if this really was the case, but if it is true then it constitutes a clear violation of the law, and is another example of the thumbscrew method (see p. 118) which seems to find favour among many of those working on street-level intervention (see also Upplands-Väsby kommun, p. 9).

Still another measure taken was that school principals would inform parents that their children were on a list of suspected drug abusers. Teachers were also notified. One of these adolescents said: 'I didn't exactly feel like a success in school after that. I worried about how it was going to affect my grades' (Sjöstedt, p. 11).

Another example of disturbing consumers is the so-called Rave Commission, founded in 1996 and consisting of approximately 20 police officers. It got its name from one of its principal means of operation, going to raves and arresting anybody who looked like they might have taken narcotics. As not only possession but also consumption is illegal in Sweden, and carries a possible prison sentence, the police can force individuals suspected of having taken a drug to take a urine test. Two researchers evaluated Rave Commission activities during the first half of 1997. In this period 200 youths aged 15–20 were apprehended. There are results from urine tests for two-thirds of them. Of the 90 who tested positive, about half were already known to the authorities (Lindström and Svensson, p. 23). In other words, 20 policemen working for six months uncovered less than 50 previously unregistered adolescents for whom it was proven that they had taken narcotics on one occasion.

A Dutch researcher who did an in-depth analysis of Swedish drug policy, Tim Boekhout van Solinge (p. 116f), believes that the function of urine tests is harassment:

> many 'suspected' drug users who are taken from the street to undergo a urine test, are in fact the 'old' drug addicts who were already by and large known to the police as such. Hence, in daily practice, the tests are used to disturb the market and to make drug use more difficult. It is only in rare cases that these drug addicts are directed to treatment after the test, as the official policy indicates. ... police officers who work on the street level know that few new drug users are now found through the tests.

Naturally the police don't interpret disturbing consumers as harassment. When explaining police tactics former police chief Björn Eriksson repeatedly stated: 'it should be hard to be a drug abuser'. This expression is also the title of an article in an anthology published by the Swedish government, written by the coordinator of the Stockholm street-level police groups, Hans Strindlund (pp. 11–17). Strindlund explains that by eliminating street dealers the police make it difficult for all but the most initiated customers to find drugs, thereby saving newcomers from (the horrors of) narcotics. He also tells us that when the police disturb consumers it's for their own good. He exemplifies this with a teenage girl from Lidingö (a suburb with many wealthy inhabitants) who after her arrest, and the police informing her parents, was never seen on the scene again. We are brought to understand that this adolescent was saved by police activity.

Strindlund's interpretation is based on Bejerot's theory of the epidemic spreading of drug abuse. An alternative interpretation, based on my fieldwork is that *by its very nature it is extremely hard to be a problematic consumer*. Neither the police nor anybody else need make things worse to scare off all but the very few people with the kinds of backgrounds described in this book. Therefore, the net result of this kind of police activity is not humane, as many in Sweden seem to believe, but rather as Danish criminologist Jørgen Jepsen (1996, p. 17) put it: 'a harmful increase in the misery of addicts'.

Getting Teenagers off Drugs

Bankel and Hermansson (p. 8) feel that there is good reason for the authorities to ignore the rights of clients:

> As an excuse for not taking action many social workers refer to the principles of the Social Services Act; i.e. help should only be given when the client requests it, and then with respect for the individual's integrity and right to make the final decision as to what should be done. These principles guide us as well, but we are also aware of the unavoidable conflict between social workers' responsibilities and these principles. *When working with drug abusers reality collides with the principles and then we must let reality be our guide*. (my italics)

'Social workers are caught between their superior's demands that they adhere to *principles which are out of touch with reality*, and the family's demands for active intervention' (ibid., p. 59). Another principle which evidently also is 'out of touch with reality' is one of the fundaments of Swedish law, *praesumptio innocentiae*; i.e. a person is assumed innocent until proven otherwise. According to this tenet the burden of proof is on the prosecutor. However, Bankel and Hermansson don't believe that this should be the case for adolescents suspected of using narcotics. 'Urine tests have two goals, to discover drug abuse, and to prove that one is not taking drugs while being treated' (ibid., p. 48).

What can happen when these ideas are put into practice in social work? One of the authors of the book just quoted, Ulric Hermansson, was responsible for a project known as ARA (which stands for work, revenge and responsibility). Its official goal was to help teenagers with social problems, such as drug abuse and criminality. One of the means to achieve this was for these adolescents to be given jobs, i.e. working in the kitchen of a home for the elderly, under the guidance of people who had been trained to work with drug abusers. They were also given support by social workers. Thus far the project seems reasonable, as does most of the content of Bankel and Hermanssons's book; if one doesn't examine it carefully.

In a radio programme an ARA staff member was asked if the teenagers and their parents had been informed that participation in the project was voluntary. The answer was: 'If they ask, we'd have to tell them. But it's nothing we talk about, as the project is built on people not knowing the law.' Furthermore, the same social worker explained that even those youths who didn't abuse alcohol were forced to take Antabuse, as an act of solidarity with the others. And finally, although it was against the law, urine tests were obligatory.

The National Board of Health and Welfare, which is responsible for supervision of this kind of project, initially took the position that the statements made in the radio programme were inaccurate. When they finally investigated the matter they concluded the project was guilty of all of these transgressions and several others as well, such as being manipulative, using illegal coercion, concentrating on mechanical control rather than building up a reciprocal relationship, not basing treatment on an individual evaluation of each client, etc. (see Socialstyrelsen, 1990, pp. 3ff).

I don't believe that the social workers who committed these transgressions are particularly evil people. Ideas are formed within the framework of an intellectual and political climate. In Sweden where narcotics are seen as capable of destroying an individual's willpower, and where what once was a debate has given way to national unity behind the drug policy, the normal checks and balances which otherwise characterize the country have been put out of function, paving the way for over-zealousness and undemocratic methods. In the words of Professor of Social Work, Rosmari Eliasson (p. 52f): 'In organizations where people are looked upon as objects, we often find, *in the name of our responsibility for the weak*, coercion, not allowing people to attend to their own affairs, and infringements on the individual's right to make his own decisions' (emphasis in original).

Care and Treatment

During the 1980s relatively large amounts of resources were allocated in Sweden for residential care. This was partially due to genuine humanitarian concern and a general optimism that treatment centres could rehabilitate problematic consumers. Another important factor was the fear of HIV/AIDS. It was known that substantial consumers often share needles, and that many earn money through prostitution. There appeared to be a significant risk of an AIDS epidemic which would first spread among problematic consumers, then to the clients of prostitutes, who in turn would spread it to their sexual partners, who would spread it to their partners, and so on. Providing treatment to problematic consumers was seen as a means of preventing this chain reaction. Although not explicitly stated, the idea was that many substantial consumers would get off drugs and those who didn't would at least be off the streets and therefore incapacitated during the period they were in treatment. However, by the 1990s several factors led to a change in policy:

- the feared AIDS epidemic didn't materialize;
- serious economic problems led to both a withdrawal of national government funding for the treatment of problematic consumers and municipal budget cuts;
- the rehabilitation rate achieved by residential care provided little reason for enthusiasm.

As a result most of the caring bases were dismantled, and many residential care units closed as the municipalities were no longer willing/able to pay for their services. The goal of providing residential care for everyone thought to be in need of it has now been abandoned.

To a great extent the once proud chain of specialized care units has been reduced to outpatient centres. According to the official narcotics policy report these outpatient centres offer 'counseling, motivation work, crisis treatment and psychotherapy' (SNIPH, p. 25). However, the National Board of Health and Welfare has done a special study on outpatient care and paints an entirely different picture:

> Both residential care, and outpatient care with high intensity contact and an ambition to bring about behavioral change ... are now offered to fewer drug abusers than in the past. Our study indicates that the specialized outpatient alternatives which have been built up do not come close to compensating for the reduction in the use of residential care.
>
> (Socialstyrelsen, 1996, p. 116)

This quote gives the impression that residential care had been efficient in helping problematic consumers; and indeed many people in Sweden believe this to be the case. However, there is little scientific evidence that a significant number of substantial consumers received extensive help. Although many institutions contend that they had been evaluated and had achieved good results, most of the evaluations referred to have not been published and therefore cannot be assessed. For instance, Hassela, the largest and most influential drug treatment movement during the 1970s and 1980s, claims: 'Hassela has been investigated and evaluated by a number of government agencies as well as by others' (Westerberg and Andersson, p. A4). 'Our methods are one of the very few with positive results' (ibid.). However, no evidence is given to support these statements. In reality there is only one scientific study, BAK/SWEDATE, which compares a number of residential treatment centres in Sweden. This study does not name individual institutions, but rather groups them in categories according to the philosophy behind the treatment offered. The most positive statistic in BAK/SWEDATE is that 59 per cent of the adolescents who had been at one of these categories of institutions, had not been registered for narcotics consumption during the first six months after treatment (Bergmark et al., p. 68). However, we must ask if this is a sufficient criterion to judge the effectiveness of residential care? In a summary of their findings for all of the treatment centres BAK/SWEDATE's researchers write:

> If we, for instance, with the term good results mean that a client doesn't abuse narcotics we can say that positive effects have been noted for about half of the clients. But if we include the abuse of alcohol or any other drug, the number of successful clients is reduced to under 40 per cent. If we also add that they haven't been committed to an institution or participated in criminal activities the number diminishes to a little over a fifth. If we require that they should be socially integrated in the sense that they are supporting themselves, have a place to live and something to do, only 15 per cent are successful, and if we also include the client's psychological status and need for some type of support from society, only one client in ten can be considered successfully rehabilitated. (Ibid., p. 152)

If we also were to demand that these results should last for a longer period of time, for instance a few years instead of six months, the number of successful cases would most probably be reduced still further.

Nor do the results from coercive care units give reason for optimism. The official narcotics policy report points out that compulsory care is a last resort in a desperate situation and we therefore cannot expect the same results as voluntary care.

> A six-month follow-up of 102 drug or multiple abusers who received compulsory care in three institutions showed ... that 9% had discontinued their abuse and 18% had reduced it. The same study showed that 28% had been motivated for further institutional care on a voluntary basis.
>
> (SNIPH, p. 29)

After reviewing the available research and doing a study of his own Åke Bergmark (p. 475) concludes that a considerable proportion of the clients who have been in compulsory care relapse into very heavy drug abuse after release, and have not become motivated for voluntary care. Director of drug research at the City of Stockholm's R & D department, Gunnar Ågren (p. 24) writes: 'data from several studies show that the death rate among Swedish heroin addicts is remarkably high; as much as 10 per cent in a year in some of them. Especially high is the death rate among those who have been in LVM care.' Anna Fugelstad found a death rate of 14 per cent within one year after realease from LVM care, while the rate for those in voluntary care is 3–4 per cent (Hasselgren, p. 30).

As coercive care implies that we at least temporarily disregard personal integrity and the right to self-determination, its use can only be justified if it has humanitarian effects. However, there is no proof of such results. On the contrary Bergmark (p. 479) argues that LVM has not had a favourable influence on the lives of problematic consumers, and Ågren summarizes: 'there is no evidence that LVM saves lives or is positive for the health of those who have been in treatment' (see Hasselgren, p. 31).

Harm Reduction Measures in Sweden

Needle Exchange

The official narcotics policy report states:

> The restrictive line taken on needle exchange programmes is prompted by fears of such programmes conveying an ambiguous message about society's attitude to drug abuse. Widespread exchange activities could be taken by drug abusers, by potential abusers, and by the general public, to imply a cachet of social approval (or at least acceptance) of i.v. drug abuse.
>
> The programmes for methadone maintenance treatment of opiate abusers are heavily circumscribed for the same reasons.
>
> (SNIPH, p. 24)

Once again we can see the importance given to getting the message across that society does not accept narcotics.

In spite of this a needle exchange programme was started in southern Sweden in the 1980s, and is currently in operation in both Malmö (Sweden's third largest city) and Lund (a nearby university town). It was established to see if it could prevent what many believed to be a rapidly approaching HIV/AIDS epidemic. Researcher Dolf Tops (p. 19) summarizes the results of several evaluations: 'Sufficient scientific evidence of positive effects on transmission of contagion have not been shown: the same can be said for any negative effects of the programme.' Since the HIV/AIDS epidemic did not materialize anywhere in the country, needle exchange is not needed for the purpose for which it was created. Logically it should be terminated, unless it serves some other purpose; in which case more such programmes should be started. However, Sweden has done neither; presumably because any change would start a new debate.

Methadone Maintenance

Currently there are three methadone maintenance programmes in Sweden. All of them are high-threshold and the total number of patients is restricted (currently to 600). To qualify to receive methadone a person must:

- be at least 20 years of age;
- have used opiates intravenously for at least four years;

- have failed to remain free of opiates after at least three attempts at drug-free treatment;
- test positively for opiates and have abstinence symptoms during detoxification, upon entering the programme;
- have medical records showing no significant multiple substance abuse;
- be in an acceptable free-choice situation, i.e. not arrested, sentenced to prison, etc.

Attempts have been made to evaluate methadone programmes in a scientifically acceptable manner. A well-known study by Grönbladh et al. (pp. 225ff) found the death rate among methadone patients to be 1.4 per cent as compared to 7.2 per cent in the control group. And an evaluation by the National Board of Health and Welfare where a sample of 205 methadone patients were interviewed found that 'a majority of both male and female patients reported distinct improvements with regard to housing, employment/educational activity, social relations, health, family relations and use of alcohol and narcotic drugs. Thirty-eight per cent of the patients showed a significant improvement in six out of the above seven areas' (Socialstyrelsen, 1997, p. II [p. 96]). A register study found that the number of hospital admissions declined markedly, as did arrests and indictments. No such improvement occurred in the comparison group, which also had a higher mortality rate (ibid.).

But methadone doesn't work for everybody. A register study based on 655 individuals who had been in methadone treatment found that 39 per cent had been prematurely discharged and not returned, 7 per cent had been prematurely discharged but returned later, and almost 6 per cent died while in the programme (ibid., p. I [p. 95]). Men with a serious criminal background, and who are under 30 when they enter the methadone programme, have the worst prognosis (ibid., p. III [p. 97]). This is compatible with my career model, and fits the pattern in my discussion of spontaneous remission (see p. 58f).

PROBLEMS WITH SWEDISH POLICY

Repression within the Framework of Care and Treatment

Not only is there no scientific proof that residential care in Sweden has been particularly successful in rehabilitating its clients, a number of reports have shown that this 'humanitarian counterbalance' to restrictive control policies has often been repressive in its own right. Due to lack of space I cannot present a thorough review of all the reports,[6] but I will use Hassela as an

[6] I furnish a more thorough account in Goldberg, 1993, pp. 303–37.

example. I choose this movement because it has been extremely important in shaping current Swedish narcotics policy. Both of the founders of Hassela have played significant roles: K. A. Westerberg became an ideological mentor for a host of treatment centres and social workers, and Ove Rosengren became the head of RNS which for well over two decades has been a major lobbyist for restrictive control policies. Widar Andersson, former head of the first Hassela treatment centre, was a Social Democratic MP, and in the late 1990s served as the prime minister's adviser on narcotics policy. And Torgny Petersson, long time director of the Hassela movement, is employed by ECAD and has represented Sweden at a large number of international meetings and conferences. It is therefore important to examine the kind of treatment offered by this movement.

A number of former Hassela clients (Hassela calls them pupils) have contacted social worker Kristian Tilander and allowed themselves to be interviewed. Tilander has also interviewed former personnel and a psychotherapist who has treated some of the people who have been in the Hassela programme. I will summarize their criticisms of Hassela by classifying them into four types of abuse.

However, first a few words of caution. It is important to emphasize that Hassela is not alone in having used these methods. Secondly, not all former Hassela pupils would agree with the criticisms presented; some feel they have been helped there. What follows is not an attempt to scientifically evaluate Hassela. I am merely systematizing what some clients report that they have been subjected to. The pages in parentheses refer to Tilander.

Physical Abuse

Swedish law forbids corporal punishment in the raising of children. In spite of this law, and the fact that Hassela works with adolescents, and that they claim that their method should be considered upbringing rather than therapy, corporal punishment is used. Pupils can be hit (p. 460), smacked across the face (p. 460), punched (p. 462), knocked down (p. 461), thrown against the wall (p. 461), have their hair cut off (p. 359), choked (p. 362), have their heads banged against the floor (p. 176), etc. As one former employee put it:

> The atmosphere was brutal, especially during group confrontations. Particularly older pupils and students doing their fieldwork placement were encouraged to scream at and humiliate new pupils. The brutality was also physical. Those who got tired – i.e. during sports activities – were shoved roughly. If you didn't want to get out of bed, you were dragged out. The personnel were taught to be strong, distinct and authoritarian. Sometimes this led to violence. (p. 232)

When criticism of the physical abuse was brought up for discussion, the headmaster replied: 'It's better that they get hit here, than go down to Stockholm and take drugs' (p. 234). Once again we see an example of either/or thinking. The choices are reduced to two, and one's own negative behaviour is justified by presenting something even worse as the sole alternative.

Psychological Abuse

Psychological abuse at Hassela takes many different forms, but the message is clear. Pupils are neither permitted to have a will or ideas of their own, nor to believe that they are of any value as human beings. Some of the methods of achieving this are:

1. *Avoid dialogue*

Most often the personnel did not see any reason to explain why they acted in a particular manner. That the adolescent's 'addict identities' were to be eradicated was the explanation for everything (p. 110). Youths were taught to 'take punishment and be thankful' (p. 115). That pupils would allow themselves 'to be attacked, accused, humiliated, stepped on, subjected to manifestations of power, etc., while remaining silent and not questioning anything, went without saying. He is the leader and he has power' (p. 115).

> Right from the start ... I noticed that he was different from the others. ... He could tease you but in a humorous way, human. You never felt that he saw you as a lower form of life. You never felt humiliated by him. He never put me down and I think the others felt the same way as he's the only one we're still in contact with. He was the only one you could talk to. Every now and then there were a couple of minutes when you could sit with him and tell him a little about how you were feeling. Actually there was no place for this, but the little space he made pretty much saved the day. You felt that he was a 'possible' adult. (p. 121)

2. *Psychological isolation*

Pupils quickly learned that they could gain favours for themselves by reporting others. As every pupil understood that at any moment anyone might turn you in, it became a matter of survival not to let anybody get close to you. As one pupil put it: 'You couldn't trust a soul. You were soon suspicious of everybody' (p. 394).

A former employee related: 'the "smart" pupils quickly learned that the best way to defend yourself was to place yourself on the side of the personnel'. She adds: 'Close relationships between pupils were not accepted. ... All forms of intimacy between pupils was seen as a threat by the leaders and was attacked ferociously' (p. 232). In the words of one of the pupils: 'We didn't dare to talk to each other after a while. We didn't dare to talk even when we were alone. ... That was the climate of the place' (p. 107).

A pupil describes a survival strategy: 'If I attack E [another pupil], I know I won't catch any flak for the rest of the day' (p. 145).

3. *Might makes right*

As the personnel have all the power, their interpretation of any given situation is automatically true. A refugee from a South American dictatorship, who did his field placement at Hassela, commented: '[The personnel] were always right, even when they weren't. Pupils were always in the wrong. Given my background it is not surprising that I associated this with prisons and all that goes with them. The military junta always think they're right because they're in power. They know what's best for everybody. Nobody else knows anything' (p. 289).

4. *Collective punishment*

One method of getting a pupil to do something was to threaten that others would be punished if he doesn't do as he is told. For instance a girl with a punk hairdo was told that if she didn't get her hair cut, another pupil would be punished (p. 155).

By threatening collective punishment, the personnel prevent pupils from expressing their needs. For example; 'we had decided to go to a discotheque. But suddenly something happened. Charlie looks really depressed. Maybe he's going to freak out. ... It may sound crazy, but they didn't let any of us go to the discotheque' (p. 305).

5. *Labelling*

A recurrent theme in the messages given to pupils is that they are worthless.

'Much of what we were told was that we were good-for-nothing, and that we were fucking junkies who didn't have any rights. We weren't worth a damn' (p. 177).

'When you're sitting in a room and maybe 15 people are staring at you and shouting that you're worthless and trying to break you down, you can't take it for very long. You agree to anything they say, just to get out of there' (p. 182).

'Then they told me "we're going to sit here until you go in there". So we went in and they stayed with me until I saw the doctor. It was a late abortion. I didn't get to talk to a social worker. They told me it wasn't necessary. ... I had an abortion and I regret it terribly. They forced me to do it' (pp. 373ff). 'A girl who had had an abortion was called a murderer and things like that. They called her a fucking murderer' (p. 464).

A person who did his fieldwork placement at Hassela relates: 'You have to get behind their [the pupil's] masks. ... Not by motivating them but by being tough and saying things like "shut up you little shit, you've never done anything worthwhile" ' (p. 290).

6. *Double-bind*

The principle behind the double-bind at Hassela is to say one thing but mean another, the result being that pupils learn that they can't trust the spoken word.

> They say that they want us to be honest, they really do, and when you're honest they can't take it because it doesn't fit in with their way of thinking. ... Instead of using the honesty you show them for something good, they punish you. When you tell them what's on your mind, if you confide in them, they tell you you're a fucking drug whore. Instead of working with what you give them, bang, they hit you over the head and turn the whole group against you. (p. 380f)

Another example occurred in connection with the highly touted requirement that all pupils at Hassela must be able to dance without being under the influence of alcohol:

> so the girls dress up. Look really good when they go out. The female staff members maybe haven't been asked to dance as much as they had hoped, and they haven't had a good time. But we've been dancing. Then the female personnel blow up at us and tells us we've been 'playing sexual games'. 'You fucking whore, where do you come off with those sexual games, and that kind of stuff.' But if the girls haven't been dancing they're called 'fucking cop-outs'. (p. 303)

7. *Sexism*

'The girls can be told that they are drug whores, that they have "fucked for their drugs" and "look at your clothes, you look like a whore" and "where did you get that jewelry, who did you pussy them off" and "you walked the streets for them". They talked like this all the time' (p. 462).

'The group sat there for a whole day, as I remember it, until they got me to say that I had had sex with R. We have a sexual relationship. That's right, I've decided to become the wife of the inspector. It was my only way out. I wouldn't have survived otherwise, they were using advanced mental torture' (p. 463).

Sexual Abuse

As we can see from the above quotes, one of the methods of psychological abuse was to make negative allusions to the girls' sexual behaviour. This can be interpreted as a form of sexual abuse. Sometimes the sexual abuse was not merely verbal.

> T was a girl who had been a prostitute before coming to Hassela. He started pawing her. He said things like 'show me what you can do'. He was really revolting. I think it was awful. Then he was put in charge of his own treatment centre. It's really disgusting. (p. 161)

> For instance when we were on an overnight hike in the mountains we came to a cabin with a shower and sauna, and everything was obligatory. Everybody had to take a sauna, both sexes at the same time. And if a

> guy went in wearing a towel they made him a laughing-stock. Teased him. And suddenly while all of us were sitting in there the headmaster came in and took pictures in the sauna.
>
> Then when I was naked in the shower he came in and took a picture. Afterwards several of the girls were really upset and I told him I wanted the negative. He said: 'what negative?' Later on he told me I overrated my breasts. (p. 399)

This is the way teenage girls, many of whom most likely have been subjected to sexual abuse in childhood, and all of whom have degrading sexual experiences as adolescents, are treated by those who claim to be acting as parents and teaching the girls how respectable members of society behave.

Legal Abuse

Laws and legal precedents were broken at Hassela. The handling of mail sent to and from pupils provides an example. A teenager describes how the personnel 'wrote down the addresses of those we wrote to and who wrote to us. Then they checked up on the people before sending the letters' (p. 170).

Another pupil relates: 'They read our letters. ... Some letters were never given to us. I saw how the personnel kept the mail they didn't want us to have' (p. 170).

Still another pupil explained: 'I was given the letters, but they opened them and read them before letting me have them' (p. 331). In some cases private letters were read aloud in front of all the pupils (p. 365).

According to the Parliamentary Ombudsman (JO, 1989/90, p. 266), personnel are not permitted to censor letters sent from someone committed to an institution. Letters sent to the individual may be inspected if they are suspected of containing drugs or something else which is not permitted. A separate decision to open mail must be made for each and every letter. *It is neither necessary nor permissible to read the letters*. Letters should always be opened in the presence of the person they are addressed to, and preferably in the presence of a witness (my italics).

Another example of legal abuse is encroachments of the Secrecy Act. 'They give our names and pictures to strangers. ... They use our pictures when they give talks. We don't know how long they'll be using our pictures. They never asked us for permission to use our faces' (p. 171).

The following incident was described by a pupil. I can't say whether or not it is against the law as it hasn't been tried in court, but at the very least it is an encroachment of personal integrity. 'I kept a diary ... until they found it. ... Then the shit really hit the fan ... Afterwards I asked myself what business they had looking in my diary?' (p. 116). The pupil herself gives a pretty good answer to her own question: 'It was one of the few safety valves I had so they shut it' (p. 116f).

Hassela's official goal is to rehabilitate their pupils and help them get off drugs. But from the statements of these pupils we can observe other goals, the operative goals. One of these is to close off all safety valves as a means of eliminating all opposition. The personnel's power to make all decisions must not be threatened. When something stands in their way, the staff have shown themselves ready and able to put themselves above the law, with the motivation that what they are doing is in the best interests of the pupils. In other words they attempt to disguise the abuse of power by calling it altruism.

How far the personnel are capable of going can be seen in still another situation. A teenager who had been sent to Hassela on a court order asked her attorney to appeal the case. The courts did in fact change the decision and the lawyer called Hassela to tell her she was free to leave whenever she wished. The personnel didn't tell her of the call (p. 355). Only the police may detain a person against his will in Sweden. However, I can't say if this should be classified as a criminal offence as it was never brought to trial.

How Did Hassela Respond?

I shall briefly describe two ways well-known people associated with the Hassela movement reacted to the criticisms put forth in Tilander's book.

Gunnar Bergström (p. 24), one of the leaders of the Örträsk treatment centre, writes:

> Although none of our pupils were interviewed by Tilander I must admit that some of the accounts could have come from us.
> Tilander's book ... contains accurate observations about our treatment centres. They aren't automatically invalid simply because they are expressed by someone who is critical of us. (Ibid.)

> There are two reasons for us to be self-critical. The first concerns infringements of the rights of our pupils. I saw this happen at other treatment centres, and similar things happened at Örträsk during the early years. In our ambition to save lives we went overboard. As time passed and our personnel became more competent and mature this kind of abuse, which cannot be defended regardless of what methods one believes in, ceased. (Ibid.)

> ... I, and many others as well, have met many former pupils who told us of their feelings of humiliation and restlessness at the treatment centres. My impression is that it was the girls who were most frequently humiliated. (Ibid.)

> ... our treatment centre was built on shame. (Ibid.)

> We must find a way for coercive treatment to function while treating pupils with respect and dignity. (Ibid., p. 25)

Even K. A. Westerberg and Widar Andersson seem to admit that at least some of the criticisms are justified (but they appear to be more interested in attacking their critics' personalities and motives, than using the criticisms as a basis for changing their methods). They write:

> Our critics ... have put themselves on the side of 'good' and Hassela on the side of 'evil'. *It's easy to be 'good' when you've chosen to place yourself on the outside, not having to assume power; chosen not to 'get your hands dirty' with the daily responsibility, the compromises and the decision making.*
> (Westerberg and Andersson, p. A4) (their italics)

To claim that Tilander has 'placed himself on the outside' is misleading; he has been a social worker for many years. Yet there is a point worth noting in Westerberg and Andersson's comment. If you go to a football match it seems there are always people in the stands who know how to play the game better than those on the field. The truth of the matter is, it's not easy to work with problematic consumers of narcotics. But this fact does not give anyone permission to infringe the rights of others. We need an open discussion of both the methods used and the ethical limits for personnel at treatment centres. The criticism put forth in Tilander's book can be a good point of departure.

Threats to Constitutional Safeguards

Aside from the illegalities and questionable methods described in the examples above, there are several direct threats to basic civil liberties which can be put in conjunction with Sweden's restrictive control policies, and which must be added to the list of secondary harm.

Wire-tapping, in certain circumstances, is legal in Sweden. If the police have reasonable suspicion against an individual a court can grant permission to tap his phone. But what the public is unaware of is that even public phones can be tapped. For instance if a suspected drug dealer is thought to be using a public phone to promote illegal activities, the police can get permission to tap it. Everyone using it, whether they are suspected of crime or not, will have their conversations recorded. And if the police should thereby become party to information which can be used in another case, it will be admitted as evidence by the courts.

Bugging goes even further and involves the placement of hidden microphones so that everybody in the vicinity (whether they are suspected of wrongdoing or not) will have their conversations clandestinely recorded. Bugging is illegal in Sweden, but since the 1970s there have been recurrent demands to legalize it as some believe it to be an important tool in fighting crime, especially narcotics. The Social Democratic Party has traditionally been against bugging. In the late 1980s Attorney-General Laila Freiwalds wrote to the Parliament that she agreed with the Narcotics Commission when they state:

> In an open society there must be a limit to the means of coercion which can be accepted. It would be a great loss if society were to broaden its tolerance for the use of force. A feeling – even if it is unwarranted – that one may at any time be overheard may spread among the populace. The commission is of the opinion that the positive effects of bugging ... do not compensate for the negative consequences.
>
> (Regeringens proposition, 1988/89:124, p. 38f)

Former assistant to the Attorney-General, Sten Heckscher agrees:

> Bugging is a very serious violation of personal integrity, and this disadvantage outweighs the advantages. Protecting personal integrity must have its price, in the form that some who are guilty will go free. Another disadvantage is that experience shows that drug problems have not diminished significantly in countries which make use of bugging.
>
> (Schüllerqvist, p. 12)

However, the Social Democratic government which came into power in 1994 appointed a committee to see if bugging is sufficiently effective to motivate allowing it, in spite of the threat to personal integrity. And in 1997 both the Liberal Party and the Conservative Party voted during their national conventions to accept bugging under certain conditions (Karlsson, p. A10).

The committee was also instructed to 'investigate the possibilities of expanding the areas of application for clandestine camera surveillance, wire-tapping and secret telephone surveillance' (Kommittédirektiv, p. 1). The road for new legislation is already paved, as from 1996 all larger companies producing telephone systems to be sold in Sweden must include built-in methods for telephone surveillance in their products.

In 1998 the committee recommended that bugging be allowed (SOU, 1998:46, p. 343). Presumably a law permitting bugging and other extraordinary forms of police surveillance will be passed in 1999.

A basic constitutional right in all democracies is that those who are indicted for crimes are entitled to a fair trial. This implies that the accused is assumed innocent until sufficient proof is presented to remove all reasonable doubt of his guilt. A well-known Swedish criminal lawyer, Peter Althin, states: 'The level of evidence deemed sufficient for a conviction in narcotics cases is low. It is so low that in some cases the accused must prove his innocence. And there is a risk that the low level of evidence will start to be applied in other types of cases' (see Fälth, p. 7). Professor of Law Ulla Jacobsson gives an example: a man was convicted of aggravated drug offences, in both the lower and appeals court, on the basis of evidence given by one informer. The informer had not witnessed under oath and was himself involved in the same drug offences as the accused (ibid.).

In other words, the precedents being established in narcotics cases deviate in a repressive direction from previous legal procedure. This in itself is bad enough, but if these precedents are applied to non-narcotics cases, the constitutional safeguards of all citizens are in danger.

In another case a man was convicted on narcotics charges principally on statements made to the police by a person who later refused to repeat what she said in court (and therefore could not be cross-examined) and on evidence which may have been gleaned by illegal bugging. In short the police had been tapping the woman's phone. When the man came to her apartment she took the phone off the hook and the wiretapping apparatus turned itself on. It was now functioning as a hidden microphone. The evidence so gleaned was accepted in both the lower and appeals court, even though the defendant's attorney claimed it was obtained by illegal bugging. In an official statement to the legal authorities, the National Swedish Police Board (RPS) declared that 'this method of collecting evidence been used by the police for decades and no objections have [heretofore] been raised' (Heckscher and Groth, p. 2).

This case raises a number of important legal questions, such as:

- What exactly is bugging?
- What is admissible evidence?
- By destroying tapes they consider irrelevant, are the police denying the accused access to material which might weaken the prosecution's case?
- What constitutes a fair trial?
- What is the significance of Article 8 of the European Convention which grants the right of privacy to all citizens?

Based on these questions an appeal was filed in the Swedish Supreme Court; which refused to hear the case. It is currently under appeal in the EU courts.

In this particular case the phone was taken off the hook by its owner. However, if we return to the statement from the National Swedish Police Board above I find it bewildering that drug dealers have been willing to aid the police for decades by voluntarily putting themselves into a situation where their residence can be bugged. Criminal lawyer Ola Salomonsson, who has defended many of these clients, has told me that he believes that in many instances it is the police themselves who have taken the phones off the hook. If this is the case the police are clearly guilty of breaking and entering, but would they also be guilty of bugging? Is the evidence so gathered admissible in court? And what if the police go into a restaurant and take a wiretapped public phone off the hook?

Another threat to fundamental legal safeguards concerns searches. In Swedish law every citizen is protected against infringements of their integrity, i.e. body searches, and searches of their homes without a warrant. However, a police district established a street-level group 'to do something about the increasing criminality in the district through active preventative measures. Narcotics was to receive special attention' (JO, 1992, p. 14). In practice this meant that the police classified some private apartments as 'hangouts' on the basis of their knowledge of the people renting them. Having done this, the authorities felt that they could search both the apartments and the people in them without a warrant, whenever officers felt they could gather evidence about some (undetermined) crime. The Parliamentary Ombudsman (JO) has declared that these police activities are illegal (ibid., p. 21).

In the cases where wiretapped phones have been taken off the hook, there are grounds for suspicion that the police have been illegally breaking and entering people's homes for decades in order to gain evidence through illegal bugging. In permitting searches without a warrant there can be no doubt that those responsible for an entire police district have accepted that officers of the law blatantly and repeatedly violate constitutional rights. How is this possible? One conceivable answer is that every profession has a number of rotten apples. However, I don't believe the matter should be individualized in this way. Instead I would argue that all government agencies, including the police and the courts, are sensitive to attitudes and social currents in society. In the climate in Sweden, where some political parties try to win votes by calling for 'law and order' and all parties try to outdo each other on who is toughest on drugs, the authorities are under great pressure to show results. As the demand that something be done about narcotics increases, so does the temptation to cut corners. This enhances the risk of repressive and even illegal measures. The war on drugs in general, and restrictive narcotics control policies in particular, are important factors determining the climate in which government agencies work.

The official goal is to rid the country of narcotics. The methods being used, such as granting exceptional powers to the police, censorship, putting oneself above the law, lowering the level of proof needed for conviction, demanding that people prove their innocence, etc., undermine constitutional safeguards. The frightening thought arises that making society more totalitarian may be the operative goal of some of those demanding ever increasing repressive measures in the name of combating narcotics. For those who do not have this aim, it is important that they be aware of the serious threat to vital democratic principles posed by the war on drugs in its current guise.

Secondary Harm – Summary

The secondary harm in conjunction with prohibition as it is practiced in Sweden is extensive. The following points should be added to the list presented in the previous chapter:

- In their eagerness to put a stop to drugs some social workers, school and recreation centre personnel, policemen, staff at residential treatment centres, etc. have shown themselves willing to be manipulative, untruthful, use coercion and even violate the law.
- By concentrating our attention on individuals who conduct themselves in undesirable ways, the environments which shaped these people remain intact and produce a never ending stream of new offenders.
- People remitted for treatment have been subjected to physical, psychological, sexual and legal abuse.
- In our attempts to control narcotics we have shown a willingness to disregard some of the most important principles for a democratic society, such as individual integrity, the right to privacy, and the right to make personal decisions concerning one's own life.
- Fundamental legal safeguards are threatened by measures such as wire-tapping, accepting information illegally gleaned as evidence in court, disregarding the Secrecy Act, illegal searches, etc. Most likely bugging and clandestine camera surveillance will soon be legal.
- Censorship jeopardizes freedom of speech; one of the cornerstones of democratic society. Accepting censorship is a major step on the road to a totalitarian state.
- Another cornerstone of democratic societies, the juridical principle that people are innocent until proven otherwise, has been put into question and curtailed in the name of our need to fight narcotics.
- The level of proof deemed necessary for conviction in narcotics cases has been reduced, thereby threatening the fundamental right of citizens to a fair trial.

In sum, the manner in which the war on drugs has been fought constitutes a threat to democratic values and institutions. In the words of Nils Christie and Kettil Bruun (p. 13): 'One of the most dangerous uses of narcotics is the political.'

13 Harm Reduction – Dutch Narcotics Policy

THE EVOLUTION OF DUTCH DRUG POLICY

As in other western countries, narcotics emerged as a growing problem in the Netherlands during the 1960s. Two committees were appointed to clarify the situation and make policy recommendations.

The Hulsman Report

In 1969 a working group within the state-sponsored Institution for Mental Health was appointed under the chairmanship of Law Professor Loek Hulsman. As the committee did not have an officially recognized political status it had a great degree of latitude.

> The Hulsman Committee warned strongly against putting more than very little reliance on the penal law in controlling drug problems. It predicted that the threat of law enforcement would not only fail to deter people from engaging in vice (victimless crime) in their private life, it would for various reasons also fail to control the supply side of the drug market. When penal law action is considered, so they reasoned, its possible or actual benefits should always be weighed against the costs, both in terms of money and law enforcement capacity, and in terms of the harmful social effects of law enforcement. Among the undesirable side-effects they mentioned the amplification of deviance and marginality of drug scenes; the symbiotic development of vigorous and violent specialized police forces and (organized) drug traffickers as opponents in an escalating war; and the gradual undermining of civil liberties and the legitimacy of penal law. In short,
> ...law enforcement against the world of illegal drugs would be costly, would fail to really control the supply, would make the social and health problems of drug-taking worse than necessary, would reinforce the growth of powerful criminal organizations, and would undermine constitutionality. (Leuw, p. 29f)

The Baan Committee

The second commission, the 'Working Group on Narcotic Substances' (the Baan Committee), was appointed by the government and had official status.

Publishing its report in 1972 it proposed a revised form of the strictly prohibitionist 'Opium Act' with its roots in 1928. The report was accepted almost in its entirety by the centre/conservative coalition government and further developed by the centre/left government which came into power in 1973. However, the proposal for the revised Opium Act was not brought before parliament until 1976.

> The four-year time lapse between the development of the legal proposal and the ultimate passing of the legislation has probably been quite functional; the proposed decriminalization and relaxation of drug control were already introduced in social practice during this period. Consequently, the effects of the proposed law could first be tested in practice even before the official new legislation was to be adapted. This was perfectly consistent with the committee's view that for the proper evolution of drug policy, frameworks for experimentation should be created. These experiments should be carefully evaluated: when sufficient faith in the safety of new positions exists, then the old ones can be left. (Ibid., p. 32)

A major tenet of the Baan Committee was that if society 'stigmatizes deviant behavior by punitive measures, the probability of intensification of this behavior is a serious danger. This will initiate a spiral that will make return of the individual to a socially accepted life style increasingly difficult' (Cohen, 1996b, p. 3).

Both the Hulsman and Baan Committees discussed what should be considered an *unacceptable risk* in conjunction with drugs. As opposed to Sweden, where all non-medical consumption of narcotics is placed in this category, in the Netherlands unacceptable risk is a floating concept and how to define it is the subject of repeated debate. It is interesting to note that while what constitutes unacceptable risk is discussed in official documents, what should be considered acceptable risk is not.

The Revised Opium Act

> In 1976 the proposed revised Opium Act was discussed in parliament. Although formally this was a penal law bill, its primary endorser was the Minister of Public Health, Social Democrat Irene Vorrink ... The Minister of Justice, Christian Democrat Dries van Agt, was the secondary endorser... This order reflects the central notion in Dutch social drug policy that drugs are, first and foremost, a public health and welfare issue, where criminal law and law enforcement is of limited and secondary importance. (Leuw, p. 34)

The Revised Opium Act 'satisfies all demands of the international conventions, stating the punishability of possession, trade, cultivation, importation and exportation and a number of other acts and omissions in relation to narcotic drugs (including cannabis products)' (Silvis, p. 44). However, the Netherlands has two 'schedules' of drugs: schedule 1 (hard drugs) and schedule 2 (soft drugs). Maximum penalties for illegal activities concerning drugs on schedule 1 are much harsher than for the drugs on schedule 2 (ibid., p. 45).

Some of the more important provisions of the Revised Opium Act are:

- Drug addicts should be offered treatment, and not prosecuted.
- Penalties for wholesale international trafficking in hard drugs were greatly increased; the maximum sentence is 12 years' imprisonment, and multiple convictions can lead to 16 years' incarceration. Officially this was to 'balance' the bill showing that the Netherlands was taking measures against supply as well as demand. However, some researchers argue that this provision was a concession to international opinion. 'The legislature feared negative international economic consequences, especially from its neighbor Germany, a country of extreme economic importance to the Netherlands. It was partly because of [*sic*] this reason that the revised legislation introduced a substantial increase of the maximum sentences for (inter)national trafficking in hard drugs; there should be absolutely no question that the Netherlands would be backing out of its international obligations' (Blom and van Mastrigt, p. 257).
- The possession of cannabis is defined as a minor misdemeanour, while drug dealing is a felony. However, cannabis was given a pseudo-legal status, allowing for possession of 30 grams for personal use. This was considered enough for two weeks' consumption and for sharing with friends. In effect the provision also protected small-scale dealers from prosecution and paved the way for coffee shops.
- The *house dealer* is 'a person who is permitted by the staff and the board of a recreational or educational youth center to sell limited quantities of cannabis to the members and visitors of such a youth center' (Leuw, p. 36). House dealers were seen as a way of separating drug markets and drug cultures, thereby lowering the risk that hard drugs would be diffused to vulnerable groups of adolescents.
- Ban on advertising: promoting the sale of illegal substances is not permitted.

After a long debate in parliament the Revised Opium Act was passed into law by a vote of almost three to one. How was this possible? While I can't give a complete explanation, one important factor was that even before narcotics became an issue the Dutch had decided to try to keep lawbreakers out of prison as much as possible. So when the Hulsman and Baan Commissions presented the idea that the role of criminal law should be diminished, they were applying a principle which had been previously established and accepted in relation to other forms of illegal behaviour, to narcotics (see Cohen, 1996b, p. 4f).

Another important factor was that the issue had not been heavily politicized. Comparing the two countries, Scheerer concludes:

> In Germany, the political parties, the police and the medical profession used the drug issue to further their own institutional objectives by a process of problem amplification. A contrary process of de-escalating the significance of the drug problem ... occurred in the Netherlands. The Social Democrats were allowed to realize their 'liberal' interests in moral issues because their Christian Democratic partners in the coalition cabinet did not choose to use the drugs issue 'as a self-serving socio-political symbol'. (Leuw, p. 39)

Kraan (p. 299) offers another explanation. He believes that socially conservative politicians who in principle might have preferred a more prohibitionist approach may have refrained from advocating it either because they have been convinced of its non-feasibility or they view it as an unacceptable burden on state finances.

Whatever the reasons, the Dutch managed to create a situation where 'there are no votes to be won or positions to be conquered by rallying on the anti-drug theme' (Leuw, p. 39).

AHOJ-G Regulations

In 1991, as a result of a number of problems in conjunction with coffee shops, the State Attorney put into effect the 'AHOJ-G' regulations which prohibit coffee shops from:

- advertising the sale of soft drugs
- selling hard drugs
- causing a nuisance
- selling drugs to minors
- trading in large quantities.

Municipalities have the power to take action against managers who break these regulations, and are also permitted to formulate further policies to control the coffee shops (Bieleman et al., p. 1). Local authorities have the power not to permit any coffee shops at all in areas under their jurisdiction; which in fact some have done.

Dutch Government Memorandum on Drug Policy

In 1995 the Dutch government published a memorandum on drug policy. The central aim of Dutch policy is still 'the *prevention* and *reduction of harm* caused by drugs by reducing the dangers of their use both to the community and to the individual' (Maris, p. 81) (emphasis in original). One of its major objectives is to present a flexible response to rapidly changing social and cultural developments at home and abroad.

The memorandum discusses a number of changes in regard to coffee shops:

- no coffee shops are to be permitted near schools;
- one-arm bandits are banned from the premises;
- the maximum quantity of soft drugs which can be purchased for personal consumption was reduced from 30 to 5 grams;
- bona fide coffee shops with a stock of a few hundred grams will not be investigated;
- alcohol may not be sold.[1]

The memorandum envisions a model where home-grown cannabis, cultivated by small-scale Dutch licensed growers would be transported under government supervision to bona fide coffee shops for distribution (ibid.). Ideally the government would like to replace current legal sanctions against soft drugs by types of control similar to those on alcohol. But as the international situation makes this impossible the government opted to continue its 'pragmatic' course (ibid., p. 82).

In regard to hard drugs:

> addicted users are viewed as patients requiring treatment rather than criminals to be punished.... The proposals for prevention and care are extremely abstract. In the case of addicts there is talk of programmes of 'personally customized care' geared both to the individual and to the group, 'with attention being paid to every area where help may be needed – for instance housing and social skills'.... Addicts who are convicted of crimes can choose between a prison term and voluntary treatment in an open or closed institution. (Ibid., p. 84)

However, at the same time the memorandum opens the possibility of treatment under coercion.

> It will also be possible to impose a legal restraint on addicts, forcing them to undergo a maximum of 2 years treatment on being found guilty of a series of minor crimes amounting to great harm being done to others. Because such offenses are mainly committed by a comparatively small and easily identified group of 5000 extremely antisocial criminal addicts, the government hopes to book a quick success with this policy. (Ibid.)

[1] This rule isn't uniformly applied. In Rotterdam it has been used to close down most of the coffee shops. By demanding that no alcohol be sold before granting a licence to sell cannabis, most coffee shops became bars as the owners had borrowed money from breweries and were obligated by contract to continue selling alcohol. In this manner the number of coffee shops was reduced from over 300 to 52 in a short time. In Amsterdam alcohol and cannabis are still being sold in the same establishments which are sometimes called hash cafés, to differentiate them from coffee shops which only sell cannabis.

Compared to the 1970s this can be interpreted as a shift in the balance of power on drug issues between the Ministries of Justice and Health; apparently the former is gaining influence. Another example of this change is that *public order* is becoming an increasingly important concept in the Netherlands, and greater emphasis is being placed on counteracting drug-related nuisance.

Furthermore the memorandum calls for measures to deal with criminal trafficking in drugs, i.e. a nationwide criminal investigation team and improving international cooperation.

THEORETICAL FOUNDATIONS

The theoretical foundations of Dutch narcotics policy differ from prohibition on almost every major point. Prohibitionist thought is based on a biochemical understanding of drug consumption; people are seen as objects in relation to narcotics. The basic assumption behind harm reduction is that drug consumers are subjects. Dutch policy,

> painstakingly balances between the reciprocal notions of freedom and responsibility. This involves, on the one hand, the personal freedom of the individual (i.e. the right to self-determination) to use drugs and even to be addicted, on the other hand, it involves the personal responsibility of drug users for their own (mental) health and their own social behavior (criminality included). (Leuw and Marshall, p. xiii)

While prohibitionists see narcotics as a problem with basically unlimited growth potential, capable of smiting anyone and everyone, and which therefore must be totally eliminated, the official view in the Netherlands is that problematic consumption is a 'limited and manageable social and (public) health problem of modern society' (ibid., p. xv). Drug policy is based on 'combating large-scale drug trafficking (through law enforcement) and prevention and assistance to the drug user (through public health)' (ibid., p. xviii). While the US emphasizes criminal justice, in the Netherlands the primary focus is on public health. Officially Swedish narcotics policy is based equally on both, letting them balance each other. However, as we have already seen this has not been realized in practice.

In the Netherlands drugs in themselves are not seen as an urgent problem. Drug policy is expressed in terms which avoid fear arousal and/or moral appeals. For instance:

1. Instead of claiming that 'soft drugs' (i.e. hashish and marihuana) are the gateway to hard drugs (and in the long run annihilation), cannabis is seen as 'just another stimulant' comparable to alcohol (Jansen, p. 169).

2. 'Reduction of drug consumption is not a policy objective *per se*. Consequently, there is no official policy with respect to non-problematic drug consumption' (Kraan, p. 299).
3. Repression on the demand side is generally considered to 'only add to the damage that drug addiction will do to users and the general society alike' (Kaplan and Leuw, p. 80).
4. There is no drug testing in the workplace and there are no fear inducing information campaigns (Marshall and Marshall, p. 228).

In sum, the Netherlands is attempting to shift to different goals; to reduce problematic consumption and to reduce harm. 'The Dutch strategy, built on post-material value orientation, involves a process of incorporation rather than alienation of the social groups linked to drug-related problems' (Kaplan et al., p. 321).

As opposed to Sweden, where policy makers, on the basis of an analysis of 'the drug problem', created a programme which they felt would deal with it, 'Dutch drug policy is not solely the result of a preconceived policy goal, rather it reflects the process of "muddling through", a process of trial and error' (Jansen, p. 180).

Some Dutch researchers argue that international drug treaties are stifling; every country must make its own innovations; adapting its drug policies to local conditions (Cohen, 1993, p. 3). American social psychologist Donald T. Campbell (p. 291) uses the concept *the experimenting society* to denote a country 'that would vigorously try out possible solutions to recurrent problems and would make hard headed, multidimensional evaluations of outcomes, and when the evaluation of one reform showed it to have been ineffective or harmful, would move on to other alternatives'. 'To learn about the manipulation of relationships one must try out manipulation. The scientific, problem-solving, self-healing society must be an experimenting society' (ibid., p. 301). Kaplan et al. (p. 323) state: 'The apparent uniqueness of the Dutch drug policy is largely the outcome of applying the principles of the experimenting society to drug problems.' It is a matter of trying to find 'the right balance between prohibition and legalization, between a "drug free" and a "free drug" society' (ibid., p. 332).

CENTRAL CONCEPTS IN DUTCH NARCOTICS POLICY

Normalization

'The concept of normalization entails a gradual process of controlled integration of the drug phenomenon into society.... Current drug policy is explicitly aimed towards trying to remove the exciting, the dramatic, and the deviant images of drug use and users' (Marshall and Marshall, p. 207). 'Normalization does not imply condoning drug use; indeed, drug use should be discouraged, but preferably through measures other than the criminalization of the user. Normalization represents some type of compromise between decriminalization and legalization on the one hand, and a repressive "war on drugs" on the other' (ibid., p. 208).

By using the concept normalization the Dutch indicate that narcotics:

> should be viewed as a 'normal' problem, one of the several health and social problems a society faces and tries to control. Moreover and importantly, criminalization of the consumer is considered a harmful way of discouraging the use of hard drugs. Consequently, the normalization process requires de-stigmatization of drug users. (Wever, p. 64)

Engelsman states that normalization implies that:

- drugs shouldn't be considered as a too specific social issue (Engelsman, p. 215);
- drug use should be shorn of sensational and emotional overtones and be made more amenable to an open discussion (ibid.);
- drug takers or even addicts should neither be seen as criminals nor as dependent patients, but as normal citizens of whom we make normal demands and to whom we offer normal opportunities. Addicts should not be treated as a special category (ibid.);
- primary attention is not given to ending addiction as such but to improve addicts' physical and social well-being and to help them function in society (ibid., p. 216);
- the addict is seen more as resembling an unemployed Dutch citizen than a monster endangering society (ibid., p. 217).

Normalization is central in the Dutch attempts to create what they call a *pragmatic drug policy*, 'which involves managing the risks of psychotropic substance use in society, rather than getting involved in futile attempts at its complete elimination' (Wever, p. 64).

Harm Reduction

While the principal goal of the war on drugs is to prevent all consumption of psychoactive drugs, the major objective of Dutch drug policy is to minimize problems with use. The emphasis is placed on individuals making well-informed choices. In harm reduction, as opposed to prohibition,

> it is not implied that the *only* right choice is *never to try illegal drugs*; education programs allow for the fact that some people will make the choice to use particular drugs. Prevention programs aim to provide the

> (potential) user with clear and useful information that allows the person to use or experiment (if he/she chooses to do so) with drugs in a manner that minimizes the risks to themselves and their environment.
> (Marshall and Marshall, p. 209) (emphasis in original)

In the Netherlands it is accepted that total abstention may not be a realistic goal for problematic consumers, who are seen as suffering from a chronic disease. Reducing consumption to a level where these individuals can survive and live a reasonable life is considered an acceptable aim for drug policy.

Decriminalization

'Decriminalization means that drugs remain illegal, but that the *use* of drugs, and to a certain degree possession of drugs are not prosecuted as a criminal offense' (Grapendaal et al., p. 235).

> The police and the Public Prosecutor's Office are explicitly instructed not to act against possession of hard drugs for personal use. This means that only those Dutch addicts who are involved with dealing and/or trafficking are caught up in the criminal justice system (not counting drug-related property crimes, of course). (Ibid., p. 235f)

The Expediency Principle

The expediency principle has its roots in one of the basic foundations of Dutch criminal procedure; empowering the Public Prosecutor's Office to refrain from initiating criminal proceedings if it is in the public interest. To prevent each public prosecutor from creating his own policy, guidelines were issued by the Public Prosecutions Department (Horstink-Von Meyenfeldt, p. 97).

> These guidelines are interpreted at a local level in the different judiciary districts of the country through a process of 'triangular consultation' (i.e. consultation between the Public Prosecutor, the Mayor, and the Chief of Police). This decentralized approach results in a variable prosecution policy, ranging from rather strict to lenient. (Jansen, p. 170)

Soft Drugs – Hard Drugs

In many countries all drugs classified as narcotics in international conventions are treated in the same manner; but not in the Netherlands. The Baan Commission was aware of the fact that all drugs are potentially dangerous, but argued that some involve less hazards than others and therefore should be treated differently. It proposed the criterion *socially acceptable risks* as the basis for placing drugs in different categories. However, this concept has never been officially defined. Instead it was merely stated that the dangers of using *soft drugs*, such as hashish and marihuana, were socially acceptable, while *hard drugs* such as heroin, amphetamine, cocaine and LSD expose users to unacceptable risks and therefore must be subjected to greater regulation.

Separation of Drug Markets

To minimize the social deviance caused by illegal drug consumption, the soft drug market had to be spatially separated from the hard drug market. The basic assumption is that consumers of soft drugs would no longer come into contact with hard drugs and thereby not be tempted to take them. The separation of drug markets was achieved by allowing the establishment of outlets, i.e. *coffee shops* and *house dealers*, where small quantities of hashish and marihuana for personal consumption can be bought and sold without risking prosecution. 'This policy is reflected in the *de facto* decriminalization of trading and possessing small quantities of marihuana' (Marshall and Marshall, p. 210).

DUTCH NARCOTICS POLICY IN PRACTICE

The Law in Practice

The Expediency Principle and Triangular Consultation
Silvis makes a distinction between *law-on-the-books* and *law-in-action*.

> Possession of marihuana and hashish is forbidden, but in virtually every town one can find coffee shops where consumers openly buy their illegal products without fearing interference from the police. Also, in the big cities one can easily spot the places where heroin and cocaine are sold, although this takes place in a more tense atmosphere. Here the police may suddenly show up and make arrests. (Silvis, p. 43)

> Contrary to the principle of legality ... the Dutch have committed themselves to the principle of expediency (or opportunity) which formally allows discretionary powers to the police and the prosecution. The use of this principle of expediency is not limited to the necessity of setting priorities in order to cope with scarcity of resources. In fact the main function of the principle of expediency is to prevent prosecutions that are

> not in the best public interest. Originally, this legal principle gave prosecutors an almost unlimited degree of personal discretion, but presently there are officially published guidelines on how to deal with certain cases under specified conditions.[2] (Ibid., p. 44)

The guidelines are the responsibility of the Minister of Justice and are 'a kind of pseudo-legislation, intended to guide officials, rather than clearly defined legal rules for citizens' (ibid., p. 46).

The expediency principle gives a degree of latitude in the application of the law. Some of this latitude is regulated by the guidelines which in turn are locally interpreted in a process called 'triangular consultation', which means that prosecutors discuss with local mayors and police chiefs before deciding on a course of action, the result being that the law-in-practice is dependent on local circumstances, and varies significantly between different communities. 'Typically, the policy is less strict in major cities than in the smaller towns and villages, reflecting differences in community standards, extent of drug problem, and so on' (Jansen, p. 170). Even the personal preferences of district court prosecutors and judges can affect the way the law is applied (Kraan, p. 287).

Local policies can also vary over time. Even when the limit on the sale or possession of cannabis was 30 grams, it was not always strictly enforced. But in 1987, Amsterdam tightened its policy; the police occasionally raided coffee shops and checked their inventory. However, shortly before the guideline limit was reduced to 5 grams, Kraan concluded: 'it cannot be said that, at the present time, the limit of 30 grams is strictly enforced in Amsterdam or elsewhere. Much depends on the good relations of coffee shop owners with the neighborhood and the responsible police officers' (ibid.).

Relations between the drug scene and its neighbours play a significant role in how the law is enforced. In the 1970s and early 1980s much of the heroin retail trade in Amsterdam took place in *heroin cafés* and their surroundings on the Zeedijk. Because the heroin scene was considered a nuisance, the police cracked down on it, closing the cafés and increasing surveillance in the neighbourhood. But this kind of reaction is not necessarily the norm. Although it is a felony to possess any quantity of heroin, major suppliers are the first priority and consumers and small-scale dealers are usually not arrested and prosecuted unless they commit property crimes. The policy practiced well into the 1990s can be summarized as: 'In general, no judicial action is taken against the majority of problematic consumers who do not harm other people. Nevertheless, there is a gray area in the sphere of repeated and extensive petty drug peddling, in combination with creating a

[2] Discriminatory powers are given to prosecutors under Swedish law as well. In the late 1960s and early 1970s 'åtalseftergift' (not bringing an offence to trial) was regularly applied in cases involving small amounts of narcotics. However, in the face of prohibitionist attacks, the policy was abandoned in about 1980.

public nuisance; local circumstances determine the kind of response these drug consumers face' (ibid., p. 294). However, in the late 1990s this started to change towards less willingness to accept drug nuisance.

Dutch Practice and International Law

In the light of international narcotics conventions it may seem strange that it is possible to have official guidelines which differ from the law. However, these UN treaties only demand that the laws are on the books, not that they are enforced. 'The Single Convention acknowledges explicitly that enforcement of statutes may be limited on the basis of principles that are a fundamental part of a nation's sovereignty. This clause provides the latitude the Dutch have been using in their drug policy' (Silvis, p. 48).

The Schengen Agreement, on the other hand, demands that the laws be put into practice. But at the same time it also acknowledges national sovereignty. As yet no international court has passed a ruling as to which of these two principles is to be given precedence.

Discrepancies between Laws and Applications

Dutch narcotics policy is based on an understanding of the problem significantly different from the prohibition-based approach of international conventions. These treaties and the threat of international political, economic or other sanctions makes the application of Dutch drug policy problematic; and there are many inconsistencies. A few examples are:

- Possession of small amounts of cannabis can result in a sentence of one month in prison or fines, but following guideline recommendations it usually does not lead to any punishment at all. In fact when the guideline limit was 30 grams, in practice it had been extended to 50 grams (ibid., p. 49). When guideline recommendations were reduced to 5 grams in 1995, it was not because the Dutch themselves felt that 30 grams was too much, but to placate French critics (Cohen, 1996b, p. 6). This concession was easy to make as 'most consumers never buy more than a few grams, let alone 30' (ibid.).
- Despite the legal differentiation between hard and soft drugs much of the tolerance for the possession of soft drugs has been extended to hard drugs. 'Actual sentences for possession of up to 10 grams of heroin (or other "hard" drugs) are considerably below the guideline term of one year' (ibid., p. 49f).
- The growing of cannabis seed is legal, as long as the cultivator does not intend to produce a crop of marijuana. Yet home grown cannabis (so-called Netherweed) is sold in just about all of the coffee shops in Amsterdam (Jansen, p. 175).
- A major tenet of the Revised Opium Law was that drug consumers should be offered treatment instead of being sent to prison. Although people

aren't put behind bars for using narcotics many problematic consumers are sentenced for ancillary crimes such as theft and burglary; the result being that addicts constitute a large percentage of the prison population (Silvis, p. 50).

Harm Reduction Measures

Introduction

The basic assumption behind harm reduction is that at least to some extent drug consumption is inevitable. Harm reduction includes all the measures taken to help both consumers and abstainers live with narcotics with a minimum of adversity.

Dutch policy is based on the idea that as far as possible drug consumption should be normalized. For instance, policy makers recognize that to a great extent problematic consumers' lack of ability to function socially is the result of labelling and a negative self-image.

> Junkie unions and other forms of drug user self-help organization were created in order to provide drug users with the resources to take more responsibility for their own impairments and to define the kind of help they needed. In this way, drug users were coaxed into a process of normalizing their problems and seeking solutions in the sphere of the conventional rather than the criminal world. (Kaplan et al., p. 329)

This implies that the reliance on criminal justice measures to be found in prohibition countries had to be reduced as a means of showing drug consumers that society had not closed the door on them. For instance 'tolerance zones' have been created by the police, where small-scale drug dealing is accepted (ibid.).

Soft Drugs

Soft drugs are considered to have social consequences comparable to those of alcohol. Guidelines have been set up regulating the sale and possession of these narcotics. Judgements handed down by different courts acknowledge that coffee shops should not be prosecuted if they refrain from:

- selling to youngsters under 18
- advertising
- selling large quantities
- selling other illegal drugs
- selling to foreigners
- causing public disturbances
- dealing in stolen goods
- violence.

In the mid-1990s there were over 1000 coffee shops in the Netherlands, and more than 300 in Amsterdam. The country's largest city used both the carrot and the stick to get the coffee shops to comply with these regulations. Owners were offered the opportunity to make a profit and conduct business with relatively little intervention if they followed the rules. If they didn't, for instance if they sold hard drugs, they risked being incarcerated and/or having their establishment closed down. Sometimes owners had to break one rule to enforce another. For instance, in the early days some coffee shop owners hired enforcers to physically remove hard drug dealers from the premises (Jansen, p. 170).

Apparently the expressed aim of separating the hard and soft drug markets has been realized: over 95 per cent of the sale of soft drugs in downtown Amsterdam takes place in coffee shops (ibid., p. 192).

As the number of coffee shops grew, they started to establish themselves in different niches in the market. Some cater to young adults, others to somewhat older people, to different immigrant groups, to the richer neighbourhoods, etc. Some are 'take-away' places, while others provide in-house activities such as chess or pool. Coffee shops have increasingly come to resemble bars, with the distinction that their primary product is cannabis instead of alcohol.

Methadone and Heroin Prescription Programmes

Even for problematic consumers of opiates, the goal is to keep them as integrated in society as possible. A major instrument for realizing this aim is methadone, which is offered both on a reduction basis (the dose is gradually reduced) and on a maintenance basis (a constant dose). Methadone is provided to approximately 7000 problematic consumers in about 60 different municipalities (Wever, p. 69). This can be compared to Sweden where methadone is given to a maximum of 600 individuals in three cities.

There are several different kinds of methadone programmes in the Netherlands. Originally the idea was that problematic consumers could be 'promoted' from lower to higher threshold programmes, when and if they became more motivated (Grapendaal et al., p. 242).

The *methadone busses* are a low-threshold programme. The goal was not to establish a first step towards a drug-free life but to reduce health risks associated with illicit drug consumption (Korf, p. 123). The methadone bus programmes 'do not aim at blocking all heroin use, but at substituting acceptable drugs (e.g. methadone) and activities (contact with a social medical professional) for unacceptable drugs (e.g. heroin) and unacceptable activities (contact with criminal dealers)' (Kaplan et al., p. 325).

Every day of the year the busses follow predetermined routes; stopping at special bus stops at set times and for set periods. There are barely any requirements a client must meet to be able to register with a methadone bus programme: i.e. no urine tests for illegal drugs, addicts are not required to show up every day and nobody tries to force them to change their lifestyle. (Grapendaal et al., p. 241).

On the high-threshold level were the community stations, which were only open on working days; clients were given pills for the weekend. As their explicit aim was abstinence from illegal drugs, urine tests were conducted twice a week, contact with doctors and social workers was obligatory and active support was offered (ibid.).

The highest threshold was that some general practitioners prescribed methadone pills for two weeks at a time. Patients were entrusted with going to their local pharmacy to fill their prescription. In this respect methadone is treated as just another medicine.

In the mid-1990s the system of distribution was changed. 'Urine tests at the community stations have been stopped. This means that the health authorities have moved away almost entirely from the graduated model. Community stations are now meant to cater to addicts who need extra attention, the extremely problematic cases' (ibid., p. 253). Thus for instance at a clinic run by the Drug Abuse Treatment Department of the Municipal Health Service in Amsterdam there are three different levels of treatment goals:

1. Harm reduction – Clients are encouraged to safe use, safe sex and low doses of methadone (less than 60 mg/day). They are offered general medical help, food and clothes, needle exchange, chest X-rays for tuberculosis twice a year, etc.
2. Stabilization of drug consumption – If the staff manages to make deeper contact with a client he is offered therapy, i.e. psychotherapy. He is given drugs in quantities sufficient to help him feel normal but not to get high. The goal is to help clients gain control over their consumption and limit taking hard drugs to twice a week. When this is accomplished they are given medication in a more normal way, such as going to a pharmacy with a prescription or going to a general practitioner. In 1998 50 per cent of the clients at this clinic ($N = 857$) were referred to one of the 216 general practitioners who prescribe methadone. All prescriptions are registered centrally to ensure that nobody is being given multiple doses.
3. Abstention – Those who abstain from heroin/cocaine while they are on medication are offered the chance to gradually lower their methadone doses if they themselves choose to do so.

Leuw and Marshall (p. xix) conclude that the Dutch policy on methadone maintenance may keep people addicted for longer periods of time, but it keeps them more socially integrated.

The government memorandum of 1995 opened the door for the supervised provision of heroin to long-term addicts (Maris, p. 84). However, it was in 1998 that such programmes were first initiated, and then on a small scale. Twenty-five patients in Amsterdam and an equivalent number in Rotterdam were chosen from among the approximately 1000 individuals who had been on hard drugs for many years and did not appear to be helped by any of the treatment previously offered. These patients are now prescribed heroin and their progress is being monitored scientifically in comparison with a matched control group. The experiment will continue for two years and may be expanded to more individuals as it progresses.

Needle Exchange Programmes

Based on the principal assumptions of Dutch drug policy – that drug use cannot be completely eliminated and that the ranks of potential problematic consumers are small – it was decided that needle exchange programmes would be an effective method of modifying one type of risky behaviour; using other people's 'works'.

With needles provided by the Municipal Health Service:

> the first needle exchange program was set up by the junkie-union. A few years later, the project was adopted and extended by the Drug Abuse Treatment Department of the Municipal Health Service. Several other treatment and assistance services also started to include free needle exchange programs, sometimes within the context of methadone maintenance programs. At the present time, some police departments even provide needle exchange facilities for arrested addicts. . . . Needle exchange programs appear to lead to safer injection practices. Feared negative side-effects, such as increased use of needles because of increased availability, have not occurred. (Wever, p. 67)

Assistance and Treatment

Both the Netherlands and Sweden are modern welfare states. Both have a tradition of large-scale governmental participation in social and health care services and have fairly similar welfare systems and commitments. Yet in the field of drugs the government's role has been defined very differently. Whereas Sweden has set as its goal to *cure* problematic consumers (i.e. get them off narcotics), the Netherlands directs its efforts towards *care* (i.e. making their lives as satisfactory as possible, without demanding that they abstain from drugs).[3]

[3] Swedish alcohol researcher Lars Lindström (1993, p. 29) writes that all experience shows that 'concepts such as "care" and "suitable environments" say more about what is possible when working with homeless alcoholics than "treatment" and complete rehabilitation'. He therefore calls for changes which are theoretically close to the Dutch model. In fact there are several examples in Sweden of this approach being put into practice in the fields of alcohol, narcotics and psychiatric care, but the official goal of Swedish narcotics policy remains 'a drug-free society'.

For various reasons the Dutch came to the conclusion that traditional health care services could not provide adequate measures for the somewhat special needs of problematic consumers. Therefore *client-centred facilities* were developed.

> In the bigger cities in particular, grassroots organizations and 'alternative' youth assistance institutions (such as 'Release' and the 'SDI', the 'Amsterdam Foundation for Drug Information') provided assistance directed at the immediate needs of people in trouble, such as providing shelter, day-care services and basic medical care.... The more informal, low threshold, peer-oriented care and assistance approach competed with the more traditional, medico-therapeutic approach. The latter soon lost ground to the former. (Wever, p. 60)

In the early 1980s,

> drug addiction had become increasingly a problem of the lower socialeconomic groups – groups that already were confronted with other social problems, such as unemployment, bad housing and crime. Ethnic minority groups, in particular, appeared to be hit hard by both drug addiction problems and unemployment, crime and poor housing. Many drug treatment services were still only focusing on abstinence, without much regard for the social needs and manifest demands of the addicts. (Ibid., p. 61)

It was in this context that a radical policy shift took place towards more direct and immediately ameliorative measures. Funding was granted to ambulatory, outpatient and low-threshold facilities, focusing on improvement of the physical and social situation of problematic consumers. Problems, as they were defined by clients, were given priority, i.e. acute health problems such as withdrawal symptoms, lack of money, unemployment, etc.

> Crisis- and detoxification centers were created, which also functioned as a connection between ambulatory and residential treatment. Treatment modalities – which typically had been of a long-term nature – became diversified; a variety of conceptual frameworks were introduced. Short-term treatment and part-time treatment was established. (Ibid., p. 62)

Efforts are also being made to integrate problematic consumers into regular care units. For instance the Drug Abuse Treatment Department of the Municipal Health Service in Amsterdam has a programme to help hospital personnel learn to communicate with drug patients. In 1998 all hospitals were accepting problematic consumers as patients.

When the risk of HIV/AIDS was added to all the other dangers of substantial consumption, Dutch policy became even more committed to harm reduction. As the goal of total abstention was deemed unrealistic, efforts were directed towards adjustments in conduct while allowing for continued drug consumption. Therefore it was considered important to have a large variety of easily accessible low-threshold assistance services. The services available are:

1. outpatient Consultation Bureaus for Alcohol and Drugs (CADs)
2. methadone and heroin programmes
3. social welfare services
4. residential treatment facilities
5. hospital treatment for addiction
6. municipal support is given to general practitioners who care for AIDS patients
7. three institutes for research, information and development of expertise.

All of these services are provided by private agencies. At first, funding was provided by the central government but now municipalities must bear some of the cost.

Drug Education

Dutch policy is based on the assumption that drug consumption cannot be dealt with by using the criminal justice system. Instead public health aspects of the problem are stressed. Great emphasis is placed on education; but the goals for this information are very different from drug war propaganda. Instead of trying to scare people into not even trying drugs the focus is on teaching youth how to deal with potentially dangerous behaviour.

Whereas before current drug policies were initiated 'drug education was an extension of rather old-fashioned information about alcohol, threatening and rigid, and aiming for total abstinence' (Van Amerongen, p. 93) the Netherlands has now changed strategies: 'young people, *knowledgeable* young people, who want to experiment should get [*sic*] the latitude to do so and not be thought immoral having made that choice' (Marshall and Marshall, p. 211). 'Consistent with the pragmatic philosophy, most drug education efforts are devoid of moralizing messages and value judgments; rather, they stress the need to be able to rationally calculate the "costs" versus the "benefits" of using drugs' (ibid.). Furthermore, illegal drug consumption is not considered a separate topic but rather is integrated into the general education on developing healthy life-styles and making healthy choices.

However, theory does not always correspond to practice: 'as the ideas and values of prevention efforts "trickle down" from government policy makers, scholars, and legislators to individual police officers, school teachers, and health education staff, a substantial part of their non-moralizing character is often lost' (ibid., p. 212).

The role of the police in drug education has been particularly controversial in the Netherlands. 'Beginning in the 1970s numerous police officers started to provide drug education to schools. Typically, education by the police tended to emphasize the sensational tales and the horror-stories of drug use' (ibid., p. 215). In 1984 the Ministers of Justice, the Interior, and Welfare Health and Cultural Affairs distributed an order to end police involvement in drug education; but this order was never executed. Many Dutch drug experts still question the value of the drug education being given by law enforcement officers.

As a type of secondary prevention the Jellinek Prevention Department provides courses to teachers on how to deal with young people who take drugs. They are also taught the differences between problematic and recreational drug consumption.

Yet another kind of drug education has evolved from a governmental decision to put an end to the production of ecstasy in the Netherlands; the result being that pills are sold and consumers don't know what they are buying. For instance in January 1997, 60 per cent of the analysed pills marketed as ecstasy were in fact what they were claimed to be, while 7 per cent were amphetamines. In 1998 these statistics were reversed. So now, for a minimal fee, people can leave in the pills they buy for analysis so they'll know what they are taking.

Self-Help

Several self-help groups have been started in the Netherlands. These were originally called *junkie unions* but the concept is now somewhat controversial. In Amsterdam the MDHG sees itself as an interest group for drug users and considers the word junkie derogatory. In Rotterdam, on the other hand, they proudly call themselves a junkie union. Whatever the name, their major goal is self-help. According to Dany Kesteloot of the MDHG the major means to achieve this are:

1. Individual support – Information, help with how to communicate with the social welfare authorities, meetings once a week where people are given a chance to discuss their experiences, etc. The goal is to help the individual solve his own problems, not solve them for him.
2. Collective support – Meetings are arranged with substantial consumers to see if there are problems common to many individuals and if something can be done about them collectively. For instance many of those who have served terms in prison, where everything is taken care of for them, have trouble adjusting to having to fend for themselves upon release. The MDHG has organized a buddy system where their members help newly released prisoners take responsibility for their lives.
3. Lobbying – As these interest groups are officially recognized they are in contact with politicians and try to influence political decisions. For

instance they were instrumental in getting some Dutch cities to set up *user rooms* where drugs can be taken safely. They are also working on trying to get suitable housing for substantial consumers. In Rotterdam I visited a house owned by the city but run by the junkie union where problematic consumers were taken off the streets and allowed to live until they were in good enough shape to find housing of their own and take care of themselves.

The Role of the Police

To exemplify how Dutch emphasis on care rather than cure has been put into practice I will briefly describe three steps in the evolution of care in the city of Rotterdam, giving extra attention to the role of the police.

The first phase was Project Central Station (see Bieleman and Bosma, pp. 196ff). Rotterdam's central station was a hangout for marginalized people; to the chagrin of many passengers. In an attempt to relieve (but not cure) the problem a portable cabin, which came to be known as *Platform Zero*, was placed at the east end of the station, giving problematic consumers a place to sit down, drink coffee and spend some time together. Different kinds of games were made available, as were activities such as drawing and painting. It was also possible to exchange needles. However, using or selling drugs or alcohol, and buying or selling goods, was not permitted. 'The visitors consisted mainly of young addicts of ethnic minority groups, Surinamese, Antilleans and Moroccans. In later days people from other problematic marginal groups, such as the homeless and ex-psychiatric patients, began to frequent Platform Zero in increasing numbers' (ibid., p. 198).

The establishment of Platform Zero was supported by the municipal police and by the St Paulus Church, and was fully funded by the local government. Two full-time professional social workers and about ten volunteers worked there. However, many passengers, people working in the vicinity and occasionally the local mass media remained critical. The Dutch Railways was afraid that Platform Zero served as a magnet drawing still more problematic consumers to the station. In response to public pressure Platform Zero was closed in 1994.

The second phase is known as Project Victor. In the words of Deputy Chief Constable C. M. Ottevanger (p. 3): 'our pragmatic and tolerant approach is limited to non-criminal users. Although we treat ordinary addicts with understanding and empathy, that certainly does not apply to addicts who commit crimes or to those causing a nuisance.' In Project Victor, the Rotterdam-Rijnmond police have developed a strategy to deal with problems such as drug tourism (people coming from other countries to buy/consume drugs in the Netherlands), drug nuisance (i.e. harassment, vomiting/urinating in public places, etc.) and drug crime (i.e. property crimes, 'drug guides' on roads and trains who lead buyers to dealers, etc.). The police have divided these people into two groups: local residents and others. Law enforcement agencies cooperate with the social authorities to try to help people from the region moderate their behaviour. There are various experiments providing care for addicts involving training, work and housing. Since 1998 heroin is prescribed on medical grounds to some of the older problematic consumers for whom nothing else has worked.

Drug consumers from out of the region are dealt with more brusquely: 'drug tourism is fought by means of repression, if and where possible in co-operation with the tourists' countries of origin' (ibid., p. 8). The means used are:

- making it difficult to find dealers
- increasing the risk of arrest and prosecution
- taking people into custody
- initiating deportation proceedings
- increasing penalties for repeated offences.

The third phase started in the late 1990s and consists of intensified cooperation between the police and other municipal agencies. For instance once a week there is a four-party consultation between the District Attorney, the probation authorities, a city government official and the police to discuss what should be done in specific cases. All are in agreement that problematic consumers are a mutual problem which cannot be solved by any one profession. To take a concrete example, a policeman who participates in these deliberations, Jaap de Leeuw, told me that when complaints were made that someone is using their apartment as a shooting gallery the police used to close the place down, the result being that eight or ten addicts were on the street and nobody knew where they were until the next time they got into trouble. Now the police do not shut down a shooting gallery until after the four-party consultation has decided upon a plan for who is going to do what with the inhabitants once they are evicted. In other words the police see that they have a role to play but they cannot do anything constructive on their own.

The police have felt frustrated as all care is voluntary and some substantial consumers have been arrested time and again for property crimes without leading to change. This is because they can choose prison rather than treatment. Therefore the police have been calling for legal provisions for compulsory care (Ottevanger, p. 11). The treatment programme the police advocate consists of approximately six months in an inpatient unit, before returning to Rotterdam. Then the individual will be given a job during the day and have to report to the police or some other authority every night for half a year. If this works well they will continue to work and report only once a week for another six months. During the entire period they will have the same probation officer who will get to know them personally.

Another role for the Dutch police is to combat organized crime and large-scale smuggling. Rotterdam is the world's largest inland port and over 360 containers *per hour* are handled there. Chief Constable J. W. Brinkman (p. 4) comments:

> The price of drugs in the Netherlands hardly fluctuates as a result of seizures – even large ones. This indicates the possibility that only a relatively small proportion of the illegal transports are intercepted.... Given the volume of the goods flow and the economic interests involved, it is impossible to curb illegal transports by means of physical controls only.

Therefore the police in the Netherlands are attempting to devise new methods.

> By means of information gathering and risk-analyses we are obtaining a wider and better insight into what is imported as cargo. The country of origin and the consigner, the cargo transported and its final destination may raise suspicions about whether a particular cargo is legal. In the process, cooperation and information exchange with domestic and foreign agencies are vital.... The growing number of drug finds should lead to more targeted investigations, eventually resulting in more arrests and convictions. The database on illegal transports, growing slowly but steadily, enables us to discover the interfaces between linked cases.
>
> (Ibid., p. 5)

As these methods, even when they result in seizures, usually only lead to the arrests of those who carry out the shipments, not the kingpins behind them, the Dutch authorities also concentrate on 'tracing and confiscating vast assets, which cannot be shown to have been earned legally' (ibid.).

PROBLEMS WITH DUTCH POLICY

Researchers in the Netherlands are aware of many of the problems and inconsistencies in the current Dutch approach. Some of these will be presented here.

Low-Threshold Treatment Centres

Critics of low-threshold treatment centres point out that while such facilities make it relatively easy to establish contact with problematic consumers, this kind of care is expensive and as a rule does not bring about positive changes. On the contrary, some substantial consumers are permitted, even aided, in continuing to slide downhill. Wever (p. 72), for instance, reports that:

there is a small but growing group of 'revolving door' patients with a long addiction career and often psychiatric problems. Poly-drug use has become more prevalent, which makes drug abuse treatment more difficult (e.g. there is no substitution therapy available for cocaine addiction or heavy use of tranquillizers).

Criticisms of Coffee Shops

Critics believe that coffee shops, by making narcotics readily available, increase the quantity and severity of consumption. While cannabis is not addictive (it doesn't give rise to physical abstinence symptoms), it can be taken in a problematic way and used as a means of (not) dealing with just about any life situation. Detractors maintain that the ready accessibility of drugs encourages problematic consumption; and there is some evidence that they may be right. A psychotherapist at the Amsterdam Jellinek Center (an alcohol and drug treatment clinic) noted an increase in the number of people treated for what he calls 'addiction to cannabis' (presumably problematic consumption). Approximately 200 individuals who seek help at the clinic each year are given this diagnosis; typically highly educated people, i.e. students, doctors, lawyers and journalists. It's unusual for substantial consumers of cannabis with a lower socioeconomic background to make use of the clinic (Jansen, p. 179).

There are contradictory reports as to the effects of the coffee shops on the number of cannabis consumers. On the one hand Sandwijk et al. (1992) found no increase in cannabis consumption in Amsterdam during 1987–90, despite the establishment of more coffee shops. On the other hand, a national survey of 11 000 high school students by the Netherlands Institute on Alcohol and Drugs in the early 1990s found a significant increase in cannabis use (Kaplan et al., p. 326). Some researchers interpret this as an indication that consumption levels in non-metropolitan areas are catching up with the cities.

If we look at the Amsterdam household population aged 12 years and older, a study by the Centre for Drug Research at the University of Amsterdam shows that in 1997 the life-time, the last-year and the last-month rates were 36.3, 13.1 and 8.1 per cent, respectively. All three rates had increased by approximately 50 per cent since 1987 (Abraham et al., p. 55). How should this be interpreted? Some researchers point out that other countries, such as the UK, have similar figures although they don't have coffee shops. Another argument is that it is not the number of consumers which is of primary importance, but the way the drugs are used. Fifty-five per cent of those who have tried cannabis in Amsterdam have used it less than 25 times in their lifetime; that is, they are clearly recreational consumers. At the other end of the scale; among those who had taken cannabis in the last month,

23 per cent had used it on 20 days or more. Some of these (but not all; see p. 21 above) are problematic consumers. This figure has remained stable between 1987 and 1997 (ibid., p. 50). If we, for the sake of argument, accept that all of the individuals in the 50 per cent increase are problematic consumers, their numbers rose from 1.3 to 1.9 per cent of the population during the ten-year period. However, the increase is not as great as these figures seem to indicate, as we must take the *generation effect* into consideration. In 1987 there were a greater number of people in the population who had passed the age of recruitment when cannabis first became generally available. In 1997 ten cohorts of these people had left the population and ten cohorts of potentially recruitable people had joined it.

As the coffee shops are believed to have helped separate drug markets and thereby reduce harm from other narcotics, some researchers consider the level of problematic cannabis consumption acceptable. But even among those who otherwise support Dutch narcotics policy, some have called for a comprehensive re-evaluation of the coffee shop system (Kaplan et al., p. 326). The measures in the government memorandum of 1995 (see p. 20) can be interpreted as reflecting a growing concern about the effects coffee shops may be having on adolescents (although some researchers ascribe the memorandum to political pressure from other countries).

Bieleman et al. (1995, pp. 3ff) point out several other problems with coffee shops:

- traffic problems, including parking problems and noise pollution;
- customers hanging around outside, disturbing neighbours and vandalizing cars and gardens;
- pollution: i.e. garbage, urine, vomit, etc. in gardens and doorways in the vicinity;
- many residents who live near coffee shops feel insecure and attribute these feelings to coffee shops (although the feelings of insecurity may well have other roots);
- the enforcement of all the rules regulating coffee shops requires intensive supervision and therefore drains police resources;
- some coffee shops have been closed for selling hard drugs and/or criminal activities.

It is important to note that all of these difficulties also occur in conjunction with bars selling alcohol. Regardless of whether it occurs near a bar or a coffee shop this kind of nuisance is not tolerated and if it continues the establishment will be closed. Arjan Roskam, the owner of several coffee shops, and the head of the officially recognized union of coffee shop owners, told me that neighbours sometimes more or less blackmail coffee shop proprietors, threatening to file complaints if their demands are not met.

There is also a potential for police harassment in conjunction with coffee shops. In Amsterdam there are two different *hit teams*, one a central unit composed of officers from different departments in the police force. The other is a part of the neighbourhood police. Roskam described how coffee shops are raided to see if they have more than the permitted 500 grams of stock, and if anybody on the premises (including customers) is carrying hard drugs. In one coffee shop I visited there were eight video cameras inside and two outside so the staff could observe and intervene in any illegal behaviour.

The hit teams sometimes go to the homes of coffee shop personnel and check the serial numbers on TVs and bicycles to see if they were stolen. Sociologist Peter Cohen remarked that one wonders if these hit teams have their own drug policy.

Another issue is the so-called *backdoor problem*. According to Arjan Roskam on the average a coffee shop sells in the range of 0.4–2 grams of cannabis to 50–300 customers/day (usually about 50 per cent marijuana and 50 per cent hash). As coffee shops are only allowed to stock 500 grams of cannabis, and may have as many as 35 different kinds, they can't keep very much of each sort. This means that they have to have a *stash* somewhere else, from which they can quickly replenish supplies. There are no rules or guidelines decriminalizing these stashes and a coffee shop owner I interviewed had been arrested the night before. An apartment where he had a stash of about 7 kilos was raided after a hit team had kept him under surveillance for several weeks.

Another aspect of the backdoor problem is where are coffee shop owners to buy their supplies? Until the mid-1990s there were many small cultivators of cannabis. A coffee shop owner told me that he used to buy from these people, but after penalties for cultivation were increased most of them were scared off. 'In recent years *organized crime* has increased enormously, concerning itself not only with hard drugs but also with large-scale cultivation, trade and export of Dutch homegrown' (Maris, p. 83). Arjan Roskam confirmed that this is the case and much of the cannabis being sold in coffee shops has its origin in organized crime. Roskam is of the opinion that the only way to change the situation is to encourage small-scale cultivation by decriminalizing it.

Yet another problem is that the coffee shops are a magnet for foreign *drug tourists*, bringing sharp criticism from abroad (ibid.).

And finally it is unrealistic to believe that coffee shops will only stock Netherweed when about half of the current demand for cannabis is for foreign grown products. (ibid., p. 84). In other words, the coffee shops provide an easy outlet for organized criminals, both those dealing in Dutch homegrown, and those involved with international smuggling.

Inconsistencies

C. W. Maris, Professor of Legal Philosophy at the University of Amsterdam, points out many of the inconsistencies in Dutch policy revealed in the government memorandum of 1995. The authors of the memorandum are themselves aware that Dutch drug policy contains inconsistencies, but defend themselves by claiming that 'drugs policy is not an exercise in logic' (see Maris, p. 80).

> If it contains inconsistencies, they argue that this is because their policy is not in every respect based on the principles behind it; rather it is sensibly and pragmatically tuned to a changing situation. Politics after all is the art of the possible, not an abstract philosophy of norms. (Ibid., p. 81)

One of the inconsistencies Maris discusses concerns Dutch attempts to control hard drugs. 'The gist of the argument for prosecuting the traffic in hard drugs is that this forces up the price, thus keeping them off the open market' (ibid., p. 85). However, the government also acknowledges that:

> combating the drugs traffic has not had any effect on the supply or price of hard drugs – in other words, the policy has not been very effective. It admits that it is this very prohibition that forces up underworld profits, thus threatening to infiltrate legal economic and administrative institutions. ... At the same time it stresses that decriminalization would lead to a significant lowering of prices so that criminal organizations would lose their main source of revenue. Despite this admission it declares its resolve to intensify its legal fight against organized crime. In doing so, it brings about the very harm to society that it aims to combat. (Ibid.)

The government defends its policy of tolerating coffee shops with the argument that soft drugs users would otherwise be forced to maintain contacts with criminals. Maris points out that 'the same argument is also applicable to hard drugs users' (ibid.). In other words, if the coffee shop system really does work, why isn't a similar system applied to hard drugs? And if it doesn't work why hasn't it been abandoned?

By taking another look at the quotes in the beginning of this section we can see that a possible answer lies in the fact that in the realm of politics logic is not the most important principle. The Dutch stand firmly behind harm reduction but feel they must be pragmatic. There is little international support for the decriminalization of hard drugs, and to do so would probably result in overwhelming international opposition, endangering even the decriminalization of soft drugs. Furthermore, the government wishes to continue to fine tune their soft drug model, before applying it to other drugs. So in the eyes of Dutch policy makers, the best course of action for the time being implies living with inconsistencies.

Threats to Constitutional Safeguards

As we have already seen, prohibition poses serious threats to constitutional safeguards. Not even the less repressive Dutch approach guarantees that the rights of citizens are protected.

Wever (p. 64) maintains: 'It is a fundamental Dutch legal principle that no-one can be forced into accepting treatment.' Yet as we have seen, the government memorandum of 1995 has apparently abandoned this principle.

Silvis gives several more examples of threats to constitutional safeguards:

- Anybody present in a place generally known for drug use and dealing, i.e. a railroad station, may be searched by the police. 'This move from individualized to generalized suspicion is a major breakthrough in norms of criminal procedure' (Silvis, p. 52).
- A person suspected of dealing can be convicted without being caught with drugs in his possession. A conviction can be based on statements from several drug consumers implicating him as a dealer. 'The normally required objective grounds for suspicion and prosecution are reduced to a minimum, which opens the risk for manipulation of the criminal justice system' (ibid.).
- An undercover agent may incite a person to commit drug crimes if the individual is considered predisposed to do so. 'The presumed predisposition of a person is based on his criminal record and on facts drawn from the operational reports of the undercover agent' (ibid.). In other words, the law is applied differently to different people.
- The number of wire taps is increasing. As it is difficult to gather information on narcotics, more than half of the taps in the Netherlands are related to drug cases. 'Very often these taps are used in a prospective manner and not as a means to solve cases that have already occurred. This makes sense, since dealers are not likely to evaluate past transactions by phone; however, constitutionally the Dutch police should only use phone taps as a tool for solving (not preventing) crimes' (ibid., p. 53).
- Racial discrimination may play a role in drug cases. 'The Dutch Supreme Court has decided that contact between a "German white and a Dutch black person in the Warmoesstraat Amsterdam" may serve as a ground for police action on the suspicion of drug dealing' (ibid., p. 54).

Silvis concludes: 'The Netherlands has not been exempted from the gradual retreat from the norms of due process resulting from the criminal justice fight against illegal drugs. And yet there is no indication that this has contributed to solving drug problems' (ibid.).

It seems that even in the Netherlands the need to combat narcotics is used as an excuse for undermining civil liberties.

Summary of Swedish and Dutch Drug Policy

Sweden	*The Netherlands*
	Primary Goals
free society of narcotics	minimize problematic consumption and reduce harm
protect society and the individual from drugs	find a balance between freedom and responsibility
cure	care
	Theoretical Foundations
all non-medical consumption is problematic	most consumption is non-problematic
narcotics have a vast growth potential	limited growth potential for problematic consumption
the drug consumer is an object	the drug consumer is a subject
narcotics are a problem of themselves	problematic consumption is primarily a result of societal conditions
supply creates demand	supply in itself does not create problematic consumption
drugs are an urgent problem in need of immediate and drastic measures	drugs are not an urgent problem – the war on drugs is politically motivated
biochemical and behaviourist models	psychological and sociological models
	Central Concepts
narcotics-free society	harm reduction
negative attitude to drugs	decriminalization
mobilization of public opinion	normalization
restrictive control policy	pragmatism, expediency principle
drug-free treatment	integration of drug consumers into society
caring chain	soft drugs – hard drugs
street-level intervention	separation of drug markets
	Policy in Practice
information as primary prevention (teach people not to take drugs at all)	information as secondary and tertiary prevention (learn to live with drugs with a minimum of harm)
fear arousal	appeal to the intellect – avoid emotional overtones
strictly enforced laws against trade, possession and consumption	discretionary enforcement based on pragmatism, expediency and local morays

street-level intervention by both police and social authorities	police measures against large-scale drug trafficking, public health measures directed to consumers
formerly institutional care – increasingly outpatient facilities	primarily low-threshold outpatient facilities, self-help (i.e. junkie unions), some institutional care
primarily non-drug treatment – both voluntary and coerced	primarily voluntary public health facilities which do not aim at abstention, some drug-free institutional treatment
limited use of harm reduction – three high threshold methadone clinics, two needle exchange programmes	harm reduction, i.e. comprehensive opiate prescription and needle exchange programmes, shooter rooms, separation of drug markets
repressive measures against both supply and demand	repressive measures against supply but not demand
extensive threats to constitutional safeguards	threats to constitutional safeguards

WHICH NARCOTICS POLICY IS BEST?

Inevitably all drug policy must balance between gains in some areas and losses in others. The degree to which any given drug policy maximizes benefits and minimizes costs is a judgement which can only be made in relation to the values of the beholder. From a purely ethical point of view there is no objective way to decide which drug policy is best.

What can be attempted is an evaluation based on a comparison of the number of problematic consumers in countries with different drug policies. However, collecting statistics on narcotics consumption involves many difficulties. Of primary importance is the way concepts are defined. For instance, in some countries all consumption is problematic, while in other countries this is not the case. This means that studies in different countries are not measuring the same thing, even if they may use the same terms.

The validity of research findings is also affected by a number of other factors: i.e. the sample chosen, loss of data, the willingness of research subjects to give accurate information and their ability to recall, changes in the law and the ways it is enforced, changes in resources allocated for measures in the drug sector, etc. This implies that there is a great degree of uncertainty in all drug statistics, and we cannot simply compare different years and different studies. Furthermore, we can never be sure what the patterns of drug consumption would have looked like if the narcotics policy of the country hadn't been implemented.

The matter is further complicated when making international comparisons. The European Monitoring Centre for Drugs and Drug Addiction is attempting to develop methods for making comparisons between nations within the EU. In their first annual report they present a review of the difficulties involved (EMCDDA, 1996, Chapter 5) and the matter is discussed in greater detail in EMCDDA, 1997a.

Extremely briefly, each country has its own specific way of collecting data on drug consumption. This is due to such factors as different

- cultural norms regarding drugs
- definitions
- types of agencies collecting data
- methods of compiling data
- drug political situations.

Due to the uncertainty of all narcotics statistics, there is leeway for different interpretations, and any conclusions drawn or comparisons made must be seen as tentative. However, until more standardized methods of data collection are developed and implemented, the alternative to making use of the figures we have is not to use any figures at all and merely guess. I shall therefore be so bold as to present the data for Sweden and the Netherlands. Given the similarities in political and social welfare systems in the two countries, and the vast differences in narcotics policies, perhaps we can see a clear difference in results. If we limit ourselves to problematic consumption, the most reliable statistics we have, and the ones quoted by the EMCDDA (1997b, p. 19), are that the rate/1000 in Sweden is estimated as being in the range 1.6–2.3, while the Dutch figure is 1.6–1.8. Once again these figures may not be measuring the same thing. However, until such time as we have more accurate and comparable figures which show otherwise, I would argue that our best guess is that the rates in the two countries are on a similar order of magnitude.

However, drug policy in itself is not the sole nor even the major determinant of the number of problematic consumers in a country. I shall now turn my attention to some of the other factors.

14 Demand Reduction

> Creating a society with a better and more just distribution of income, housing, education, work-environment and culture is a way to prevent the social maladjustment which often causes criminality; and thereby is certainly of greater importance than use of the penal system against crimes which have already been committed.
>
> (From a proposal for a new law sent by the Swedish government to parliament, Regeringens proposition, 1982/83:85, p. 30)

INTRODUCTION

The Vienna United Nations International Conference on Drug Abuse and Trafficking in 1988 signalled a somewhat new direction in drug policy. Instead of primarily concentrating on reducing supply (production and distribution) the conference called for an emphasis on demand reduction (consumption). Since then demand reduction has become an increasingly important concept, although much remains much to be done. For example, EMCDDA (1997b, Chapter 2) devotes an entire chapter in its second annual report to demand reduction efforts within the EU. Yet when it comes to allocation of resources there seem to be other priorities. For instance in 1995 the EU spent about 27.9 million ECUs on anti-drug actions. Of this sum approximately 4 per cent was spent on the alleviation of poverty. This is 20 per cent less than what was spent on drug-related telecommunications (EMCDDA, 1996, p. 4:2).

EMCDDA (1997b, p. 49) is well aware that a macroanalysis of narcotics consumption is necessary but as they themselves put it: 'Across Europe school programmes are the major primary prevention measure.' Based on my theoretical understanding, school programmes may be relevant for reducing recreational consumption in the short run but do not prevent problematic consumption in the long term. As this latter goal is of primary importance, this chapter will be concerned with some of the implications of my theory for practical policy in this area.

However, before I begin it must be emphasized that to be effective measures must be relevant for the culture in which they are implemented. It is not possible to mechanically transplant steps taken in one country to another. The discussion in this chapter should therefore be seen as a way of illustrating the implications of my theoretical model for reducing problematic drug consumption in the context of European welfare states, most notably Sweden. To be applicable elsewhere the ideas must be modified to fit local conditions. Furthermore, in some cultural contexts the suggestions simply aren't relevant. In other words this chapter should not be seen as presenting concrete measures to be universally applied, but rather as an illustration of a way of thinking.

THREE APPROACHES

In their criticism of Scandinavian prohibitionism, Christie and Bruun (p. 246) write:

> Current narcotics policy is conducted in a way which is inconsistent with what is known about drugs and those who take them. It damages groups which cannot endure more punishment, and strengthens tendencies within the state control apparatus which should not be encouraged. But worst of all: it distracts us from dealing with the real and very serious problems of highly industrialized societies.... In the larger framework, drugs are of minor importance, blown up into something big, a major problem. We wish to make them small again, just as trivial as they in reality are.

How can Christie and Bruun claim that narcotics are trivial? My interpretation is that what is considered important depends upon how one construes cause and effect. In prohibitionist thinking drugs are the root of much evil, while Christie and Bruun believe that narcotics consumption does not cause any of the major problems of society, but rather are the result of much more important and deeply rooted societal processes and decisions. By regarding narcotics as *the explanation* for many negative aspects of society we lose perspective.

> Those who have lost out – in school, in the work place, have been placed in institutions and punished – take drugs. Their failures are blamed on the drugs. Drug consumption is seen as the reason why generally poor conditions exist in society. If the lumpenproletariat takes drugs, we have explained why there is a lumpenproletariat. The use of drugs accounts for their misery: there is no need to analyse alternatives.
>
> (Ibid., p. 187)

Narcotics as an explanation is a deception, diverting our attention from the deeper problems of society.

But what are these deeper problems?

> Class differences are lost... Innate privileges, arenas adapted to only the strongest, the lack of solidarity in a society which claims to be taking its responsibility for the weak – all disappears in the haze of drug smoke. In

> this way the war on drugs helps to maintain the status quo. Some of the welfare state's visible deficiencies become easier to live with ... The enticing and destructive power of drugs provide good explanations in the sense that they do not demand painful self-examination – or social criticism. (Ibid., p. 187f)

Drugs as an explanation neither disturb centres of power nor the population at large, and make it less urgent to deal with other, more deep-seated social problems. As Ethan Nadelmann (p. 114), Director of the Lindesmith Center in New York succintly put it: 'Drugs, crime, and race problems, and other socioeconomic problems are inextricably linked.'

Claes Örtendahl (p. 18), former head of the National Board of Health and Welfare in Sweden, writes:

> the number of people no longer needed in the work force, the number forced into early retirement, and those with psychological problems are increasing. Working life, social life and society has in some way or other overwhelmed them. If this continues our social welfare is threatened and so is our narcotics policy.

Dutch researchers Ed Leuw and I. Haen Marshall (p. xiv) give a similar analysis of the macrobasis of 'the drug problem':

> Perhaps more than with any other social problem, the extent and quality of drug problems are a reflection of a particular society's moral priorities and preoccupations, its political processes, the (in)equalities of its distribution of wealth and welfare among (ethnic) classes and the integrative (in)adequacies of its culture. Illegal drug taking, addiction and the viability of the legal drugs trade are all symptoms and logical consequences of a national socialeconomic and cultural order.

They conclude:

> Dutch drug ideology has rejected the idea that present day drug addiction and drug trafficking, with its heavy concentration in socially deprived and culturally alienated population groups, could (or even should) be eradicated without reconsidering society's socialeconomic and cultural order. But obviously, staging a sociocultural revolution in order to eliminate drug addiction is just as futile as staging a 'war on drugs'.

We can identify three basic approaches on how to come to terms with narcotics:

1. Swedish prohibitionists see the consumption of narcotics as a problem in itself which can be solved without changes in society's macroeconomic institutions. The solution lies in implementing a restrictive narcotics policy.

2. Dutch harm reduction is based on an understanding of the macroeconomic basis of problematic narcotics consumption. The basic assumption is that it cannot be eliminated without extensive macrolevel measures. However, since these are considered unfeasible, the best we can hope for is a narcotics policy which minimizes harm.
3. As a third alternative I propose that macromeasures are plausible, and that this is the best way to minimize the damage in conjunction with psychoactive substances. In saying this I am not proposing a world revolution or claiming that we are capable of creating a perfect society. I am merely saying that to the extent that we can provide as many citizens as possible with the hope of a reasonable future, we will reduce the number of problematic consumers of narcotics.

In Chapter 12 we examined a system based on the first approach. The preceding chapter described a way in which the second postulate can be applied. The third alternative is in reality the foundation of all welfare states. In this chapter we shall begin to sketch an outline of some of the types of measures which might possibly be included in an attempt to create policies based on the third approach.

SOCIETAL PRESSURE

What do people have to do to survive in our society? For most adults the most basic answer is they have to work to earn a living or be supported by someone who does. When a person goes home after a long workday he bears with him what he has experienced on the job. Therefore even his free time and his ability to function socially (i.e. as a spouse, parent, friend, etc.) are influenced by his working life.

Labour markets in industrialized countries are an outgrowth of market economy. As such there are many advantages, and that which follows is by no means meant to deny this fact. But there are also a number of inherent problems, and that which is done to reduce these harmful effects is of major importance for reducing the number of problematic consumers of narcotics.

Professor of Sociology Joachim Israel (p. 191) points out two of the basic limitations of our economic system:

1. the driving force behind almost all production is profit;
2. this implies that people must earn their living in a system which looks upon them as *units of production* and treats them as such.

Profit is measured in the limited sense of business economics, and therefore little attention is paid to long-term social consequences. For instance, if an individual becomes physically or psychologically impaired on the job it usually doesn't entail extra expenses for his employer; other than those for recruiting a replacement. For instance, sometimes profits can be increased by not making investments which would lower noise levels, eliminate dangers, reduce monotony, etc. In welfare states the financial costs are picked up by the rest of the population in the form of rehabilitation programmes, hospital costs, social welfare, etc. In other systems of social policy the individual and his family bear both the emotional and economic burden.

But this is not to imply that businessmen are malevolent. The way individual actors produce goods and services must be seen in relation to international competition. Competition means that some win and others lose. To stay in business – and produce jobs – management must make a profit, which means keeping prices on a level which are competitive on the international market. This reduces options both for companies and countries, and it is unrealistic to think that in the foreseeable future we shall be able to eliminate the majority of the negative aspects of our ways of producing goods and services. However, our hands are not completely tied and we should do as much as possible.

In the space available I cannot begin to describe all the destructive forces operative in working life, but I will list some of the more important ones:

1. Powerlessness – people feel that they cannot influence their situation to a significant extent.
2. Meaninglessness – is based on the assumption that humans need to develop their own rationality and to grow intellectually. Far from everyone experiences this at work.
3. Anomie – in times of rapid changes in production and living conditions, cultural elements cannot keep pace. People are left without relevant norms to guide their behaviour.
4. Isolation – many feel a lack of solidarity, close contacts and support on the job.
5. Fatigue
6. Illness
7. Stress
8. Pollution

These are among the more important factors which comprise what I call *negative societal pressure*: the destructive processes in conjunction with modern production and our economic system.

Unemployment is an aspect of negative societal pressure which is particularly relevant for understanding substantial consumption. Correlations between unemployment and problematic consumption of narcotics have been shown in a number of studies (see for instance, Lenke and Olsson, 1996; Peck and Plant, 1986). Although the unemployed don't experience all the factors described above, they are under great pressure. Western culture emphasizes that all adult males (and increasingly females) should pull their own weight. It is devastating for an adult to feel that he has nothing to offer that others are willing to pay for; and that he cannot support himself and his family. I shall return to the negative psychological effects of unemployment shortly.

Everyone is subjected to negative societal pressure. All of us bear scars from the macroprocesses which form the basis of our existence. However:

1. some are subjected to more negative societal pressure than others;
2. everyone in similar situations does not react in the same manner. Once again it is not a matter of simple causation. We cannot mechanically state that because a person is subjected to a certain amount of negative societal pressure he will crumble and fall.

My hypothesis is that the more negative the societal pressure, the greater the number of people who will come apart, for instance in the form of problematic consumption of narcotics. To the extent that we can diminish negative societal pressure, we will also diminish the number of substantial consumers.

Some might argue that negative societal pressure, particularly unemployment, was at its greatest during the depression of the 1930s, while narcotics consumption at the time was minimal: and in the 1960s, after a long period of economic growth, problematic consumption started to increase. That narcotics consumption was low in the 1930s was almost certainly due to lack of availability. If people had knowledge of and access to psychoactive substances, it is reasonable to assume that there would have been a demand. Since the 1960s, due to increased international trade and improved methods of transportation, drugs have become widely available. As explained in Chapter 11, we have nothing to gain by dreaming of returning to a state when narcotics were inaccessible.

CREATING NEGATIVE SOCIETAL PRESSURE

In the 1960s Chein et al. (p. 55f) studied demographic variables in New York City to see what distinguished neighbourhoods with a high degree of narcotics consumption (epidemic areas) from nonepidemic districts.

> The epidemic areas are, on the average, areas of relatively concentrated settlement of underprivileged minority groups, of poverty and low economic status, of low educational attainment, of disrupted family life, of disproportionately large numbers of adult females as compared to males, and of highly crowded housing; they are densely populated and teeming with teenagers.

In the 1980s Pearson (1987b, p. 69) writes of the UK: ‘where heroin misuse has become a serious problem in recent years, those same neighborhoods are likely to suffer from a number of other problems such as poor housing, low income, a high density of single-parent families, and unemployment'. And in the Netherlands in the 1990s Wever (p. 61) concludes that drug addiction has 'become increasingly a problem of the lower socialeconomic groups – groups that already were confronted with other social problems, such as unemployment, bad housing and crime. Ethnic minority groups, in particular, appeared to be hit hard.'

The founding of welfare states can be seen as an attempt to limit, and even eliminate, negative environments. Sweden, a country which for many people has stood as a model of what could and should be accomplished to this end, has now made a number of political decisions which contribute to the creation of conditions which promote problematic consumption of narcotics. The treatment of refugees provides many examples.

In principle Sweden has generous and humane policies towards refugees. In practice there are serious problems. Many refugees have fled from their native countries after having been driven from their homes and families and/or traumatized by war, torture, rape, etc. Upon arriving in Sweden they are placed in camps until their application for asylum is processed; a procedure which often takes several years. While the camps are usually of good material standard, refugees are not permitted to work or as much as given lessons in Swedish. With lots of time on their hands and no adequate help to deal with the trauma they bear, they are in a precarious psychological situation. At the same time the prospect of being deported back to the country from which they have fled weighs heavy.

Another dilemma is how they should raise their children. They hope to be able to live in Sweden, but they know nothing about the country. What they can teach their offspring is the culture of their native land; but this may not be what's needed to function in Swedish society.

Even if they are finally given permission to settle in Sweden, their problems are far from over. To date about half of those granted asylum have never been gainfully employed in the country. And although the housing offered is of high material standard, refugees are most often referred to segregated areas, which are beginning to take on the demographic characteristics of the epidemic areas described above.

Altogether too little is being done to integrate refugees into society. The schooling provided in the refugee camps does not meet normal Swedish standards and refugee children fall behind their Swedish contemporaries. Although there are currently few segregated schools their number is rising, and there are 'integrated' schools which have some classes composed almost entirely of Swedish children, while other classes principally comprise foreign born (Björkman, p. A5). Put concisely, Sweden is making it difficult for these children to gain the skills necessary to function in Swedish society. There are already signs of criminality, and ethnic and racial conflict.

> In the light of the difficult background of many of the teenagers, and the marginal situation they are living in, one can expect that experimenting with drugs can easily lead to a pattern of drug use in which drugs will play a very dominant role. ... One gets the impression that the authorities do not realize how serious the situation is and how it might deteriorate. This may lead to an even more aggravated and violent situation, resembling the experiences of France and the UK, where riots have taken place in highly segregated and deprived areas where young people (immigrants) grow up without hope. (Boekhout van Solinge, p. 152)

Although people of foreign background represent 11.8 per cent of Sweden's population, they curently occupy over 40 per cent of the places in institutional drug care (SIS, p. 19). Neither prohibition nor harm reduction addresses the roots of the problem.

THE SOCIALIZATION OF CHILDREN

Another aspect of negative societal pressure which is important for understanding problematic consumption of narcotics is uncertainty as to how to bring up children. Rapid and dramatic changes in the workplace entail teaching the next generation numerous skills which their parents do not have. This is not to imply that parents no longer play an important role for their offspring but many adults are unsure about what knowledge and values they should convey.

While it is still true that to a large extent children 'inherit' their parents' social competence (or lack thereof), to an increasing extent, and starting from a very young age, a large part of the socialization process takes place outside of the home. As women increasingly join the workforce more children are placed in some form of daycare. As a result of a combination of economic problems and the application of business economic rationality to the daycare and school systems, many communities have reduced allocations to these sectors. This often means that the staff has neither the time nor the energy to satisfactorily attend to the needs of children and adolescents with special problems. When functioning properly daycare and schools can provide a degree of compensation for those children who are psychologically deprived at home. But the more we limit resources, lower the adult/child ratio and overwork the personnel, the greater the risk that their level of aspiration recedes from high pedagogical ideals towards merely attempting to make it through the day. Children who have ample and adequate contacts with relatives and other grown-ups will manage anyway; but those who are starving for positive relationships to adults suffer the loss.

A closely related problem is that in spite of the official rhetoric, our schools are not designed to develop the capabilities of each and every child. A host of studies clearly show that those who come from the middle and upper classes do best in school right from the start.

> This is true regardless of whether one measures grades, teachers' assessments, or pupils' evaluations of themselves and each other. Measuring students' attitudes to school and desire to continue their education gives the same results. ... Why this is so has now become clear. It has to do with *what is being taught in school*, with *the pupils' experiences before starting school*, and with *the functions schools have* in society.
>
> (Christie and Bruun, p. 28f) (emphasis in original)

It is not without reason that many sociologists consider school to be a sorting station where some are favoured and primed for success while others are weeded out and taught that they don't make the grade. During approximately twelve of their most formative years children are obliged to go to school. At first glance it appears that everybody begins their formal education from square one and that it is the individual's biological capabilities that determine who will prevail. It appears to be fair play and many of those who don't succeed blame themselves for not doing so. That the language used, the tasks to be done, the demands made – in fact, everything – is created by the middle and upper classes for the middle and upper classes is not evident to those who have trouble competing. School is often one of the most important components in the societal labelling process.

ONE-WAY COMMUNICATION

Another component in societal labelling is one-way communication. Following the tenets of symbolic interactionism, sociologist Sten Andersson (p. 103) writes: 'To be able to see, I must first be seen by others. For me to hear, others must listen to me. Before I can speak, others must speak to me. I cannot love, until I have been loved. To understand, I must be understood.' Put succinctly, to develop we must have close relationships and two-way communication with other people who thereby help to bring forth and confirm our aptitudes. But as we have already seen, all children do not receive this at home, and it is becoming all the more difficult for daycare and school personnel to 'see' each child, as the work-load has escalated with every budget cut. As stress increases so does the risk that adults will lecture instead of interacting with the children.

Modern mass media, such as TV, radio, magazines and music, constitute another form of one-way communication. The media can neither confirm the child as an individual nor answer his questions. The average adolescent in Sweden now spends as much time watching TV as in school.

ASSISTING PARENTS

The demands of the modern workplace create role conflicts for parents. As more women work outside the home, the traditional mechanisms for the socialization of children are no longer functional. Many people have to commute a long way, are expected to work overtime, travel on the job, must learn new skills, be more productive, etc. Parents often feel stressed and tired, and it has become all the more difficult to meet the demands of others – and the demands we place on ourselves. It has somewhat jokingly been said that in modern society people either have three jobs or none at all.

Some fail to maintain a reasonable balance. This may be a result of primary and/or secondary resource deficiency (see p. 52), or giving some functions priority at the expense of others. For instance, there are people who spend so much time at their jobs that we speak of *workaholics*, others are obsessed with keeping up with the Joneses, while still others can't miss a ball game. Some just abdicate from their parental role. In other words, there are people who can't seem to give their offspring the emotional support they need to develop a positive self-image. Such parents label their children, and far from all of these youngsters have access to other adults who are willing and able to fill in the gaps.

The nuclear family (especially those with only one parent) needs support. Without aspiring to be exhaustive I shall name a few possible measures which may lighten the burden. It is important to note that all of the suggestions presented require a transfer of resources.

Six-Hour Workday with Full Pay for Parents with Small Children

If we look at the immediate costs, this is an expensive reform. The principal gain is that it allows the parents of small children to remain in the workforce, while giving them more time and energy for their children. In the short term this entails an economic burden for those who bear the costs (presumably taxpayers). In the long run we hope that fewer children will grow up lacking the necessary skills and emotional security to become respected members of the community.

Community Planning

Residential neighbourhoods can be built so as to avoid segregation, allowing people with different incomes, education, ethnic backgrounds, etc. to live near each other. This allows for integrated schools without bussing. Those who currently live in relatively problem-free areas and whose children go to schools which function satisfactorily may well be making a sacrifice in the short term. The gain is that we avoid ghettos where each individual's problems and lack of resources further diminish the already precarious living conditions of their neighbours.

Societal Support for a Broad Range of Recreational Activities

Much support is given to the next generation through the work of recreational centres, athletic associations, different kinds of clubs, cultural societies, etc. However, many of these are limited by lack of funds. Increased public funding would allow them to reach more youths.

Weekend Parents

This is a type of individual support for children in families which need assistance. For example, a male role model is lacking in many families. By giving support to the child, and temporarily relieving the burden on the parent(s), the family situation may improve even during the rest of the week. At the same time the weekend parents themselves receive much personal satisfaction through their relationship to a child who needs them.

Parents' Walking Tours

In Sweden some adults participate in organized walking tours at night in the central parts of cities and towns. The purpose is to establish contact with the teenagers who are hanging out. By being physically present these adults reduce the risk of violence and criminal activity, and most importantly, show an interest.

Individual Measures for Children with Problems

Anyone who has come into contact with a child in trouble can try to help. For instance one of my neighbours noticed that a boy at the same daycare centre as their son often wandered alone in the local mall in the evening. This family decided to invite this boy to their home and let him come along when they took their own children to different activities.

Some studies on *resilience* or *super kids* (i.e. those who have grown up in extremely disadvantageous environments, yet manage to do fairly well) have shown that in their childhood there had been an adult (i.e. a relative, teacher, scout leader, coach, etc.) who supported them. When parents don't fulfil their responsibilities, other adults must step in.

THE SOCIETAL FUNCTIONS OF CITIZENS

Three of the most important functions citizens in a modern industrial society have are:

1. *Production* – The production of goods and services is a prerequisite for the continued existence of any society.
2. *Consumption* – Modern market economies require a large number of consumers so that enough profit is made to motivate continued production.
3. *Reproduction* – As life isn't everlasting, there must be a continual socialization of new individuals.

Ideally all adults should participate in all three functions, but obviously such is not the case. If we begin with reproduction, not everyone becomes a parent. Biological problems prevent a number of couples from having children of their own, and some people choose to remain childless. Of those who become parents a few lose custody by court order. This is often the case for problematic consumers.

For others, especially women who live in areas of high unemployment, reproduction may be seen as a way of avoiding some of the negative psychological effects of not being gainfully employed. For instance some teenage girls choose to become mothers rather than be without work or move far from home to look for a job. But at least in Sweden, where over 80 per cent of the adult females belong to the workforce, it is becoming increasingly difficult for women to consider themselves completely adequate without being gainfully employed.

We have more people who want jobs than we can accommodate in the labour force. This gives rise to two central questions:

1. What do we have to offer those who are not needed in production?
2. What happens to the self-image of these people?

FOUR CATEGORIES

Based on the two societal functions, production and consumption, the adult population can be divided into four categories.

1. *Both producer and consumer* – I have placed everyone who is gainfully employed in this category, and call them producers. The money producers earn makes it possible for them to also be consumers.
2. *Potential producers and consumers* – The usual state of industrial economies is that the labour market cannot accommodate everyone who is willing and able to work. In periods of economic upswing, the demand for labour increases, and it is necessary to have a reserve with the

necessary skills to immediately take a position should one become available. These are the people in category 2. They are often offered some kind of labour market programme, such as education, on-the-job training, etc. and are paid. This permits them to be consumers, albeit with less buying power than those in category 1.

3. *Only consumers and accept this role* – When the demand for producers and reserves is satiated most often there are people left over. These are offered the role of consumer (although with not very much to spend). If they don't make trouble or show symptoms which disturb other people, they are given welfare and/or other benefits and permitted to live their lives with a minimum of intervention from society's repressive apparatus.
4. *Only consumers but do not accept this role* – These people are unwilling/unable to accept a little money in exchange for not disturbing the rest of us. They commit crimes, take drugs, behave in a bizarre manner, etc., and thereby evoke further action from the community.

In the following I will consider category 1 unproblematic. In doing so I am making a gross oversimplification as such is obviously not the case. As previously mentioned, even those who are employed are subjected to negative societal pressure. But in order to more readily make my point I shall assume here that those who belong to category 1 are able to maintain a positive self-image. When a person has a job and contributes to society, he has a basis for holding his head high; which the unemployed lack.

Category 2 lives in the hope of someday soon belonging to category 1; and some will achieve this goal. But others finish their training courses and apprenticeships without finding employment. These are now offered category 3.

Category 3 is a relatively inexpensive solution – for those who belong to category 1. In exchange for not disturbing the rest of us, the unemployed are offered a minimal standard of living. But the price they pay is high. I shall return to this shortly.

People in category 4 disturb us. They infringe upon our integrity when they break into our homes, make us feel insecure, and give us guilt feelings when we see them sleeping on park benches or poking in trash cans. They also cost a lot of money for publicly financed medical care, police, courts, penitentiaries, psychiatric centres, social workers, etc. They make us uncomfortable and raise taxes. Something must be done – but what?

WHAT SHOULD BE DONE ABOUT THE PEOPLE IN CATEGORY 4?

Some believe that the answer is rehabilitation. Let's say that we manage to successfully treat a problematic consumer of narcotics. After leaving a specialized programme he is willing and able to work, and with the help of an energetic social worker he manages to find a job. What happens then?

This person may very well continue to improve (although some setbacks are to be expected). But we still haven't solved the basic problem because now that this individual has found work, another person who otherwise would have had this job is without.

One could argue that this can be a solution, for if we could maintain a rotation, so that those who become unemployed do not remain in category 3 for very long, nobody would fall into category 4. In this way no one would be seriously hurt during the relatively short period they do not belong to category 1.

However, much of the unemployment in modern societies is not temporary. First of all there are structural problems and cyclical slow downs in the economy which tend to make unemployment in certain segments of the population permanent. This is especially true of those who are a little older, are not well educated and/or belong to a minority group. These people have great difficulty finding a job after even a relatively short period of unemployment.

Secondly some people believe that a certain degree of unemployment is in the best interest of society, as it tends to keep wages and prices down, and gives competitive advantages. It also guarantees a sufficient labour reserve so that sectors in an expansive phase can quickly recruit personnel without losing pace. Indeed the stock-market usually reacts negatively when unemployment decreases.

The bottom line of any cost–benefit analysis is dependent upon what factors are included. The psychological and economic problems which afflict the unemployed and their families affect the rest of society in the long term in the form of drugs, criminality, school problems, vandalism, fear, security measures, etc. These costs should be weighed against the benefits, but this is almost never done. It is certainly more humane, and may very well also be economically sound, to eliminate unemployment, although this idea contradicts current market-economy reasoning.

How many will be left out of the workforce is partially beyond human control; for instance we have thus far been unable to fully regulate business cycles and prevent recessions and even depressions. But to some extent it is also dependent upon our will and determination. From my point of view our choices are:

1. Attempt to prevent problems from arising by taking measures which allow as many people as possible to feel they have a function in society; thereby helping them to maintain a positive self-image.
2. Wait until difficulties arise and then try to alleviate them through treatment, welfare benefits and/or repressive measures.

3. Leave those who haven't been able to compete on the labour market to fend for themselves, knowing that some will not take this lying down.

REDUCING UNEMPLOYMENT

I propose that instead of simply giving welfare to the unemployed, thereby making them feel superfluous, we should be hiring them to do *meaningful work*, which otherwise would not be done. For instance we can increase the number of people working in daycare, schools, recreational centres, the environment, etc. Those so employed should be given the *same wages as others in similar positions*.

But won't this lead to increased inflation? The answer is yes as long as these jobs cost more than we already pay for social services. If we accept that inflation is a more serious problem than unemployment, then we cannot offer full-time jobs. But since we already have expenses for the unemployed, it will not increase inflation if they are hired part time at the same cost. If for instance social benefits are equivalent to working half-time, we should offer time-limited half-time jobs. The time limit is to make it easier to get people on to the open labour market should the need arise, i.e. in an economic upswing.

This idea may awaken negative feelings in some people; arousing associations to programmes where people with social problems were bunched together and assigned some meaningless task to keep them off the streets. I emphasize that I am suggesting real employment, where people feel they are making a meaningful contribution to society; not merely something to do, which is a parody of a job, and therefore more likely to be experienced as labelling than something positive.

It is also important that these positions be spread among the ordinary workplaces in the region. Nobody should feel himself singled out by having to go to a place known as a dumping-ground for social outcasts. Furthermore, to avoid labelling, people should be assigned these jobs through an employment bureau, not the social welfare services. To summarize, I suggest that:

1. People should be offered meaningful work so they feel they are making a contribution to society.
2. To avoid inflation the jobs may have to be part time; equivalent in expense to social benefits. Calculation of how much money is available should include all current and projected costs. We know, for instance, that the unemployed use public medical services to a significantly greater extent than others of the same age.
3. The positions opened should be spread among the ordinary workplaces, making it possible to associate with people who do not have social problems.

4. The wages offered should be equivalent to those paid to others doing similar work.
5. Placement should be arranged through an employment bureau.
6. Funds to finance the job are transferred from the social welfare authorities to the workplace, but wages are paid out by the employer in the same way as to all other employees.
7. Employment is time limited so that people will be available on the open labour market if the need should arise. If such does not occur, the time limit should be extended.

Two further problems must be discussed. Due to physical and/or psychological impairments, some people are not able to take the kinds of positions suggested here. These individuals should be given a job which suits their capabilities, but otherwise under the same conditions as described above.

Secondly, there are people who apparently don't want to work. This is a problem, although I don't believe there are very many who completely reject the idea of having a job. To do so implies that they have entirely neutralized the very strong norms of western society that adults should pull their own weight. I don't believe this is easily done. However, people can become passive after many failures and labelling reactions. I assume that what at first appears to be a completely negative standpoint, is in reality complicated and partially contradictory. With encouragement and support a different attitude may well emerge.

But there will always be a certain number of people who cannot be motivated to take a job. To decide what responsibilities society has towards these people, we must have a broad political discussion. In Sweden for instance, only those who actively seek work are legally entitled to social welfare. But in practice many are given assistance anyway, as social workers are well aware that there simply is no work available for some individuals, and see little sense in forcing them to humiliate themselves by applying for positions they have no chance of getting, or looking for jobs that do not exist.

I believe that neither moralizing nor coercion are effective in getting people who say they don't want to work on to the labour market. My hypothesis is that many of those offered a job will accept, due to the destructive effects of unemployment. This will be my next topic.

THE PSYCHOSOCIAL EFFECTS OF UNEMPLOYMENT

Psychologist Kerstin Isaksson (p. 6) writes: 'The evidence of negative effects of unemployment on psychological well-being is unequivocal and strong.' Psychiatrist Johan Cullberg (p. 28) sees unemployment as comparable to other life crises: 'it threatens the individual's physical existence, social identity and security'.

My discussion is based on the assumption that in order to maintain a positive self-image in societies with a market economy, people must feel that they have something to offer which others are willing to pay for. Merely taking without reciprocating has an extremely negative effect on a person's self-image. Being able to give, on the other hand, strengthens the individual. Adult men (and increasingly women) in the industrial world are evaluated by what they contribute to production. People in category 3 or 4 do not contribute and are judged accordingly – not only by others but also by themselves.

Unemployment has extremely negative consequences for an individual's social life. Social relationships are often related to the workplace. We earn money which enables us to be active and meet others during our leisure time. Friendships are formed among coworkers, and people acquire an expertise in their field of work which lends authority to their opinions on related subjects. Perhaps most important is that work is an integral part of the individual's identity. In several Indo-European languages it is grammatically correct to say 'I earn my living as a . . .', but people do not express themselves in this manner. Instead they say: 'I *am* a . . .'. If you *are* what you do, what *are* you when you do nothing?

When adults meet, the conversation is often related to work. In countries with a deeply rooted work ethic, the unemployed may feel left out. Avoiding social contacts is a common coping strategy; but at the cost of enhanced feelings of inferiority and of not belonging.

Marie Jahoda (1982) who has been studying the effects of unemployment since the 1930s, and who has had great influence on research in this field, believes that work fills both manifest (openly acknowledged) and latent (tacit) functions. In this latter category she includes the fact that work: structures time, activates people and gives them a sense of reality, creates social contacts outside the family, gives social status, influences the individual's identity, and makes it possible to strive towards a common goal together with others.

Work also influences a person's health. In his doctoral thesis in social medicine Urban Janlert (p. 31) writes: 'it is obvious from this and other studies that there is an indisputable connection between unemployment and poor health'. The correlation between these two variables is extremely complex and should be seen as a feedback relationship; i.e. unemployment can lead to poor health and vice versa. Furthermore many other variables play a role, i.e. 'The health of those who are unemployed in a community with little unemployment seems to fare more poorly than unemployed who live in areas with a great deal of unemployment' (ibid., p. 25). A possible explanation for this is that the less unemployment the greater the risk that personal characteristics determine who will be without work. This can lead to a vicious spiral. Negative reactions to for instance a physical or psychological handicap prevent the individual from getting a job, which leads to further negative reactions because he is unemployed, which makes him feel even worse, which makes it even more difficult to find work, and so on.

'Another explanation as to why the negative consequences of unemployment are less in a community with a high unemployment rate is that misfortune may be attributed to societal problems rather than individual deficiencies' (ibid., p. 26). Although this may well be true, we must not lose sight of the fact that it is difficult to be without work, no matter where one lives. At least initially this is an incentive for people to increase their efforts to find a job. But repeated failures often lead to self-reproach, and can result in apathy and a feeling of helplessness. A theory of 'learned helplessness' put forth by Seligman (1975) has received much attention:

> people who feel that they have no control over their life situation tend to develop helplessness, apathy, anxiety and depression. The risk of developing psychiatric problems when becoming unemployed is highest with repetitive unemployment and when the persons blame themselves for the unemployment. (Janlert, paper IV, p. 1025)

Hammarström et al. describe another vicious spiral in conjunction with unemployment.

> Adolescents from the most adverse environments run the greatest risk of unemployment. They have already felt that they lack control and fail to find school meaningful, and this has led to passivity, lack of self-confidence and depression. Unemployment aggravates the effects of lack of control. Pessimism about one's chances of ever finding a job increases. This can initiate a chain of stress reactions, which leads to various psychological and behavioural changes, i.e. more psychological and psychosomatic symptoms, increased drug consumption, etc. (Ibid.)

The correlation between unemployment and drug consumption has been the subject of numerous scientific studies. Isaksson (p. 24) found that among the unemployed men she studied there was a 'very high percent who abused alcohol and/or narcotics. According to the scale used to estimate alcohol abuse (MAST) more than half of the men had scores over the level for manifest alcohol problems. In addition, 24 per cent abused narcotics, of which one-third used opiates or CNS and the rest hash.'

Another study initially examined the drinking patterns of all 16 year olds in Luleå, a city of about 70 000 inhabitants in northern Sweden. The research subjects were followed up after two and five years. The last of these studies showed that 'the total alcohol consumption for both men and women who had been without work for at least twenty weeks was twice as high as those who had been unemployed for a shorter period or not at all' (Janlert, paper VI, p. 6). The authors conclude: 'high alcohol consumption at 16 years of age increases the risk of unemployment, but unemployment will increase alcohol consumption regardless of previous consumption levels' (ibid., paper V, p. 10).

It is most likely that the same can be said about other drugs. I shall now present British Professor of Social Work Geoffrey Pearson's discussion of the relationships between unemployment and heroin.

SOCIAL DEPRIVATION, UNEMPLOYMENT AND PATTERNS OF HEROIN USE

The heading above is also the title of a chapter Pearson wrote in a book – *A Land Fit for Heroin?* – published after eight years of 'Thatcherism' in the UK.

Pearson doesn't accept simple causation and clearly states that unemployment neither necessarily nor mechanically leads to heroin consumption. But he writes:

> on all available evidence there is undoubtedly an important and significant relationship between the problem of mass unemployment and Britain's new heroin problem... The circumstances of unemployment will make it more likely that heroin misuse will spread more rapidly within a neighbourhood, once the drug has become available.
>
> (Pearson, 1987b, p. 62f)

The pattern of heroin use in Britain changed dramatically between 1979 and 1983. First the youth of the UK's battered working-class housing estates began experimenting with heroin on a large scale: 'for the first time in the history of heroin misuse in modern Britain there were clear associations between heroin and unemployment' (ibid., p. 65). The figures doubled in the UK between 1979 and 1981 from 1.5 to 3 million people and 'there is a tendency for heroin misuse to be concentrated in localities which are also suffering from high levels of unemployment' (ibid., p. 66).

But unemployment alone is not a sufficient explanation. First, heroin must be available in large quantities, and secondly it is not only being used in deprived areas. Furthermore, there are areas with high levels of unemployment which don't have a heroin problem. To explain all this Pearson uses the term *distribution network*. Those areas which are not among the most deprived in the country yet have a high rate of heroin consumption, are situated close to communities which have well-developed distribution networks. Deprived areas without heroin are geographically remote from these networks.

In other words, supply is an important factor. Lack of access is certainly a major reason why we didn't have 'a narcotics problem' during the first half of the twentieth century. But there is little point in longing for bygone times. The steady increase in world trade coupled to improved methods of transportation make it reasonable to assume that it is only a matter of time before distribution networks are established wherever there is a potential market.

THE FUNCTIONS OF HEROIN FOR THE UNEMPLOYED

Pearson reports that when the national unemployment rate in Britain was 12 per cent, in areas with heroin problems it varied from 23 per cent to 34 per cent, with even higher levels for people under 25 (ibid., p. 71).

Heroin can fill at least three different functions for the unemployed.

1. *Escape* – Chein et al. believe that in the face of abject misery some people give up. Without hope of ever having a decent life, some try to cope by using heroin in an attempt to escape from the unbearable circumstances of their life.
2. *Activation* – Pearson argues that heroin gives problematic consumers a reason to be active. Unemployment arouses feelings of worthlessness, and makes it difficult for people to obtain things which would grant them status and a chance to maintain a positive self-image (ibid., p. 81). That is, when a person has little or no means to achieve societal goals through his position in the workforce, he looks for alternative means. A similar idea is expressed in Merton's now classic theory of anomie, where lack of access to legitimate means is seen as an important reason for turning to illegitimate methods (Merton, Chapters 6 and 7). Williams (p. x), in his study of young cocaine dealers in New York City, concludes that these teenagers have 'found a way to make money in a society that offers them few constructive alternatives'. And Sifaneck and Kaplan (p. 499) conclude that: 'Hard-drug dealing in the Netherlands remains particularly attractive to children of immigrants whose economic opportunities are limited.'

   Pearson believes that problematic consumers can gain high status with the help of heroin. As an example he describes a youth who buys a gram of heroin for £70, cuts it, and divides it into £5 or £10 bags. He sells these until he has the £70 he needs to buy another gram, and uses the rest himself. From this Pearson (1987b, p. 83) concludes: 'if this person were able to sustain his £70 daily transaction for a full year, it would represent an annual cash flow of £25 000. It would still be true that he would not be making any cash profit out of this low-level business, and would remain poor as a church mouse. Nevertheless, it takes little imagination to see that in a socially deprived area with high unemployment levels, an annual cash flow of £25 000 is a phenomenal achievement. With something like

£500 per week passing through his pockets, such a young man would be likely to be a figure of some real local standing.'

On this point I have trouble understanding Pearson's reasoning. Even if some people in the neighbourhood might temporarily let themselves be impressed, problematic consumers are disdained by most people, even among the poor. If there is any lustre at all, it doesn't last, as sooner or later problematic consumers are arrested, burned, robbed, beaten up, or simply haven't the strength to go on. At best a problematic consumer may have a short period where some people look up to him and/or he can convince himself that he is flying high. But it usually doesn't take long before he realizes that his situation is untenable; the negative aspects of his life accelerate, and he has seen what has become of others on the scene. *So he lives for the moment because he knows that in the long run he has no future.* However, I agree with Pearson that in order to be able to take heroin every day, one must be active.

3. *Structures time* – I have previously noted that work structures time, and that the unemployed often have difficulty organizing their lives. This is succinctly stated in the proverb, 'if you want something done, ask a busy man'. Those with little to do, have trouble getting anything accomplished. Pearson (ibid., p. 87) writes: 'heroin use within the contexts of unemployment can take on a new significance, as an effective resolution of the problem of de-routinised time-structures'. Put concisely problematic consumers of heroin must:

get money, in order to
buy drugs, to be able to
shoot up, so that
he won't become abstinent, which is a prerequisite for being able to
get money, etc.

This becomes the recurrent cycle which governs his life. Time does not merely drift away; he has something to keep him active.

In sum, Pearson (ibid., p. 89) believes that:

On the one hand these daily routines of a heroin habit can be seen as a dismal compulsion from which the user cannot escape. But at the same time they offered to people meaningful structures around which to organize their lives in an eventful and challenging way. In the absence of competing routines and structures of meaning and identity, such as might be supplied by work commitments, we can then say that it will not only be more difficult to 'come off' and 'stay off' heroin by breaking out of its routines and replacing them with alternative patterns of daily activity. It will also be more likely that a novice user will establish a pattern of habitual heroin use in the first place.

Pearson concludes that it is:

> highly unlikely that it will prove possible to contain the spread of heroin misuse, let alone cure it, until policies are adopted which offer to young working-class people realistic opportunities to obtain effective financial rewards and to fashion meaningful identities and life-styles through work and access to decent housing. (Ibid., p. 94)

CONCLUSION

Narcotics are not a problem unto themselves. The patterns of drug consumption in a country are deeply rooted in both the nation's history and current social and economic institutions. As problematic consumers of narcotics are primarily recruited from marginalized segments of the population, there are no easily realized measures, no declarations of war, and no therapeutic methods which will lead to a dramatic reduction in their numbers. That some people dream of finding a magic formula is understandable, but unrealistic. Narcotics are so intertwined in the fabric of society that they will most certainly always be present in one form or another.

However, this does not imply that nothing can be done. My basic assumption is that people have innate resources, among which are energy and the will to live. These have been bred and refined since *Homo sapiens* started to walk this planet. However, it is clear that the spark of life can be extinguished; the conditions of our existence can become overwhelming. Without any real prospects of a future as a respected member of the community, human energy can be turned from constructive efforts to self-destruction.

There are macrolevel processes, such as economic cycles, which nobody seems to be able to control. These limit our prospects of giving everyone the necessary resources for a decent life. By making the 'proper' political decisions, we shall not be able to accomplish miracles. But the industrial world has enormous resources, and we have a responsibility for how they are used. While political decisions cannot achieve anything and everything, they do have significant impact. If we choose to distribute our resources so that some have little or nothing, we create fertile soil for the growth of problematic consumption of narcotics and other destructive acts. To the degree that we can create a society where every person has a genuine chance of maintaining an identity as a useful citizen, we reduce the prerequisites for problematic consumption. But even under these conditions, it will take several generations before we begin to approach the elimination of socially inherited negative behavioural patterns.

A tangible and permanent reduction of the number of substantial consumers is a long-term project. Nobody knows exactly how we should go about achieving it, or how long it will take. But the arguments in this book imply that to have a chance of success, those of us who have resources must be prepared to share them. To the extent we aren't willing to do so, we have chosen to maintain a corresponding level of problematic consumption of narcotics.

Bibliography

Abraham, M. D., Cohen, P. D. A., van Til, R-J., and Langemeijer, M. P. S., *Licit and Illicit Drug Use in Amsterdam III: Developments in Drug Use 1987–1997*, CEDRO Centrum voor Drugsonderzoek, University of Amsterdam, 1998

Ågren, G., 'Metadon i Sverige', *Oberoende*, Nr. 1–2, 1998

American Psychiatric Association, *DSM-IV: Diagnostic and Statistical Manual of Mental Disorders*, Fourth Edition, American Psychiatric Association, Washington, DC, 1994

Andersson, B., *Att Förstå Drogmissbruk: Praktiken, Situationen, Processen*, Lund Studies in Social Welfare VI, Arkiv Förlag, Lund, 1991

Andersson, B-E., *Hur bra är egentligen dagis?*, Utbildningsförlaget, Kristianstad, 1990

Andersson, S., *Dubbla Budskap: Socialpsykologiskt Perspektiv på Schizofreni*, AWE/Gebers, Stockholm, 1980

Andersson W. and Westerberg, K. A., 'Hasselas Agitation', http://www.medströms.se/˜re7m8/art/veckans.htm, 1996

Anslinger, H. J. and Tompkins, W. F., *The Traffic in Narcotics*, Funk and Wagnalls, New York, 1953

Bakalar, J. B. and Grinspoon, L., *Drug Control in a Free Society*, Cambridge University Press, Cambridge, 1988

Bankel, M. and Hermansson, U., *Att Störa är att Bry Sig Om*, Mary Media AB, Stockholm, 1988

Becker, H. S., *Outsiders*, The Free Press of Glencoe, New York, 1963 and 1973

Bejerot, N., *Narkotikafrågan och Samhället*, Aldus/Bonniers, Stockholm, 1968

Bejerot, N., *Addiction and Society*, Charles C. Thomas Publisher, Springfield, IL, 1970

Bejerot, N., 'Drug Abuse and Drug Policy: An Epidemiological and Methodological Study of Drug Abuse of Intravenous Type in the Stockholm Police Arrest Population 1965–1970 in Relation to Changes in Drug Policy', *Acta Psychiatrica Scandinavica*, Supplementum 256, Munksgaard, Copenhagen, 1975

Bejerot, N., *Missbruk av Alkohol, Narkotika och Frihet*, Ordfront, Stockholm, 1979

Bejerot, N. and Hartelius, J., 'Polisens eget eviga Vietnamkrig', *Dagens Nyheter*, Dec. 13, 1980

Bergmark, Å., 'Överdödlighet och upprepade LVM-domar bland tvångsvårdade missbrukare', *Socialmedicinsk Tidskrift*, Vol. 71, No. 10, 1994, pp. 474–9

Bergmark, A. and Oscarsson, L., *Drug Abuse and Treatment: a Study of Social Conditions and Contextual Strategies*, Stockholm Studies in Social Work 4, Almqvist and Wiksell International, Täby, 1988

Bergmark, A., Björling, B., Grönbladh, L., Olsson, B., Oscarsson, L. and Segraeus, V., *Klienter i Institutionell Narkomanvård: Analyser av Bakgrund, Behandling och Utfall*, Pedagogisk Forskning i Uppsala, Pedagogiska institutionen, Uppsala Universitet, Oktober 1989

Bergström, G., 'Omvärdering av Hassela', *Narkotikafrågan*, Nr. 3, 1991, pp. 24–5

Bieleman, B. and Bosma, J., 'The Drug-Related Crime Project in the City of Rotterdam', in Leuw, E. and Marshall, I. H. (eds) *Between Prohibition and Legalization: The Dutch Experiment in Drug Policy*, Kugler Publications, Amsterdam, 1996

Bieleman, B., Schakel, L., de Bie, E. and Snippe, J., *Clouds Over Coffee Shops*, Intraval, Groningen, 1995

Björkman, T., 'Ett Litet Svenskt Pretoria', *Dagens Nyheter*, Nov. 22, 1997, p. A5

Blom, T. and van Mastrigt, H., 'The Future of the Dutch Model in the Context of the War on Drugs', in Leuw, E. and Marshall, I. H. (eds) *Between Prohibition and Legalization: The Dutch Experiment in Drug Policy*, Kugler Publications, Amsterdam, 1996

Blomqvist, J., *Beyond Treatment?: Widening the Approach to Alcohol Problems and Solutions*, Stockholm University, Department of Social Work, Studies in Social Work, 13, Stockholm, 1998

Bødal, K. and Fridhov, I. M., *Straff som Fortjent? 440 Narkoselgere Dømt Efter § 162 till Mer Enn 3 Års Fengsel i Perioden 1980–1988*, Delrapport 1, Kriminalomsorgsavdelningen, Justisdepartementet, Nov. 1989

Boekhout van Solinge, T., *The Swedish Drug Control System: An In-depth Review and Analysis*, Uitgeverij Jan Mets, Cedro, Amsterdam, 1997

Börjeson, B., *Inre och Yttre Tvång: En Principfråga vid Vården av Missbrukare*, Tidens Förlag, Borås, 1979

Börjeson, B., 'Varför är vi så öppna för repression?', *Nordisk Sosialt Arbeid*, No. 2, 1991

Börjeson, B. and Håkansson, H., *Hotade Försummade Övergivna*, Rabén and Sjögren, Kristianstad, 1990

Boström, P., *Sexuell Traumatisering*, Svensk Förening för Psykisk Hälsovård, Monografiserie Nr. 29, Stockholm, 1988

Brå apropå, No. 2–3, Brottsförebyggande rådet, 1977

Brinkman, J. W., 'Public Order and Addiction in Rotterdam', paper presented at the conference: *Cities and Addiction*, Rotterdam, 22 April 1997

Burroughs, W. S., *Tjacket*, AWE/Gebers, Stockholm, 1977

Campbell, D. T., 'The Experimenting Society', in Overman, E. S. (ed.) *Methodology and Epistemology for Social Science, Selected Papers*, University of Chicago Press, Chicago, 1988

Carlberg, A., Lenke, L. and Sunesson, S., 'Narkotikamissbruket ökar kraftigt', *Dagens Nyheter*, March 24, 1997, p. A4

Carlsson, L., *Gatloppet*, Prisma, Stockholm, 1977

Chein, I. Gerard, D. L., Lee, R. S. and Rosenfeld, E., *The Road to H: Narcotics, Delinquency and Social Policy*, Basic Books, New York, 1964

Christie, N. and Bruun, K., *Den Goda Fienden*, Rabén and Sjögren, Kristianstad, 1985

Cohen, A. K., *Deviance and Control*, Prentice-Hall, Englewood Cliffs, NJ, 1966

Cohen, J., 'Drug Education: Politics, Propaganda and Censorship', *The International Journal of Drug Policy*, Vol. 7, No. 3, 1996, pp. 153–7

Cohen, P. D. A., 'Re-thinking Drug Control Policy: Historical Perspectives and Conceptual Tools', paper presented at the *United Nations Research Institute for Social Development (UNRISD)*, Geneva, 7–8 July 1993, http://www.frw.uva.nl/cedro/library/geneva/genevaus.html

Cohen, P. D. A., 'The Case of the Two Dutch Drug Policy Commissions: An Exercise in Harm Reduction 1968–1976', paper presented at the *5th International Conference on the Reduction of Drug Related Harm*, Addiction Research Foundation, Toronto, website http://www.frw.uva.nl/cedro/library/ARF94/ARF94.html, Revised in 1996, 1996b

Cooley, C. H., *Human Nature and the Social Order*, Charles Scribner's Sons, New York, 1922 (first published in 1902)

Cullberg, J., *Dynamisk Psykiatri*, Natur och Kultur, Stockholm 1986

Dagens Nyheter, 'Facket Kräver Ny Lag', Sept. 30, 1991, p. A5

Dahlberg, R., Martinger, J., Knutson, G., Cederschiöld, C., Fridolfsson, F., Björne, E., Ekström, A., Henriksson, B., Ericsson, G., Koch, I. and Nilsson, C. G., *Ny Narkotikapolitik*, Motion till Riksdagen, 1990/91:Ju826

Dahlberg, R., Martinger, J., Knutson, G., Cederschiöld, C., Fridolfsson, F., Björne, E., Ekström, A., Henriksson, B., Ericsson, G., Koch, I. and Nilsson, C. G., *Unga Lagöverträdare*, Motion till Riksdagen, 1990/91:Ju827

Dahlström-Lannes, M., *Mot Dessa Våra Minsta: Sexuella Övergrepp mot Barn*, Förlagshuset Gothia, Falköping, 1990

Densen-Gerber, J. and Benward, J., 'Incest as a Causative Factor in Antisocial Behavior: An Exploratory Study', paper presented at a meeting of the *American Academy of Forensic Sciences*, Chicago, 1975

Dorn, N. and Murji, K., *Drug Prevention: A Review of the English Language Literature*, ISDD, London, 1992

Ehrenfeld, R., *Narco-terrorism*, Basic Books, New York, 1990

Eliasson, R., *Forskningsetik och Perspektivval*, Studentlitteratur, Lund, 1987

Ellinwood, E. H., Smith, W. G. and Vaillant, G. E., 'Narcotic Addiction in Males and Females: A Comparison', *International Journal of the Addictions*, 1(2), 1966, pp. 33–45

EMCDDA (European Monitoring Centre for Drugs and Drug Addiction), *Annual Report on the State of the Drugs Problem in the European Union*, UK, 1996

EMCDDA (European Monitoring Centre for Drugs and Drug Addiction), *Estimating the Prevalence of Problem Drug Use in Europe*, Italy, 1997a

EMCDDA (European Monitoring Centre for Drugs and Drug Addiction), *Annual Report on the State of the Drugs Problem in the European Union*, Italy, 1997b

Emerson, R., 'Heroin High', *Newsweek*, Jan 29, 1996, pp. 22–7

Engelsman, E. L., 'Dutch Policy on the Management of Drug-related Problems', *British Journal of Addiction*, Vol. 84, 1989, pp. 211–18

Ennett, S., Tobler, N., Ringwalt, C. and Flewelling, R., 'How Effective is Drug Abuse Resistance Education?', *American Journal of Public Health*, 84, 1994

Eriksson, I. and Eriksson, U. B., *Polisens Insatser mot Gatulangningen av Narkotika: Ett Utvärderingsförsök*, Brottsförebyggande Rådet, Kansli PM 1983:9

Fälth, G., 'Rättssäkerheten i Fara: Domstolarna Sänker Beviskraven', *Dagens Nyheter*, May 14, 1988

Flores, J., 'Langarna Finns Kvar', *Dagens Nyheter*, Sept. 13, 1991, p. D1

Fugelstad, A., *LVM-vård av Narkomaner: Kartläggning av Narkomaner Inskrivna på Serafens LVM-hem 1986–1988*, Stockholms Socialförvaltning, FoU-byrån Rapport Nr. 101, Stockholm, 1989

Glingvall-Priftakis, G., *Sexuella Övergrepp mot Barn och Ungdomar*, FoU-rapport Nr. 102, Stockholms Socialförvaltning, Stockholm, reviderad upplaga, 1991

Goldberg, T. (ed.), *Den Ömsesidiga Utmaningen: Sociologi och Praktiskt Socialt Arbete*, Gothia, Stockholm, 1990

Goldberg, T., *Narkotikan Avmystifierad: Ett Socialt Perspektiv*, Carlson Bokförlag, Stockholm, 1993

Grapendaal, M., Leuw, E. and Nelen, H., 'Legalization, Decriminalization and the Reduction of Crime', in Leuw, E. and Marshall, I. H. (eds) *Between Prohibition and Legalization: The Dutch Experiment in Drug Policy*, Kugler Publications, Amsterdam, 1996

Grönbladh, L., Öhlund, L. S. and Gunne L-M., 'Mortality in Heroin Addiction: Impact of Methadone Treatment', *Acta Psychiatrica Scandinavica*, 1990:82, pp. 223–7

Gutierres, S. E., Raymond, J. and Rhoads, D., *A Comparative Study of Women Heroin Abusers During and After Treatment: Needs and Attributions*, final report submitted to Arizona Department of Health Services-Behavioral Health Services, 1979

Hall, W., Solowij, N. and Lemon, J., *The Health and Psychological Consequences of Cannabis Use*, National Drug Strategy Monograph Series no. 25, Australian Government Publishing Service, Canberra, 1994

Hasselgren, S., 'Hög Dödlighet Bland Tvångsvårdade Missbrukare', *Alkohol and Narkotika*, Årg 89, Nr. 4, 1995, pp. 30–2
Heckscher, S. and Groth, E., *Hemlig Teleavlyssning Enligt 27 Kap. 18§ Rättegångsbalken: Yttrande till Justitiekanslern*, Diarienr RÄS-102–1424/97, Rikspolisstyrelsen, April 28, 1997
Hellsvik, G., Knutsson, G., Högmark, A. G., Ekendahl, M., Johnsson, J., Sundqvist, Å., Anderberg, C., Wågö, L. and Björkman, L., *Åtgärder Mot Ungdomsbrottsligheten*, Motion till Riksdagen, 1996/97:Ju909
Hessle, S., *Relationsorienterat Synsätt och Socialt Arbete med Missbrukare*, Projekt R Rapport Nr. 1, Socialhögskolan, Stockholms Universitet, 1987
Hessle, S., *Familjer i Sönderfall*, Norstedts, Göteborg, 1988
Hibell, B., Andersson, B., Bjarnason, T., Kokkevi, A., Morgan, M., and Narusk, A., *The 1995 ESPAD Report: Alcohol and Other Drug Use Among Students in 26 European Countries*, The Swedish Council for Information on Alcohol and Other Drugs (CAN) and Council of Europe Co-operation Group to Combat Drug Abuse and Illicit Trafficking in Drugs (Pompidou Group), Stockholm, 1997
Hilte, M., *Droger och Disciplin: En Fallstudie av Narkomanvård i Malmö*, Arkiv Förlag, Lund, 1990
Hilte, M., 'Narkotikakriget och det Öppna Eller Slutna Samhället', *Oberoende*, Nr. 1–2, 1998
Holmberg, M. B., *The Prognosis of Drug Abuse in a Sixteen-year-old Population*, Dept of Psychiatry, Göteborgs Universitet, 1981
Horstink-Von Meyenfeldt, L., 'The Netherlands: Tightening Up of the Cafés Policy', in Dorn, N., Jepsen, J. and Savona, E. (eds) *European Drug Policies and Enforcement*, Macmillan, Chippenham, Wiltshire, 1996
Huxley, A., *The Doors of Perception, Heaven and Hell*, Chatto and Windus, London, 1972
Inciardi, J. A., *The War on Drugs II*, Mayfield, Mountain View, CA, 1992
Isaksson, K., 'Livet Utan Arbete: Arbetslöshet och Mental Hälsa Bland Unga Manliga Socialtjänstklienter', Doctoral Dissertation, Psykologiska Inst., Stockholms Universitet, 1990
Israel, J., *Sociologi: Inledning till det Kritiska Samhällsstudiet*, BonnierFakta, Stockholm, 1984
Jahoda, M., *Employment and Unemployment*, Cambridge University Press, 1982
Janlert, U., 'Work Deprivation and Health: Consequences of Job Loss and Unemployment', Doctoral Dissertation, Karolinska Institutet, 1991
Jansen, A. C. M., 'The Development of a "Legal" Consumers' Market for Cannabis: The "Coffee Shop" Phenomenon', in Leuw, E. and Marshall, I. H. (eds) *Between Prohibition and Legalization: The Dutch Experiment in Drug Policy*, Kugler Publications, Amsterdam, 1996
Jepsen, J., 'International Narkotikakontrol – Spredning af Ideologi, Retshåndhævelse och Kontrolmodeller', *Social Kritik*, August, 1992
Jepsen, J., 'Copenhagen: A War on Socially Marginal People', in Dorn, N., Jepsen, J. and Savona, E. (eds) *European Drug Policies and Enforcement*, Macmillan, Chippenham, Wiltshire, 1996
JO, *Justitieombudsmanens Ämbetsberättelse*, Riksdagen, Saml 2:1, Band C1, 1987/88
JO, *Justitieombudsmanens Ämbetsberättelse*, Riksdagen, Saml 2:1, Band C1, 1989/90
JO, *Tillämpning av bl a 28 kap. 3 § RB vid Polisiär Störningsverksamhet i Tillhåll*, Dnr 1233–1990, Oct. 5, 1992
Jonsson, G., *Det Sociala Arvet*, Tiden/Folksam, Stockholm, 1969
Jonsson, G., *Att Bryta det Sociala Arvet*, Tiden/Folksam, Stockholm, 1973
Jospe, M., *The Placebo Effect in Healing*, Lexington Books, Lexington, MA, 1978

Kandel, D. and Yamaguchi, K., 'From Beer to Crack: Developmental Patterns of Drug Involvement', *American Journal of Public Health*, Vol. 83, No. 6, 1993, pp. 851–5

Kaplan, C. D. and Leuw, E., 'A Tale of Two Cities: Drug Policy Instruments and City Networks in the European Union', *European Journal on Criminal Policy and Research*, Vol. 4, No. 1, 1996

Kaplan, C. D., Haanraadts, D. J., Van Vliet, H. J. and Grund, J. P., 'Is Dutch Drug Policy an Example to the World?', in Leuw, E. and Marshall, I. H. (eds) *Between Prohibition and Legalization: The Dutch Experiment in Drug Policy*, Kugler Publications, Amsterdam, 1996

Karlsson, B., 'Bråk om Buggning', *Dagens Nyheter*, Aug. 30, 1997, p. A10

Knutsson, J., *Stämplingsteori – en Kritisk Granskning*, Rapport 1977:1, Brottsförebyggande rådet, 1977

Kommittédirektiv, *Hemlig Avlyssning m.m.*, Dir. 1996:64, Regeringskansliets Offsetscentral, Stockholm, 1996

Korf, D. J., 'Drug Tourists and Drug Refugees', in Leuw, E. and Marshall, I. H. (eds) *Between Prohibition and Legalization: The Dutch Experiment in Drug Policy*, Kugler Publications, Amsterdam, 1996

Kraan, D. J., 'An Economic View on Dutch Drugs Policy', in Leuw, E. and Marshall, I. H. (eds) *Between Prohibition and Legalization: The Dutch Experiment in Drug Policy*, Kugler Publications, Amsterdam, 1996

Laing, R. D., *Knots*, Penguin Books, Harmondsworth, 1970

Lasagna, L., von Felsinger, J. M. and Beecher, H. K., 'Drug-induced Mood Changes in Man', *Journal of the American Medical Association*, Vol. 157, No. 12, March 19, 1955

Lenke, L., *Multi-city Study of Drug Misuse in Amsterdam, Dublin, Hamburg, London, Paris, Rome, Stockholm: Overview and Synthesis of City Reports*, Council of Europe, Strasbourg, 1986

Lenke, L. and Olsson, B., 'Sweden: Zero Tolerance Wins the Argument?', in Dorn, N., Jepsen, J. and Savona, E. (eds) *European Drug Policies and Enforcement*, Macmillan, Chippenham, Wiltshire, 1996

Lettieri, D. J., 'Drug Abuse: A Review of Explanations and Models of Explanation', *Advances in Alcohol and Substance Abuse*, 1985:4

Leuw, E., 'Initial Construction and Development of the Official Dutch Drug Policy', in Leuw, E. and Marshall, I. H. (eds), *Between Prohibition and Legalization: The Dutch Experiment in Drug Policy*, Kugler Publications, Amsterdam, 1996

Leuw, E. and Marshall, I. H. (eds), *Between Prohibition and Legalization: The Dutch Experiment in Drug Policy*, Kugler Publications, Amsterdam, 1996

Levine, M., *Deep Cover*, Dell Publishing, New York, 1991

Liedman, S-E., *Surdeg*, Författarförlaget, Stockholm, 1980

Lindberg, J., 'De "Legala" Narkomanerna. En Studie av Dr S. E. Åhströms Patientgrupp', in Narkomanvårdsommittén, *Narkotikaproblemet: Undersökningar*, SOU 1969:53, Esselte AB, Stockholm, 1969, pp. 345–403

Lindén, G., *Byta Föräldrar*, LiberFörlag, Kristianstad, 1982

Lindström, L., *Managing Alcoholism: Matching Clients to Treatments*, Oxford University Press, Oxford, 1992

Lindström, L., 'Överambition, Uppgivenhet eller Omsorg', *Sociologisk Forskning*, Nr. 1, 1993, pp. 29–45

Lindström, P. and Svensson, R., 'Med Fokus på Ungdomar', *Apropå*, No. 2, 1998, pp. 20–4

Löfgren, B., *Alkoholismen, Människan och Samhället*, Aldus/Bonniers, Stockholm, 1972

MacAndrew, C. and Edgerton, R. B., *Drunken Comportment: A Social Explanation*, Aldine, Chicago, 1969

McCoy, A. W., *The Politics of Heroin in Southeast Asia*, Harper and Row, New York, 1972

McCoy, A. W. and Block, A. A., *War on Drugs: Studies in the Failure of US Narcotics Policy*, Westview Press, 1992

Mannheim, K., *Ideology and Utopia*, Routledge and Kegan Paul, London, 1968

Maris, C. W., 'Dutch Weed and Logic. Part I: Inconsistencies in the Dutch Government's Memorandum on Drug Policy', *International Journal of Drug Policy*, Vol. 7, No. 2, 1996, pp. 80–7

Marshall, I. H. and Marshall, C. E., 'Drug Prevention in the Netherlands: A Low-key Approach', in Leuw, E. and Marshall, I. H. (eds) *Between Prohibition and Legalization: The Dutch Experiment in Drug Policy*, Kugler Publications, Amsterdam, 1996

Mathiesen, T., *Kan Fängelset Försvaras?*, Bokförlaget Korpen, Göteborg, 1988

Menicucci, L. D. and Wermuth, L., 'Expanding the Family Systems Approach: Cultural, Class, Developmental and Gender Influences in Drug Abuse', *The American Journal of Family Therapy*, Vol. 17, No. 2, 1989

Merton, R. K., *Social Theory and Social Structure*, Free Press, Glencoe, IL, 1968

Møller, K. O., 'Eufomani i Farmakologisk Belysning', *Nordisk Medicin*, Nr. 40, 54, 1955, pp. 1533–9

Montagne, M., 'The Culture of Long-term Tranquilliser Users', in Gabe, J. (ed.) *Understanding Tranquilliser Use: The Role of the Social Sciences*, Tavistock/Routledge, London, 1991

Mossberg, L. and Änggård, E., *Missbrukskarriärer – En Litteraturstudie*, NU-serien B 1978:23, Nordiska rådet och Nordiska ministerrådet, Stockholm, 1978

Nadelmann, E. A., 'Commonsense Drug Policy', *Foreign Affairs*, Vol. 77, No. 1, 1998, pp. 111–26

Narkomanvårdskommittén, *Narkotikaproblemet: Del 1, Kartläggning och Vård*, Stockholm, 1967

Narkomanvårdskommittén, *Narkotikaproblemet: Samordnade Åtgärder*, SOU 1969:52, Esselte AB, Stockholm, 1969

Neill, A. S., *Summerhill, A Radical Approach to Child Rearing*, Hart, New York, 1960

Nilsson, I. and Wadeskog, A., *Det Blir För Dyrt*, Institutet för Socialekologisk Ekonomi, Järna, 1981

Nordegren, T. and Tunving, K., *Hasch: Romantik och Fakta*, Prisma, Borås, 1984

Olsson, B., *Klienter i Narkomanvård: En Rapport från SWEDATE-projektet*, Pedagogiska Inst., Uppsala, 1988

Örtendahl, C., 'Social Trygghet – Narkotikapolitikens Bas', in *Vi Ger Oss Aldrig!*, Rapport från Regeringens Aktionsgrupp mot Narkotika, Socialdepartementet, Stockholm, 1991

Ostrovsky, V. and Hoy, C., *By Way of Deception*, St Martin's Paperbacks, New York, 1991

Ottevanger, C. M., 'VICTOR in Rotterdam', paper presented at *European Cities on Drug Policy Conference*, Montreuil, 28 October 1997

Pauloff, A., 'Elevernas Drogvanor Påverkades Inte', *Apropå*, No. 2, 1998, pp. 25–7

Pearson, G., *The New Heroin Users*, Basil Blackwell, Oxford, 1987a

Pearson, G., 'Social Deprivation, Unemployment and Patterns of Heroin Use', in Dorn, N. and South, N. (eds) *A Land Fit for Heroin? Drug Policies, Prevention and Practice*, Macmillan Education, Tiptree, Essex, 1987b

Peck, D. F. and Plant, M. A., 'Unemployment and Illegal Drug Use: Concordant Evidence from a Prospective Study and National Trends', *British Medical Journal*, Vol. 293, 1986, pp. 929–32

Peele, S., *The Meaning of Addiction: Compulsive Experience and its Interpretation*, Lexington Books, Lexington, 1985

Perrow, C., 'The Analysis of Goals in Complex Organizations', in Litterer, J. A. (ed.) *Organizations, Vol. II*, second edition, John Wiley, New York, 1969

Ramström, J., *Narkomani: Orsaker och Behandling*, omarbetad och utvidgad upplaga, Tiden/Folksam, Falköping, 1983

Ramström, J., *Tonåringar och Droger*, Tiden/Folksam, Kristianstad, 1987

Regeringens proposition 1982/83:85, *Om Ändring i Brottsbalken, m.m. (Villkorlig Frigivning och Kriminalvård i Frihet m.m.)*

Regeringens proposition 1988/89:124, *Om Vissa Tvångsmedelsfrågor*

Rikspolisstyrelsen, *Rakt på Knarket: Ett Manifest Från Polisen om Kampen mot Narkotikabrottsligheten*, 2:a upplagan, 1991

Robinson, T. E. and Berridge, K. C., 'The Neural Basis of Drug Craving: An Incentive-Sensitization Theory of Addiction', *Brain Research Review*, No. 18, 1993, pp. 247–91

Rosenberg, C. M., 'Young Drug Addicts: Background and Personality', *The Journal of Nervous and Mental Disease*, Vol. 148, No. 1, 1969

Rosenblum, M., 'Hidden Agendas', *Vanity Fair*, March 1990

RRV, 'Missbrukarkarriärer i Ekonomisk Belysning', *Narkomanvården: Om Kostnader, Resursutnyttjande, Samordning och Statlig Styrning*, RRV-rapport F 1993:2, Stockholm, 1993

Sætre, M., Holter, H. and Jebsen, E., *Tvang til Seksualitet: En Undersøkelse av Sekseulle Overgrep mot Barn*, Cappelens Forlag, Oslo, 1986

Sandwijk, J. P., Cohen, P. D. A. and Musterd, S., *Licit and Illicit Drug Use in Amsterdam*, University of Amsterdam Press, Amsterdam, 1992

Sarnecki, J., *Sprutnarkomani Bland 'Vuxna Stockholmspojkar'*, Kansli PM 1985:11, Brottsförebyggande Rådet, Stockholm, 1985

Schmidbauer, W., *Professionella Hjälpare*, Alfabeta, Värnamo, 1987

Schüllerqvist, L., 'Dansk Buggningslag Stoppade Inte Knarket', *Dagens Nyheter*, May 21, 1989

Seidel, J., *Övergrepp mot Barn*, Studentlitteratur, Lund, 1991

Seligman, M. E., *Helplessness: On Depression, Development and Death*, Freeman, San Francisco, 1975

Shapiro, A. K., 'Contribution to the History of the Placebo Effect', *Behavioral Science* 5, 1960, pp. 109–35

Shapiro, A. K., 'Psychological Use of Medication', in Lief, H. I., Lief, V. F. and Lief, N. R. (eds) *Psychological Basis of Medical Practice*, Harper and Row, New York, 1963

Shedler, J. and Block, J., 'Adolescent Drug Use and Psychological Health: A Longitudinal Inquiry', *American Psychologist*, Vol. 45, No. 5, May 1990, pp. 612–30

Sifaneck, S. J. and Kaplan, C. D., 'Keeping Off, Stepping On and Stepping Off: The Steppingstone Theory Reevaluated in the Context of the Dutch Cannabis Experience', *Contemporary Drug Problems*, No. 22/Fall 1995, pp. 483–512

Silvis, J., 'Enforcing Drug Laws in The Netherlands', in Leuw, E. and Marshall, I. H. (eds) *Between Prohibition and Legalization: The Dutch Experiment in Drug Policy*, Kugler Publications, Amsterdam, 1996

Simon, D. and Burns, E., *The Corner: A Year in the Life of an Inner-city Neighborhood*, Broadway Books, New York, 1998

SIS (Statens Institutionsstyrelse), *Årsredovisning 1997*, Stockholm

Sjöstedt, J., 'Knarkjakten', *Socialt Arbete*, Nr. 10, 1985

SNIPH (Swedish National Institute of Public Health), *Drug Policy: The Swedish Experience*, second revised edition, 1995

Socialstyrelsen, *Granskning av ARA-projektet*, Upplands-Väsby kommun, Individ-och familjeenheten, Socialstyrelsen, Aug. 21, 1990

Socialstyrelsen, *Kursändring i Missbrukarvården – Mot Öppna Former*, Socialstyrelsen Följer Upp och Utvärderar, 1996:3, Modin-Tryck, Stockholm, May 1996

Socialstyrelsen, *Metadonbehandlingen i Sverige: Beskrivning och Utvärdering*, SoS-rapport 1997:22, Graphic Systems, Dec. 1997

Socialtjänstkommittén, *Ny Socialtjänstlag, Huvudbetänkande av Socialtjänstkommittén*, SOU 1994:139, Angered, 1994

Solarz, A., *Vem Blir Drogmissbrukare? Droger, Kriminalitet och Kontroll*, Brå-rapport 1990:3, Brottsförebyggande Rådet, Stockholm, 1990

SOU 1998:46, *Buggning och Andra Hemliga Tvångsmedel*, Stockholm, 1998

Stanton, M. D., 'The Family and Drug Abuse: Concepts and Rationale', in Bratter, T. E. and Forrest, G. G. (eds) *Alcoholism and Substance Abuse: Strategies for Clinical Intervention*, The Free Press, New York, 1985

Stenberg, B., *Rapport*, Bokförlaget Pan/Norstedts, Stockholm, 1971

Stjerna, B. E., 'Sexuella Problem – Sexuella Övergrepp – Drogmissbruk?!', paper presented at the *Nordic Association for Clinical Sexology Conference* in Saltsjöbaden, Sept., 1997

Strindlund, H., 'Det *Ska* Vara Svårt att Vara Missbrukare', in *Vi Ger Oss Aldrig!*, Rapport från Regeringens Aktionsgrupp mot Narkotika, Socialdepartementet, Stockholm, 1991

Sundelin, C. and Kjellberg, G., *Klass och Ohälsa hos Barn och Ungdom*, Institutionen för Pediatrik, Akademiska sjukhuset, Uppsala, 1991

Sunesson, S., 'Den Kemistyrde Dåren och Andra Vardagsmyter', *Oberoende*, Nr. 1–2, 1998

Svensson, B., *Pundare, Jonkare och Andra*, Carlsson Bokförlag, Eslöv, 1996

Sykes, G. M. and Matza, D., 'Techniques of Neutralization: A Theory of Delinquency', *American Sociological Review*, Vol. 22, Dec. 1957

Tham, H., 'Narkotikakontroll som Nationellt Projekt', *Nordisk Alkoholtidskrift*, Vol. 9, No. 2, 1992

Tham, H., 'Avskaffa Parollen "Ett Narkotikafritt Samhälle"', *Oberoende*, Nr. 1–2, 1998

Therborn, G., *Maktens Ideologi och Ideologins Makt*, Zenit Förlag, Malmö, 1981

Thorberg, B-L. and Hoffman, O., 'Hera-kvinnor: Incestoffer med Drogberoende', *Läkartidningen*, Vol. 94, No. 3, 1997, pp. 129–34

Tilander, K., *Bakom Vår Blindhet: Röster från Hassela*, Carlsson Bokförlag, Helsingborg, 1991

Tobler, N. S., 'Meta-analysis of 143 Adolescent Drug Prevention Programs: Quantitative Outcome Results of Program Participants Compared to a Control or Comparison Group', *Journal of Drug Issues*, 16, 1986, pp. 537–68

Tops, D., 'Rena Sprutor – En Stridsfråga', *Oberoende*, Nr. 1–2, 1998

Torstensson, M., *Drug-abusers in a Metropolitan Cohort*, Project Metropolitan Report No. 25, University of Stockholm, Stockholm, 1987

UNO (Utredningen om narkotikamissbrukets omfattning), *Ungdomar, Droger och Förebyggande Arbete*, Socialdepartementet, DsS 1981:11

Upplands-Väsby kommun, *Kommunpolitiskt Handlingsprogram mot Narkotika*, undated

Van Amerongen, B., 'Cinderella's Portrait: Some Observations on Dutch Drug Prevention Policy', in Kaplan, C. D. and Kooyman, M. (eds) *Proceedings of the 15th International Institute on the Prevention and Treatment of Drug Dependence*, Institute for Preventive and Social Psychiatry, Erasmus University, Rotterdam, 1987 von Hofer, H. and Tham, H., 'Stöld i Sverige 1831–1988', in Goldberg, T. (ed.) *Samhällsproblem*, Liber, Falköping, 1990

Weil, A., *The Natural Mind*, Penguin Books, Bungay, Suffolk, 1975

Westerberg, K. A. and Andersson W., 'Är det Fel att Ha Framgång?', *Dagens Nyheter*, Aug. 16, 1991

Wever, L., 'Drugs as a Public Health Problem: Assistance and Treatment', in Leuw, E. and Marshall, I. H. (eds) *Between Prohibition and Legalization: The Dutch Experiment in Drug Policy*, Kugler Publications, Amsterdam, 1996

Williams, T., *The Cocaine Kids: The Inside Story of a Teenage Drug Ring*, Addison-Wesley, Reading, MA, 1990

Windsløw, J. H., *Narreskibet*, Forlaget Socpol, Holte Denmark, 1984

Wurmser, L., *The Hidden Dimension: Psychodynamics of Compulsive Drug Use*, Jason Aronson, Northvale, NJ, 1995

Zinberg, N. E., *Drugs, Set and Setting: The Basis for Controlled Intoxicant Use*, Yale University Press, New Haven, 1984

Name Index

Subject Index